D0919002

DEMOCRACY AND DICTATORSHIP IN LATIN AMERICA

edited by THOMAS DRAPER

THE REFERENCE SHELF

Volume 53   Number 3

THE H. W. WILSON COMPANY

New York   1981

THE REFERENCE SHELF

The books in this series contain reprints of articles, excerpts from books, and addresses on current issues and social trends in the United States and other countries. There are six separately bound numbers in each volume, all of which are generally published in the same calendar year. One number is a collection of recent speeches; each of the others is devoted to a single subject and gives background information and discussion from various points of view, concluding with a comprehensive bibliography. Books in the series may be purchased individually or on subscription.

Library of Congress Cataloging in Publication Data
Main entry under title:

Democracy and dictatorship in Latin America.

(The Reference shelf ; v. 53, no. 3)
Bibliography: p.
1. Latin America—Politics and government—
1948–   —Addresses, essays, lectures. 2. Latin
America—Foreign relations—United States—Addresses,
essays, lectures. 3. United States—Foreign
relations—Latin America—Addresses, essays,
lectures. 4. Civil rights—Latin America—Addresses,
essays, lectures. I. Draper, Thomas.
II. Series: Reference shelf ; v. 53, no. 3.
F1414.2.D43   980'.038   80-10311
ISBN 0-8242-0655-X   AACR2

Copyright © 1981 by The H. W. Wilson Company. All rights reserved. No part of this work may be reproduced or copied in any form or by any means, including but not restricted to graphic, electronic, and mechanical—for example, photocopying, recording, taping, or information and retrieval systems—without the express written permission of the publisher, except that a reviewer may quote and a magazine or newspaper may print brief passages as part of a review written specifically for inclusion in that magazine or newspaper.

PRINTED IN THE UNITED STATES OF AMERICA

821271

LIBRARY
ALMA COLLEGE
ALMA, MICHIGAN

CONTENTS

III. In Search of Democracy: Human Rights and
      U.S. Security

PREFACE

Government by unelected military rulers, widespread violation of human rights, clashes between Left and Right sparking guerrilla warfare and terrorist assaults, sectors of the traditionally conservative Catholic Church engaged in the struggle against right-wing dictatorships and persecuted or murdered as Communist traitors, runaway inflation, population explosions, festering squatter slums, deepening chasms between rich and poor—these are facts of Latin American life, complicated and vexing issues to which must be added the influences exerted by foreign nations and multinational business. As a neighbor, the United States has, since the proclamation of the Monroe Doctrine in 1823, declared its concern for regional security, observing with special interest events south of its border. In recent years crises in Cuba, the Dominican Republic, Chile, and Nicaragua have notably affected and been affected by U.S. policies. The latest instance is El Salvador, seen by some as a potential Vietnam of the Western Hemisphere.

Whatever their roots, the problems blocking the establishment of democratic alternatives to right-wing dictatorships or Marxist satellite states—problems that stymie moderate Latin American leaders as well as U.S. policymakers eager to support constitutional governments—have long existed and are not likely to be resolved by the outcome of the Salvadoran conflict. Indeed, if El Salvador is "a microcosm of Latin America," as one of the authors represented in this volume asserts, then its grim experience may well be duplicated elsewhere in the region. Most analysts conclude that despite such encouraging developments as the restoration of civilian government in Peru, prospects for flourishing democracies throughout Latin America appear remote.

This survey of the current but swiftly changing Latin American picture begins with an inventory of democratic aspirations, starting with the Caribbean, continuing with Mexico, and proceeding southward to Central America. The second section focuses on the struggle between the opposing antidemocratic forces: communism and rightist authoritarianism. The third section analyzes the forces searching for democratic government and their impact on the interests of the United States as this nation pursues its hazardous course: striving to foster democracy among its neighbors while avoiding intervention in local politics yet without weakening hemispheric security.

The editor wishes to thank the authors and publishers of the selections that follow for permission to reprint them in this compilation.

THOMAS DRAPER

April 1981

LATIN AMERICA

Reprinted from *Latin America's Emergence: Toward a U.S. Response*, pamphlet by Abraham F. Lowenthal and Albert Fishlow. (Headline Series 243) Foreign Policy Association. '79. © Copyright 1979 by Foreign Policy Association, Inc. Reprinted by permission.

I. LATIN AMERICAN PROFILE

EDITOR'S INTRODUCTION

The effort to achieve autonomy, democracy, and viable economies in the developing—and mostly desperately poor—countries of Latin America has been an ongoing struggle since the battles for independence began in the early nineteenth century. Despite individual differences of history and geography, the countries share to a greater or lesser degree a common heritage of colonial exploitation and repression, social systems characterized by acute race and class inequities, and records of successive coups and intervals of rule by military juntas. As the rate of change accelerates, alarmed observers perceive no real change except a growing threat to the security of the United States.

It is against this background that the extracts in Section I present an overview of the critical state of the nations immediately to the south. Thirty separate political entities dot the Caribbean Sea, aptly called a Sea of Troubles in the first selection, excerpted from the Foreign Policy Association's *Great Decisions '81*. A *National Review* article follows, calling the "political infection" (communism) in the Caribbean beyond the creeping stage and setting forth the difficulties of promoting democracy in countries in which the contending sides of political power have been polarized between extremes of conservatism approaching right-wing dictatorship and extremes of socialism approaching Communist dictatorship.

Our only contiguous Latin American neighbor is Mexico, which shares a two-thousand-mile border. Mexico's unusual form of government—a regime with authoritarian features but flexible enough to retain passive popular support—is the subject of the third extract, taken from a publication on Mexico by Professor Peter H. Smith.

Two following articles—from *Great Decisions '81* and *Foreign Policy*—compare conditions in Central America to a fire storm and recent United States attempts to stave off Communist takeover as the work of a fire brigade. The facts of El Salvador's simmering crisis are cogently presented in the report that concludes this opening section: a *Foreign Affairs* analysis in which government in El Salvador is seen as a political alliance between oligarchs and officers.

THE CARIBBEAN: SEA OF TROUBLES[1]

Mare nostrum—our sea—was the proud term Julius Caesar applied to the Mediterranean when imperial Rome was approaching the height of its power. Americans were thinking of the Caribbean in much the same way back in 1898 when U.S. sea power drove Spain out of its last American colonies, Cuba and Puerto Rico.

Few Americans would call the Caribbean "our sea" any longer. The 22-year reign of Cuba's Fidel Castro, Moscow's ally, has dramatized the decline of this nation's capacity to shape events in the area. Yet important U.S. interests remain. Under the 1978 neutrality treaty with Panama the United States retains a permanent responsibility for the security of the canal. Basic materials—Venezuelan oil and gas, Jamaican bauxite—cross the Caribbean in large volume to U.S. ports. U.S. trade and investment in the Caribbean are considerable. Puerto Rico and the U.S. Virgin Islands are under the American flag. Finally, the well-being of the 30 million inhabitants of the Caribbean is important not only to American ideals but also to our self-interest in fostering security and stability in the area and slowing the tide of Caribbean migration to U.S. shores.

[1] Excerpted from *Great Decisions '81*, a book by the Editors of the Foreign Policy Association. Foreign Policy Association. '81. p 47–50. © Copyright, 1981, Foreign Policy Association, Inc. Reprinted by permission.

Caribbean Miscellany

From the jaws of the Gulf of Mexico southeast to Trinidad Island off Venezuela's coast, the thousands of islands of the Antilles and Bahamas stretch 1,750 miles across the Caribbean Sea. Divided into some 30 separate political entities, they make a bewildering miscellany—islands both large and tiny; peoples of Indian, European and African backgrounds; political systems democratic and otherwise; independence of long-standing, recent, or yet to be attained. Most populous among 30-odd political entities are Cuba, the Dominican Republic, Haiti, Jamaica and Puerto Rico. Also, usually considered as belonging to the Caribbean region are four mainland countries recently, or still, under European rule. On the South American coast are Guyana, once a British colony; Suriname, most recently a Dutch dependency; and the still-surviving French colony (officially an "overseas department") of Guiana. In Central America, wedged between Mexico and Guatemala, is the British colony of Belize.

Diverse though they are, the Caribbean states have two things in common. All, in varying degrees, are poor. And all, because they weigh little in the scales of world power, have a history of dependence on stronger states outside the region. The present era of decolonization and "third-world" economic development has raised high hopes of overcoming these conditions. But many hopes have been disappointed or deferred, tension is constant and crises are frequent.

Politically, a contrast is visible between the countries that were once colonies of Spain or France and those more recently set free from British rule. As far back as the French Revolution, Haitians began to fight for independence from France, and the peoples of the Dominican Republic and Cuba struggled for generations during the 19th century to win independence from Spain. With little experience of self-government under their colonial rulers, their history as independent states has been marked by alternating periods of dictatorship and civil strife.

In contrast, states of the English-speaking Caribbean such

as Jamaica, Trinidad and Barbados had their own parliaments long before London finally granted them independence—by peaceful agreement, not war—in the 1960s. Generations of popular education, professional training and broadening of the franchise helped to prepare their people for independence. Most, thus far, are a successful, if still delicate, transplant of British parliamentary institutions.

In economic and social terms, the histories of all the Caribbean states are depressingly similar. The key words are sugar and slavery. Sugar plantations in the region, using African slaves, date from the early 16th century. In the 18th and early 19th centuries the sugar-and-slave economy reached its peak; the total slave population was then over 1.7 million, far outnumbering the free citizens. After slavery was abolished the labor gap in some islands was filled by indentured workers imported from India and China.

Racially and culturally, this history lives on in a unique mixture of peoples, folkways, languages and dialects. Economically, heavy dependence on a single export commodity—sugar in the Dominican Republic and Cuba, coffee in Haiti, bauxite in Jamaica—is still a major vulnerability. Only for Trinidad-Tobago, whose big export is oil, has the one-commodity economy meant prosperity.

Since 1973, rising oil prices and global recession have pushed Caribbean economies into crisis. Most states in the area still suffer wrenching poverty and high unemployment rates. Their average population growth rate is high—2.4% a year. Emigration to the United States, both legal and otherwise, is constant. Even in Cuba, where population growth is slower and Castro's egalitarian policies have softened the worst edges of poverty, it was mainly economic mismanagement and discontent that led to the massive emigration of 1980.

The Postintervention Age

In the decades following the defeat of Spain, the United States began a long succession of military interventions in

Caribbean countries. U.S. troops were stationed repeatedly in Cuba, the Dominican Republic and Haiti to end civil strife, to assure payment of overdue foreign debts (lest European creditors intervene instead) and to support or install governments friendly to the United States. Underlying these immediate purposes were the basic aims of promoting U.S. business interests in the area and preventing any threat to the Panama Canal.

In the decades since World War II, with communism perceived as the chief foe, two such Caribbean ventures have occurred: the disastrous Bay of Pigs proxy invasion in 1961 of Castro's Cuba, and the landing of U.S. Marines in a chaotic Dominican Republic in 1965 to support a junta which had nullified the election of a left-wing government. The latter step, through widely condemned, had a better sequel: a gradual return to democracy, culminating in the accession of the opposition party through a free election in 1978, the first such peaceful changeover in Dominican history.

Today there is little talk of sending U.S. troops into Caribbean countries. Yet U.S. economic and strategic stakes in the region remain substantial. . . .

Cuba: Fight On, or Make Up?

Failing to overthrow Castro, U.S. policy has sought for two decades to isolate and weaken Cuba in order to lessen its influence in and beyond the hemisphere. At times, in frustration, Washington has seemed ready to admit that it cannot contain Castro and may as well bury the hatchet with him. On his side Castro, in economic trouble at home and deeply in hock to his Soviet patron, has repeatedly sought a U.S. reconciliation. But on the terms of a settlement the two sides are still far apart.

Friction with Cuba goes back as far as its independence. To secure U.S. military evacuation after Spain's defeat, Cuba had to concede to the United States the right to intervene unilaterally in Cuba—a right not relinquished until 1934—and to acquire a permanent naval base at Guantánamo Bay. These

and other arrangements made Cuba a virtual U.S. protectorate and gave Cuban nationalism an anti-U.S. tinge—intensi-
fied over time by U.S. support for a succession of dictators. It
was one of these, Fulgencio Batista, whom Fidel Castro overthrew in 1959.

Just how Communist, or subservient to Moscow, Castro's
revolution was at the outset remains to this day a matter of
dispute. But suspicion of him was strong in Washington, and
relations quickly became acrimonious. Castro complained of
U.S. plots to overthrow him. The United States reacted bit-
terly to the nationalization of U.S.-owned businesses in Cuba
and to Castro's opening of diplomatic relations with the Soviet Union—a step few Latin American countries had yet
dared to take. By 1961, the United States had broken diplomatic relations with Havana and imposed a partial trade
embargo, made total in 1963—a heavy blow to the Cuban
economy.

The failure of the CIA-sponsored invasion at the Bay of
Pigs did not end U.S. efforts to bring down the Cuban government. Throughout the 1960s, the CIA covertly trained and
armed hundreds of anti-Castro Cuban exiles to raid the
Cuban coast. Several times it tried to have Castro assassinated. Meanwhile the diplomatic and trade boycott continued.

Far from being cowed, Castro went on the offensive. He
turned to the Soviet Union increasingly for economic and political support. At home, he locked up fellow-revolutionaries
who disagreed with him. Elsewhere in Latin America his
agents did their best to export revolution to the Dominican
Republic, Venezuela and Bolivia. This strategy backfired
when all Latin American countries, except Mexico, followed
the U.S. lead in suspending Cuba from the Organization of
American States (OAS).

By the late 1960s, the quarrel had become a standoff. Castro was now solidly in the Soviet camp, unchallenged at home
and something of a hero in the third world. On the other
hand, the Soviet attempt in 1962 to threaten the United
States with nuclear rockets based in Cuba had ended in a So-

viet backdown. Castro's inept economic system was not working and his attempt to export revolution in the hemisphere had come to a halt with the death of its chief apostle, Ernesto "Che" Guevara. Many Latin Americans began to argue that if the United States could negotiate *détente* with the Soviet Union, they should do the same with Cuba. The OAS diplomatic and economic sanctions against Cuba, already crumbling, were officially relaxed in 1975.

As early as 1974, President Gerald R. Ford launched a dialogue between U.S. and Cuban diplomats looking toward a possible resumption of relations. But in 1975, when 20,000 Cuban troops turned up in Angola to bolster the new Marxist government there, Secretary of State Henry A. Kissinger suspended the talks and refused to resume them until Cuba withdrew its Angola force—which Castro refused to do.

The Carter Administration entered office intending to clean the slate and start over. Goodwill gestures were made on both sides: the Americans halted reconnaissance overflights of Cuba and permitted a resumption of tourist travel; Castro released some political prisoners and scaled down his forces in Angola.

Again, it was a false dawn. In 1978 over 15,000 Cuban troops were sent to Ethiopia as allies of the Soviet power play in that country. Soon other irritants appeared. There were charges, never fully confirmed, of Cuban complicity in a brief invasion of Zaire by Katangan exiles based in Angola. Soviet MIG-23 aircraft—capable, some U.S. experts said, of rapid conversion to carry nuclear weapons—turned up in Cuba.

Then in mid-1979 came the biggest flap of all: U.S. intelligence had discovered what appeared to be a Soviet combat brigade in Cuba. Moscow protested that the unit, in Cuba for years, was there solely to train Cuban troops. Whatever the explanation, President Carter pronounced such a Soviet presence in Cuba "unacceptable," and when no sign appeared that it would be removed, announced certain military precautions including increased surveillance of Cuba and establishment of a U.S. Caribbean Joint Task Force headquarters at Key West. . . .

Normalization: On What Terms?

The goal of U.S.-Cuban normalization holds attractions for both sides, but the problem, as always, is to agree on terms. Officially, the list of issues is the same as it was more than six years ago when the exploratory talks began: ending the U.S. economic embargo; compensation to U.S. companies for expropriated properties; compensation to Cuba for damage suffered at the hands of the CIA; Cuba's demand for the return of Guantánamo; and U.S. concerns about political prisoners in Cuban jails.

In 1980 the mass exodus of Cubans by boat to the United States, reportedly including individuals released by Castro from Cuban jails and mental institutions for the occasion, did nothing to improve the atmosphere. By mid-October, however, Cuba had made several gestures of conciliation, notably the release of some 33 American citizens held in Cuban jails.

None of these questions seems insuperable. Overshadowing the official agenda, however, is the issue that caused Washington to interrupt the normalization talks in the first place: Castro's persistent political and military involvements abroad. His troops and technicians still serve Soviet-backed governments in Africa and as far away as South Yemen; less conspicuously, he supports the rash of revolutionary movements in Central America; now he seems bent on extending his influence in the eastern Caribbean. And in Cuba itself, he continues to accept a Soviet military presence which many Americans, rightly or wrongly, suspect of being aggressive in purpose.

Essentially, the policy issue in regard to normalization lies between those who are in no hurry to normalize until Cuba retreats from all or some of these objectionable policies, and those who hold that U.S. interests call for early normalization in any case. These opposing views can be summarized as follows:

For normalization: The U.S. policy of hostility has failed. Castro has not yielded; instead he and the Cuban people have paid the economic price we exacted. If we want to modify

Cuba's behavior, we are more likely to do so through normal contacts than by pressures that merely arouse Cuban pride. It is the United States, in fact, that is likely to pay the larger cost of continuing to force other countries to choose between us and Cuba. Moreover, some countries aided by Castro, notably Angola and Nicaragua, are by no means necessarily hostile to the United States. Especially in Central America, an outcome acceptable to U.S. interests is more likely if we and Cuba are at least on speaking terms than if we remain opposed.

Viewed affirmatively, normalization would be a way to wean Cuba away from its crippling dependence on the Soviet Union and its commitment to a heavy-handed socialist economy that does not work; to show magnanimity toward Latin American nationalism; to obtain amnesty for political prisoners; and to gain some compensation at last for the U.S. properties seized in 1959.

Against normalization: The U.S. diplomatic and economic boycott of Cuba should continue until Cuba learns not to subvert other countries and ceases to act as a tool of the Soviet Union. The policy of isolating Cuba has *not* failed. Castro's economy is in a shambles, revealed to all the world by the "freedom flotilla" of 1980. His pretensions to third-world leadership have been undercut by his Soviet patron's aggression against Afghanistan, as a result of which the nonaligned nations under Castro's pro-Soviet chairmanship are split wide open and Cuba cannot round up enough third-world votes to win election to the UN Security Council. Incompetent at home and discredited abroad, Castro—or his successor—will have to come to terms with us. We should be in no hurry to reward him for his hostility.

CARIBBEAN ROT[2]

Political infections are like cancer: they creep on unnoticed, appearing here and there, then multiplying and gathering speed until deemed incurable or terminal. In both cases, surgery can work, but only if used in time.

The political infection in the Caribbean area, including the Central American mainland as well as the islands, is well beyond the creeping stage. It is hard to say whether the incurable stage has been reached. One of the most encouraging aspects of a Reagan Administration is the prospect that he would "do something" about the area, and indeed about Latin America as a whole.

A visit to San Juan, Puerto Rico the other day concentrated my mind wonderfully on the galloping infection, which it would be quite wrong to attribute to neglect in Washington when what has been happening has been active encouragement of the germs.

The Nicaragua Model

But then, what else could be expected of an Administration which appointed, as assistant to Andrew Young at the UN, Brady Tyson, the man who publicly apologized for the American role in Vietnam, and a founding member of the pro-Castro North American Congress on Latin America? Or in which the State Department's Policy Planning Department was headed by Anthony Lake, an associate of the International Institute for Strategic Studies of the Council on Foreign Relations?

Nicaragua is not a bad starting point. Now that the Sandinista government is a year old and its political complexion has become clearly visible to the naked eye, there is wry amusement in recalling how often we were told that the San-

[2] Reprint of article by Brian Crozier, British journalist and author, founder of the Institute for the Study of Conflict (London), and contributing editor of *National Review*. *National Review*. 32:1068. S. 5, '80. © 1980, National Review, Inc. Reprinted by permission.

dinista were a broad-minded lot and it was by no means certain that the Castro-oriented Marxists would come out on top. In fact, as my compatriot and colleague Robert Moss pointed out in his London column before the fall of Somoza, the guerrilla war of the Sandinista was conducted from Havana (itself controlled from Moscow). In my experience, Communists do not go to such trouble without, in the end, claiming the dividends on their investment.

The pay-off came earlier this year, when the Frente Sandinista de Liberación Nacional sent a delegation to Moscow where it swiftly concluded a number of deals, not only on a government-to-government basis but also on a party-to-party basis, with the Soviet Communist Party (CPSU). In the Communist world, party-to-party agreements imply ideological approval and are thus intrinsically more important than government-to-government deals.

About the time the Sandinista were coming home, the State Department was figuring out a way to help their government financially—that is, to get around the ban on U.S. aid to Nicaragua enacted when Somoza was still in place. The solution, with White House approval, was to divert $15 million to Nicaragua from general aid funds approved by Congress.

The worrying thing is that, for the best of "human rights" motives, the Administration may end up delivering the governments of Guatemala and El Salvador to the Marxists, despite the example of Nicaragua.

On the eve of his departure, Secretary of State Vance was telling visitors that the American ambassador to El Salvador, Mr. Robert E. White, a strong interventionist, was doing exactly what was needed to help reduce inequality in the country. Some weeks ago, Mr. White, in a speech before the San Salvador American Chamber of Commerce, accused the businessmen of financing "hit squads" to eliminate their political opponents. Such charges are music in the ears of leftist guerrillas.

Mr. Vance was saying at that time that the government of Guatemala was very "regressive" and that social inequality had created an explosive situation.

The "social justice" and "human rights" approach to international relations so often, alas, produces worse social injustice and a deeper denial of human rights. The condition of Cuba today—bankrupt, a tool of Soviet imperialism, disgorging its unwanted citizenry—is a lasting monument to the kind of policy that delivers the helpless masses from the frying pan to the fire.

It is not necessary to praise Somoza's record in social terms to point out that the advent of another Cuba is not the ideal solution. Similarly, it would be hard to argue that either social justice or a betterment of human rights has been achieved in Iran with the downfall (and now the death) of the Shah.

Revolutionary Rumblings

And still the infection spreads. In comparison with most of its neighbors, Costa Rica is (was) both stable and enlightened. Now it harbors a growing Communist infiltration, directly traceable to the Sandinista take-over in Nicaragua.

There is a growing Soviet presence in Panama and ever closer links with Castro. There are revolutionary grumblings in Haiti; in the Dominican Republic (the other half of Hispaniola island), the Communist leader, Isa Conde, is having some success in identifying the Church's calls for land reform with Marxism. Marxist Jamaica, too, like Castro's Cuba, is spewing forth refugees from oppression, unemployment, and a massive dose of socialism.

Puerto Rico, an American oasis in the surrounding Caribbean desert, has its terrorist problem (the Armed Forces of National Liberation), and I was fascinated to read lately in London's Communist *Morning Star* about "the terror and hopes of Puerto Rico." The headline was: "Island under siege for U.S. elections." That was not the way it struck me when I was there; but then, I am not part of the propaganda apparatus of what James Burnham called the "world Communist enterprise."

I don't think President Carter or Secretary of State Muskie is going to do anything about all this. What I do hope is that President Reagan will lose no time in formally denouncing the solemn commitment made by President Kennedy to Nikita Khrushchev at the time of the 1962 missile crisis to desist forevermore from attempting to overthrow Fidel Castro. That, at least, would be a start.

MEXICO: SOCIETY IN TRANSITION[3]

What is the Mexican political regime? It is a wondrously complex, intricate system that has maintained itself in power for the last half century by controlling the terms of political debate, responding to potential challenges with modest reforms, and repressing uncooperative opposition movements. As the institutional heir to the Mexican Revolution of 1910, the current government and its semiofficial party, the Partido Revolucionario Institucional (PRI), have exerted a virtual monopoloy on political power. Presidents rule for nonrenewable six-year terms, during which time they command supreme authority: they possess the final word on all major policy questions, they control vast amounts of patronage, and, despite the limitation on incumbency, they can have enduring influence on the path of national development. There is a constitution, of course, and there are regular elections. There have been political prisoners, a fact the government has often denied, and there have been moments of violent repression. In October 1968 army troops killed approximately 300 participants in a large-scale demonstration in Mexico City, a demonstration that had swelled from a student protest against university policies to a critique of police brutality and finally, as Mexico's Olympic Games approached, to a broad denunciation of social and political inequities. Scores of students

[3] Excerpted from *Mexico: The Quest for a U.S. Policy*, a publication by Peter H. Smith. Foreign Policy Association. '80. p 3–6. Copyright by Foreign Policy Association, Inc. Reprinted by permission. Professor Smith, head of the Department of Humanities at the Massachusetts Institute of Technology and president-elect of the Latin American Studies Association, is the author of numerous works on Latin American political history.

were again shot down by paramilitary thugs in 1971, as police stood casually by, and peasant leaders and labor agitators have mysteriously disappeared from time to time.

There are opposition parties, but at the moment they are fragmented and relatively powerless. For the past 40 years a handful of political parties—principally the Partido de Acción Nacional (PAN), the Partido Popular Socialista (PPS), and the Partido Auténtico de la Revolución Mexicana (PARM)—have provided the regime with loyal, parliamentary dissent: with low-to-miniscule electoral support, their leaders have accepted seats in the congress, criticized occasional decisions (but never the system itself), made frequent deals with the PRI, and, by their mere existence, strengthened the government's claim to popular support and legitimate authority. In recent years a more radical, less collaborationist party movement has appeared. Led by the Partido Comunista Mexicano (PCM) and the Partido Mexicano de los Trabajadores (PMT), a leftist coalition has stressed the unfulfilled hopes of the masses, the long-lost dreams of the Mexican Revolution, and the persistence of injustices, but it has yet to capture a large following (in the 1979 congressional elections, in fact, the coalition obtained just over 5 percent of the vote).

Outside the party structure there have been terrorist movements, both urban and rural, but their importance has diminished since the mid-1970s. Crackdowns and antiguerrilla campaigns by army and police units appear to have subdued such groups.

One of the most pervasive aspects of popular feeling, however, is apathy. Voter turnout in presidential elections ranges from 43 to 69 percent, and as a whole the Mexican people tend to perceive their government as distant, elitist, and self-serving. A sizable share of the populace, perhaps one-quarter to one-third, is underfed, underschooled, underclothed—and so marginal to the political process that it represents, in the phrase of one Mexican sociologist, an "internal colony." Apathy and marginalization do not necessarily constitute a clear and *present* danger to the regime (indeed, they often permit the regime to do what it does), but they offer ominous warnings about the potential for *future* discord and strife.

Two Carrots, Then a Stick

But if the Mexican political system exhibits authoritarian features, it possesses flexibility too. Top-heavy as it is, the PRI is organized around three distinct sectors: one for peasants, one for workers, and one, quixotically called the popular sector, for almost everyone else. This structure provides at least token representation for broad strata of Mexican society, and it helps explain the passive acceptance, if not enthusiastic endorsement, that the regime enjoys among the masses. A steady rotation of political personnel means that new people, some with new ideas, are able to gain access to high office. When signs of discontent appear, Mexico's rulers have frequently co-opted mass leaders by providing them with public positions, further broadening the base of support for the system. And every decade or so, most recently under President López Portillo himself, the system undergoes a period of self-examination that often leads to some kind of reform (in the latest instance, expanding opposition representation in the national Chamber of Deputies to one-quarter of the total seats). The results are less than dramatic, but they affirm the system's basic code, which one close observer has succinctly summarized: two carrots, even three or four, then a stick if necessary.

Such methods demonstrated extraordinary effectiveness in resolving the governmental crises that beset Mexico from the 1910s through the 1960s. The political challenges now looming before the country reflect tremendous social and economic forces, however, and they cannot be met through electoral adjustment and administrative tinkering.

World War II helped inaugurate the pattern of economic growth that has since become known as the Mexican miracle. Loans poured into the country, investment flowed, and, with both the supervision and participation of the state, the gross domestic product (GDP) increased at annual rates of 6 or 7 percent. But not all Mexicans shared in this expansion. By 1969 the top 10 percent of families received 51 percent of the national income, while the bottom half had only 15 percent—and it seems likely that the disproportion worsened in the 1970s. (In the United States, by contrast, the wealthiest 10 percent in 1970 took in about 27.5 percent of the national income, and the bottom half received 26 percent). About 40 percent of Mexico's labor force is underemployed, according to best estimates, causing a degree of social hardship usually associated with an unemployment rate of 20 percent or so—over and above the open unemployment rate of 6 percent in the urban industrial sectors. Laborers struggle for work, peasants clamor for land, one-fifth of the population cannot read or write, and poverty continues to spread in both the cities and the countryside. An especially poignant indicator of social deprivation is the persistence of infant mortality: despite great progress in Mexican medical and public health services, about 55 children out of every 1,000 still die before their first birthday, compared to 15 per 1,000 in the United States.

Especially worrisome for the future is the fact that, due to one of the highest rates of demographic growth in the world, nearly half of Mexico's 68 million people are under the age of 15. To be sure, the annual rate of population growth appears to have slackened in recent years, dropping from 3.5 or 3.6 percent to 2.9 percent or so, and this pattern may continue for some time. No matter what kind of birth control programs start now, however, the age structure of the Mexican population presents a fundamental, unchangeable reality: the pressure for new jobs from now to the end of the century will be immense. There is no convincing sign that Mexican industry, with its tendency to rely on technology instead of labor, will be able to meet this demand.

Stability and Change: a Delicate Balance

These conditions have serious implications for U.S.-Mexican relations. For in dealing with Mexico, we will be dealing with a government simultaneously beset by two kinds of challenges: first, an almost overwhelming set of socioeconomic problems; and second, the long-term need to broaden its own political support. At times these two goals may seem mutually inconsistent, if not downright contradictory. It is frequently argued that dictatorship, either reactionary or revolutionary, constitutes a necessary prerequisite for economic growth or income redistribution, as the examples of Chile and Cuba allegedly attest. To avoid such stark outcomes, Mexican leaders must strike a delicate balance. In order to maintain the peace, to meet the needs of their people, and to improve representation within their political system, they will have to adopt far-reaching, radical-appearing policies. They will continue to feel a patriotic need to protect their country's resources, assert their nation's autonomy, and insist on pursuit of their own interests—especially against pressure from their giant neighbor to the north. And yet, in the process, they will not want to frighten off the U.S. capital and technology they still want for national development. If the Mexicans cannot attain these goals, the choice will be a most unpleasant one: either a major upheaval from below, or, more probably, an increase in repression and perhaps even the implantation of a military dictatorship.

FIRE STORM IN CENTRAL AMERICA[4]

In the scales of geopolitics, the six small republics along the narrow land bridge between North and South America do not weigh very much. For the mighty United States they have been important mainly for the Panama Canal, built (1904–14) as the world's shortcut between the Atlantic and Pacific oceans but now of diminished strategic significance; for exports of, and U.S. investment in, such commodities as cotton, coffee, bananas and beef; and for delightful places to go on a

[4] Excerpted from *Great Decisions '81*, a book by the Editors of the Foreign Policy Association. Foreign Policy Association. '81. p 44–7. © Copyright, 1981, Foreign Policy Association, Inc. Reprinted by permission.

vacation. Of their history, and the life of their 22 million inhabitants, most North Americans have remained largely ignorant.

It was imperial Spain that first subdued the aboriginal peoples of Central America. For three centuries beginning in the early 1500s, Spanish kings ruled over them through royal governors and captains general. This period ended with the collapse of the Spanish empire in the Americas after the Napoleonic Wars. Panama then became part of Colombia (remaining so until its independence in 1903, a step promoted by President Theodore Roosevelt as a stratagem to prepare for the building of the Panama Canal). The remainder of the region, first a part of newly independent Mexico, settled down after much strife as five separate republics.

All six countries inherit from their colonial past the Spanish language, the Catholic religion, and a tendency for people of European ancestry to dominate the political scene at the expense of the more numerous people of Indian, African or mixed race. And all except relatively prosperous and democratic Costa Rica—the only country of the region virtually free of such ethnic divisions—have seen their republican institutions lapse repeatedly into dictatorship.

A Legacy of U.S. Intervention

Increasingly through the late 19th century and into the 20th, Central America—as well as the Caribbean—fell under the shadow of the growing power of the United States. It was the site of the strategic Panama Canal, completed in 1914, and a target of increasing U.S. business investment. Both factors gave the United States an interest in the region's political stability. But stability proved hard to attain, what with repeated civil wars, boundary wars and unpaid foreign debts.

It was then that the term gunboat diplomacy entered the language to describe U.S. policies in the area. In 1904 Roosevelt, who advised the nation to "speak softly and carry a big stick," propounded the Roosevelt Corollary to the Monroe Doctrine, asserting the right to send U.S. armed forces to collect foreign debts owed by any country of the hemisphere. Acting on this principle, Washington during the succeeding quarter-century sent its military forces repeatedly into countries of Central America and the Caribbean when instability threatened U.S. interests.

In Central America, the big stick fell most heavily on turbulent and debt-ridden Nicaragua. There U.S. Marines were landed in 1912 at the request of a pro-U.S. government, and remained with one brief respite until 1933. Under what amounted to a U.S. protectorate, order was maintained, debts were settled and economic growth resumed. But the new stability was not for long. In the mid-1920s a populist and nationalist force under General Augusto César Sandino launched a guerrilla war against the regime. In 1933, with the Marines gone at last, Sandino made peace with the government, receiving a grant of amnesty and land for his followers. A year later, Sandino was shot dead by members of the national guard—on direct orders, many authorities believe, of the then minister of war and later dictator and friend of the United States, General Anastasio Somoza.

This story of betrayal is burned into the memories of the guerrilla fighters who fought and won in the 1970s in a brutal struggle against the dictatorship of the second Anastasio Somoza, son of the first. To them the United States was the patron of their oppressors, while Sandino is a hero and martyr—his name perpetuated in the name of their movement, the Sandinist National Liberation Front (FSLN).

The record of U.S. intervention has fluctuated in Central America since the 1930s. President Franklin D. Roosevelt's Good Neighbor Policy, announced in 1933, was intended to put an end to the era of the big stick. The policy endured through World War II, when nearly all of Latin America supported the United States. But the cold war in the 1950s brought a revival of U.S. intervention in other forms. In Central America it had its most dramatic expression in Guatemala, where a freely elected left-wing government was overthrown in 1954 by an invading force masterminded by the U.S. Central Intelligence Agency (CIA). In the 1960s, with Castro eager to export his new revolution, counterinsurgency programs, with arms and military advisers supplied by the United States, were mounted by all the military dictatorships or political oligarchies that ruled most of Central America. Meanwhile the social and economic reforms that had been a central concept of President John F. Kennedy's Alliance for Progress failed to take root for lack of support.

The resulting situation raised awkward questions for U.S. policy. The governments of Central America remained so self-consciously dependent on the power and favor of the United States that as late as 1977 a newly arrived U.S. ambassador in Nicaragua was startled to find the Nicaraguan army "saluting the American ambassador as if he were a proconsul." To maintain themselves in power, some of these same governments—in Nicaragua most of all—were using U.S. weapons to commit flagrant violations of the rights of their own peoples.

In the 1970s, U.S. support of repressive governments began to draw increasing protests from Americans. Soon Congress put restrictions on aid to governments with the worst records of political torture and murder. In 1977 Carter, elected partly on his pledge to promote universal human rights, sought a region where a crackdown on human rights violators would not endanger U.S. security interests. One relatively safe region seemed to be Central America. The governments of El Salvador, Guatemala and Nicaragua came under direct U.S. pressure to improve their human rights performance.

Eruption in Nicaragua

The most consequential result, far from what the policymakers had intended, occurred in Nicaragua: a speedup in the developing confrontation between the Somoza regime and the radical, Marxist-leaning FSLN. Somoza, bowing to U.S. pressure, restored press freedom. The press responded with stinging criticism of official corruption. In revenge, the leading opposition editor, Pedro Joaquin Chamorro, was assassinated in January 1978 by gunmen widely believed to be acting for Somoza. Amid public outrage over that incident, FSLN-organized uprisings broke out in one city after another and were unmercifully suppressed by Somoza's forces.

The civil war was on. Washington, writes Latin America scholar William M. LeoGrande, found itself "caught in the pull of opposing imperatives"—its support of human rights and "the political stability long provided by a brutal but reliable ally." Amid fears lest the Sandinist alternative might become "another Cuba," U.S. policy vacillated between supporting Somoza and trying to ease him out in favor of a government of moderates. But the moderates lacked political strength. Events overtook this makeshift policy, and Somoza was driven from power by a coalition dominated by the FSLN but including some of the moderates the United States had favored.

The months of frantic maneuvering came to an end with the triumph of the revolution in July 1979. During the crisis, U.S. diplomats, leery of locking themselves in with a dying dictatorship, had opened lines of communication to the opposition, and had obtained from the new junta a pledge of respect for human rights. Washington resolved that, whatever suspicions it might harbor about Sandinist radicalism, the United States would seek cordial relations if Nicaragua would. For their part, the victorious junta seemed anxious to stay on good terms with the United States, hoping for U.S. help in rebuilding their wartorn country.

The Carter Administration lost little time in making its case for U.S. aid. "By extending our friendship and economic assistance," said Secretary of State Cyrus R. Vance to a Foreign Policy Association audience in New York in fall 1979, "we enhance the prospects for democracy in Nicaragua. We cannot guarantee that democracy will take hold there. But if we turn our backs on Nicaragua, we can almost guarantee that democracy will fail." A highly controversial request for $75 million in aid to Nicaragua inched its way through the congressional labyrinth and won by a narrow vote in May— with a proviso that the President must first certify that Nicaragua was not supporting terrorism in other countries. The

State Department and U.S. military intelligence experts promptly disagreed on whether or not Nicaragua was living up to the stipulation. In July, in an interim gesture of friendship, a U.S. delegation led by Ambassador to the United Nations Donald F. McHenry joined in the revolution's first anniversary festivities in Managua. In mid-September the required presidential certification was finally made.

By then the issue had been swept up in the presidential campaign. The Republican party platform called for a cutoff of aid to Nicaragua. U.S. aid, its advocates argued, could influence the Nicaraguans in the direction of pluralism, while refusing it could drive them into the arms of Castro and his Soviet patrons. Conservatives replied that the new regime in Nicaragua is openly Marxist and immune to U.S. influence. Political observers predicted that, whoever won the presidency, the battle would be joined again in Congress in 1981.

Central American Dominoes?

The Nicaraguan revolution set in motion a full-scale review of U.S. policy toward the whole Central American region. Priority attention went to El Salvador and Guatemala, already approaching the boiling point.

In El Salvador, it was none too soon. In October 1979, alarmed by the Nicaraguan events and by rising insurgency in their own country, a junta of Salvadoran colonels and civilians ousted the country's right-wing military dictator. With U.S. and Venezuelan encouragement, the junta instituted a sweeping land reform designed to take the wind out of the sails of the radical left. By the fall of 1980 the reforms, extended to nearly a million peasants, had seriously undercut the left-wing guerrillas—but also pushed hard-line conservatives inside and outside the government into violent opposition. The junta, shedding its reformist complexion, picked up some key business support and strove to maintain a fragile center-right coalition against both extremes. But violence still flared both from the guerrillas and from right-wing "hit squads," and the number of Salvadorans killed by the army in

1980 rose to an estimated 7,000. El Salvador seemed still in danger of sliding into full-scale war.

Next door in Guatemala, Mexico's neighbor and historically the chief power of Central America, the story was depressingly similar—except that here nobody had been able to devise a middle-ground stategy. In a nation of exteme contrasts between a ruling class of rich landowners and entrepreneurs and an Indian underclass—almost half the whole population—that lives in grinding poverty, political violence has been endemic since the U.S.-sponsored coup of 1954. Since the Nicaraguan revolution, according to Alan Riding of *The New York Times*, significant numbers of the traditionally passive Indians have begun to fight alongside a fragile coalition of left-wing and politically moderate groups against the regime and its American-trained forces. Political murders and reprisals are increasingly common on both sides. "Guatemala," wrote the U.S. ambassador . . . [in June 1980], "is a bloodbath waiting to happen." Under U.S. pressure, the military government of General Romeo Lucas García last year started a few highly visible public works in Indian provinces, but the main strategy seemed to be to ignore the Carter Administration and lobby for a Reagan victory in the U.S. elections—then, if Reagan should win, seek U.S. military aid against the insurgents. Meanwhile the mutual killings went on in both city and countryside and no middle ground was in sight. "What we'd give to have an Arbenz now," said one U.S. official, referring to the populist president whose overthrow Washington had engineered in 1954.

Where, in this turbulent region, might U.S. policy help to build a backfire against extremism? If Nicaragua's revolution can keep and strengthen its seemingly moderate posture, that might be the place. Costa Rica, a relatively prosperous democracy, is too untypical of the region to be a model for the others, though its cooperation is valued on regional problems. Perhaps the best choice of the moment, suggests historian Richard Millett in a 1980 article in *Foreign Policy* quarterly, is Honduras, the poorest and least-developed nation of the region, still relatively untroubled by left-wing violence but by no means immune to it. Following a 1980 election in which the ruling military party lost, the country was preparing to return to civilian rule. It is a key moment, Millett suggests, to offer highly visible development aid such as a national literacy program—almost half the nation's 3.6 million people cannot read—and to press for wider political participation. [See the following selection.—Ed.]

Central America: U.S. Options

Sketched below are arguments for and against four broad directions which U.S. policy toward Central America could take in the years ahead. Since conditions vary from country to country, the U.S. response may likewise vary; but the broad thrust of policy is what counts most.

1. *Hold the middle ground.* This is the strategy most congenial to U.S. ideals of pluralism and tolerance. The aim is to dampen revolutionary violence and undercut the extreme left and extreme right through timely reforms. If successful, this policy would create the best conditions for both civil liberties and private enterprise to flourish. But the political situation in much of Central America is already so polarized that moderate governments, as in El Salvador, are likely to find their reforms sabotaged and their power destroyed by extemists of both right and left. Thus a heavy investment in this strategy would be a major gamble—except perhaps in a country like Honduras where political polarization is not far advanced.

2. *Work with the left wing.* This is the policy which Washington ended up adopting in Nicaragua when the Sandinist victory became inevitable. It means cooperating with governments and political groups which are predominantly leftist or Marxist wherever their eventual victory appears probable. Its aims would be to help such regimes through difficult years of social transformation; to influence them toward tolerance of individual rights and respect for U.S. interests; and to reduce their dependence on powers hostile to this country. Advocates see in this policy the best chance to serve U.S. interests in the long term. Opponents see it as a sellout to the Marxist enemy.

? *Crush Marxism.* This approach would jettison U.S. sup-
‸ˑ˙˙ and social reform as an unaffordable
‿ ˙˙‿ aid for the surviving
la and Hon-
ild have the
al interests.
s country on
ighout Cen-

ction is a de-
al American
of some ob-
t. Only time
a the regimes
e notion that
of history in
anyway. Fi-
artments and
mbering to be
however, can
vhen its ideals
and interests aˑ‿ ‿‿

[handwritten call numbers on overlaid card:]
F 1402 .S53   F 1418 .C613   F 1418 .57

CENTRAL AMERICAN PARALYSIS[5]

U.S. efforts to respond to revolutionary change in Central
America resemble those of a fire brigade during the London
blitz. American officials rush frantically from place to place,
trying to contain the damage and save what they can of existing structures. But they seem unable to deal with the basic
sources of their troubles. Problems abound: an incipient civil
war in El Salvador, a flailing economy and a Marxist-in-

[5] Reprint of article by Richard Millett, professor of history at Southern Illinois University at Edwardsville. *Foreign Policy.* no 39, p 99–117. Summer '80. Reprinted with permission from *Foreign Policy* magazine #39 (Summer 1980), Copyright 1980 by the Carnegie Endowment for International Peace.

fluenced government in Nicaragua, increased political violence in Guatemala, and lagging economic and political development in Honduras and Costa Rica. To forge a policy capable of dealing with Central America, the United States
must drastically revise its approach to the region.

When Jimmy Carter took office, any suggestion that Central American affairs would emerge as the primary U.S. policy
concern in Latin America would have seemed absurd. Since
the 1954 Central Intelligence Agency-sponsored overthrow
of Guatemala's left-leaning government, the United States
has largely ignored Central America. The important canal
treaty negotiations with Panama received some attention, but
Panama has few historic ties with Central America, and the
State Department does not group Panamanian relations with
Central American affairs.

The Office of Inter-American Affairs was in fact a State
Department backwater, usually manned by undistinguished
individuals with little, if any, experience in the area. Political
upheavals, such as the 1969 Honduran-Salvadorian war, or
natural disasters, such as the Nicaraguan and Guatemalan
earthquakes, invoked occasional flurries of activity. But for
the most part, U.S.–Central American relations were simple
and controlled. If any region could have been safely ignored
by the United States in early 1977, it was probably Central
America.

Both economic and political realities supported this assumption. With underdeveloped, basically agricultural economies, the five small countries and their 20 million inhabitants hardly threatened U.S. interests. The total area of
Central America is just over 163,000 square miles; the republics range in size from Nicaragua (57,200 square miles, about
the size of Iowa) to El Salvador (8,100 square miles, just larger
than New Jersey). Guatemala has the largest population (6.9
million), followed by El Salvador (4.5 million), Honduras (3.6
million), Nicaragua (2.6 million), and Costa Rica (2.2 million).

The republics are poor relative to the United States: Costa
Rica, the most prosperous of the Central American states, had
a gross domestic product (GDP) per capita estimated at only

$1,540 in 1978; Honduras, with a 1978 GDP of $480 per capita, was the poorest. The prime exports of Central America—cotton, coffee, bananas, and meat—could be easily obtained elsewhere. The Panama Canal's declining importance to U.S. policy and scheduled transfer to Panama diminish the area's strategic significance.

Central American politics were equally unobtrusive. In the three northern republics—Honduras, Guatemala, and El Salvador—pro-Western military dominated the governments; in Nicaragua a 40-year-old family dynasty seemed firmly entrenched: and in Costa Rica, which had no army, democracy seemed to be flourishing. All five nations usually supported the United States in international forums. None had formal relations with Cuba or China. Only Costa Rica, after long debate, had established diplomatic relations with the Soviet Union.

The American Proconsul

While the United States gave low priority to Central American affairs, Central American leaders devoted much of their energy to predicting, interpreting, and adapting to U.S. goals and interests. This subordination placed American ambassadors in the region in a very special and, at times, awkward position. Their traditional role was described in a 1927 State Department memorandum by then Under Secretary of State Robert Olds:

Our ministers accredited to the five little republics, stretching from the Mexican border to Panama . . . have been advisers whose advice has been accepted virtually as law in the capitals where they respectively reside. . . . We do control the destinies of Central America and we do so for the simple reason that the national interest absolutely dictates such a course. . . . Until now Central America has always understood that governments which we recognize and support stay in power, while those we do not recognize and support fall.

Dr. Mauricio Solaun, U.S. ambassador to Nicaragua from 1977 to 1979, found that Nicaraguans, at least, partially retained this perspective, with the army even "saluting the American ambassador as if he were a proconsul." Ironically, it was in Nicaragua that the U.S. loss of power in Central America first became evident.

Shortly after taking office, Carter pressured the regime of Nicaraguan dictator Anastasio Somoza Debayle and the military governments of El Salvador and Guatemala for improvements in human rights and expansion of political freedoms. In El Salvador and Guatemala, the most visible result was the angry cancellation of military assistance pacts with the United States. Somoza responded with cosmetic changes that elicited a complimentary letter from Carter in summer 1978; but when revolution broke out, Somoza abandoned all pretense of reform and returned to brute force to maintain his dictatorship.

To the surprise of virtually every politician and military officer in Central America, Somoza defied subsequent U.S. pressure to give up the presidency. Unwilling to resort to force, U.S. policy drifted for several months while Venezuela, Panama, and Costa Rica increased their support for the revolutionary Sandinistas.

The extent to which the United States had lost control over Central America became evident when the Sandinistas began their final offensive in late spring 1979. Not a single Central American nation supported the Carter administration's proposal for sending an inter-American peace force to Nicaragua. When the United States then approved an Organization of American States resolution calling for the replacement of Somoza with a totally new government, only Costa Rica, among the Central American republics, voted with the United States.

By mid-July 1979, when Somoza fled to Miami and control of the nation passed to the Marxist-influenced Sandinista Liberation Front, old patterns of U.S.-Nicaraguan relations— and therefore U.S.–Central American relations—were destroyed. The heritage of U.S. supremacy collapsed with Somoza.

Nicaragua—once a kingpin of American operations in

Central America—was now warmly disposed toward Cuba, deeply suspicious of the United States, and committed to radical change at home and a nonaligned position abroad. Within Central America, the Sandinista triumph frightened conservatives, who in turn directed sharp expressions of anger at the Carter administration. Facing growing, increasingly violent opposition from the left, military governments in El Salvador and Guatemala feared that Nicaragua would provide inspiration and arms to revolutionary groups at home. Honduras, where thousands of Somoza's troops had fled for refuge, faced the possibility of serious clashes along its long, poorly defended border with Nicaragua. Increased conflict seemed certain in Central America. The State Department was forced to begin developing a new policy in the midst of spreading turmoil.

Lost Credibility

At this point, U.S. influence in Central America was at its lowest level in this century. Carter's human rights policy and his refusal to intervene to prevent a Sandinista victory confused and alienated much of the right, including the military, but failed to diminish the suspicions and hostility of the left. Moderate reformists, such as Christian Democratic and Social Democratic parties, appeared to be losing ground as forces became increasingly polarized. Decimation of their leadership by ultrarightist hit squads further compounded their problems.

Inability to control violence and contain Marxist influence in a region only two hours flying time from Miami contributed to an image of U.S. weakness in dealing with Central America in particular and the Third World in general. While most U.S. officials involved with Latin America policy recognized the urgency of formulating an effective program for Central America, their ability to do so had been consistently constrained by domestic and foreign political realities. There was no quick or cheap way to overcome 25 years of neglect or to restore the credibility lost during the Nicaraguan crisis.

High-level administrative attention to the region was easily diverted by problems in areas of greater strategic significance, such as the Persian Gulf; and the willingness of Congress to appropriate significant funds for any effort in Central America was questionable at best.

In formulating a response to Central America's new political environment, the Carter administration had three basic options. It could decide that the costs of attempting to reverse the revolutionary process so outweighed the region's actual worth that the United States should withdraw and, at least for the present, allow events to run their course. Fear of domestic political consequences should a second or third Cuba emerge mitigated strongly against this option. Or, the United States could help prop up existing governments with military assistance and support. This would mean abandoning the human rights content of Latin America policy and would require isolating and perhaps even trying to reverse the revolutionary process in Nicaragua. A possible upshot would be U.S. military intervention.

The final option was to promote and identify with the process of basic change within the region, hoping at the same time to preserve a fair degree of political and economic pluralism. While discarding the traditional client-state approach to Central America, this option would actively seek to restore a modicum of U.S. influence and insure that none of the republics became dependent upon nations hostile to U.S. interests.

With little public debate, the Carter administration apparently chose the last option. Then Assistant Secretary of State for Inter-American Affairs Viron P. Vaky summarized this approach in September 1979 testimony before the House Foreign Affairs Committee:

. . . Defense of the status quo will not avoid change; it will only radicalize it. . . . Failure on our part to identify with the legitimate aspiration of the people in these countries, and with those democratic elements who seek peaceful, constructive change, respect for human rights and basic equity will put us on the wrong side of history.

Our task therefore is how to work with our friends to guide and influence change, how to use our influence to promote justice, freedom and equity to mutual benefit—and thereby avoid insurgency and Communism. Nowhere will this task be more crucial than in Nicaragua.

Unfortunately, attempts to implement this approach have thus far failed. Administration efforts to restore credibility to U.S. policies and stability to Central America have been consistently overtaken by events or undermined by congressional budget cuts. This has been most notable in El Salvador, Central America's smallest nation.

Assaults and Kidnappings

Since the early 1930s, the armed forces have dominated Salvadorian politics. As the population density of this agricultural nation increased, pressures for basic social and economic reforms mounted. Urged on by the handful of powerful families that controlled the economy, the military responded by using massive fraud to deny the moderate Christian Democrats victory in the 1972 elections. Throughout the 1970s the government encouraged the rise of right-wing, paramilitary groups that terrorized peasant and labor organizations, destroyed the Christian Democratic party's infrastructure in the countryside, and even murdered socially active priests. These events, in turn, led to the steady growth of armed, radical forces on the left that financed their efforts through spectacular assaults and kidnappings. By fall 1979 the nation seemed on the verge of civil war.

Encouraged by the United States, younger army officers ousted the hard-line military government in October 1979 and replaced it with a military-civilian junta. Their proclaimed advocacy of democratic reforms attracted strong U.S. support. Caught between violence from both right and left the new regime never gained full control of internal politics. The first junta collapsed in January 1980 when its civilian members quit in protest of military opposition to basic reforms.

Christian Democratic participation in a second junta led to a split within that party. Nationalization of banks, adoption of a new labor code, and promulgation of a far-sweeping agrarian reform law have failed to appease left-wing opposition and have infuriated powerful forces on the right. Only strong, direct pressure from the United States prevented a February 1980 countercoup by angry conservatives. By spring 1980 El Salvador was clearly in danger of drifting into civil war, a process accelerated by the brutal murder of Archbishop Oscar Arnulfo Romero, a heroic spokesman for justice for most Salvadorians.

While not as dramatic, events in the rest of the isthmus have been almost as frustrating for American policy makers. Guatemala, where internal violence has escalated considerably in the past few months, is a case in point. For well over a decade, bloody conflicts between left-wing guerrillas and government troops—supplemented by private far-right terrorist organizations such as the Mano Blanca—have been a recurrent facet of Guatemalan life. By 1979 murders of moderate and leftist political leaders had become so common that even Vice President Francisco Villagrán Kramer declared that "death or exile is the fate of those who struggle for justice in Guatemala."

Three factors have helped the right maintain control of Guatemala. While the population is the largest in Central America, nearly half of Guatemala's citizens are Indians, traditionally outside of active politics and impervious to appeals from the left. Furthermore, Guatemala's Central American neighbors, El Salvador and Honduras, also were under firm military control, insulating Guatemala from external subversion. Finally, high coffee prices and conservative economic policies produced a strong economy that reduced middle-class discontent. The recent growth in domestic petroleum production, which could enable Guatemala to reach self-sufficiency in a few years, contributes to the financial well-being of the country.

In the past year, the first two factors have changed considerably, thereby threatening economic stability. For the first time, substantial elements of the Indian population have shown signs of supporting and even joining the guerrillas. In March 1980 a confrontation between stone-throwing Indian women and army troops resulted in the machine-gunning of several women and the bitter condemnation of the army by the normally conservative bishop of El Quiché. Growing opposition has undermined control of two heavily populated highlands departments, Huehuetenango and El Quiché, and has produced a sharp drop in army morale.

The turmoil in El Salvador has created acute anxiety over regional stability, leading many Guatemalan officers to talk openly about staving off subversion at home by fighting revolution in El Salvador. Also, the dispute between Guatemala and Great Britain over governing rights of the small Central American territory of Belize has increased regional tension. To date, mounting problems in Guatemala have precluded any intervention, but right-wing groups have funneled aid to their Salvadorian counterparts.

Frustrated and angered, the Guatemalan right has purchased full-page advertisements in local newspapers to denounce what they view as a weak U.S. policy that encourages left-wing uprisings and to charge members of the Salvadorian junta with membership in the Communist party. Rumors of a possible coup by the far right within the military have begun to circulate. But nothing is likely to happen before the U.S. presidential elections in November: Many right-wing Guatemalan politicians and military officers fervently hope for a victory by Republican candidate Ronald Reagan, believing this would remove U.S. opposition to their continuing or even escalating violent repression of the left.

Honduras and Costa Rica have escaped the violence and polarization found in the other nations, but both are plagued by accelerating inflation, mounting labor troubles, and weak political leadership. Prospects for stability in Honduras, Central America's least-developed nation, are further clouded by strong public resentment of the flagrant corruption in the higher military ranks. This outlook is somewhat offset by the surprisingly honest results of the April 1980 Constituent

Assembly elections. Although left-wing parties were excluded, the Liberal party defeated the military's traditional ally, the National party, and initiated a return to civilian rule. Overall, the mixture of reform and corruption makes difficult a balanced U.S. response.

Costa Rica's democratic traditions and its relatively advanced social programs help insulate it from the region's violence, but the consumerist orientation of its increasingly middle-class society makes it especially vulnerable to mounting economic problems. Those problems could reverse the usually cordial U.S.–Costa Rican relations.

Frenetic Search

Events beyond Central America also hamper efforts to forge an effective policy. Historically, the United States has not given consistent attention to the problems of small, poor nations. Many Costa Ricans saw the U.S. actions in the controversy over tuna-fishing rights as demonstration that the United States is more concerned with the interests of a few Californian fishermen than it is with the well-being and dignity of a small, democratic ally.

Crises in more vital areas divert American attention and resources and diminish any sense of urgency. Currently, Iran and Afghanistan overshadow Central America; they also reduce U.S. tolerance of foreign attacks on past American policies and promote domestic acceptance of possible U.S. military intervention. The priority given to issues in the 1980 U.S. elections further obscures efforts to develop a consistent Central American policy.

Establishing a responsive American policy is complicated by the [Carter] administration's frequent inability to deliver promised aid. Nicaragua is a case in point. Despite efforts by Ambassador Lawrence A. Pezzullo and his staff, attempts to moderate the course of Nicaragua's revolution have enjoyed only limited success. A key element of the American approach was to be the demonstration that the United States could not only tolerate but also could actually support basic social and economic changes in Nicaragua. This required combining verbal assurances of support with significant amounts of reconstruction assistance. Other nations, notably Venezuela, Panama, and Costa Rica, were counted upon to promote political pluralism and reduce potential Cuban influence.

The initial scenario was optimistic. Congress quickly approved the reprogramming of over $8 million in emergency aid for Nicaragua. Other nations offered substantial credits, and multilateral agencies, such as the Inter-American Development Bank (IDB), began processing major new loans.

The recent situation is less hopeful. Rebuffed in initial efforts to moderate the revolution, Costa Rica, Panama, and to a lesser extent, Venezuela have reduced involvement in Nicaragua. The processing of IDB and other multilateral loans has slowed dramatically. U.S. government efforts to provide a $75 million aid package have been cramped by a seemingly endless series of congressional roadblocks. Originally projected for late 1979, this package has been the subject of sharp debate; amendments, highly objectionable to Nicaragua, have been added to the authorization bill. Finally, the entire appropriation has been further delayed by the congressional mood of budget slashing.

These setbacks contributed to growing demoralization within Nicaragua's private sector and increased suspicion among the Sandinista leadership that the United States will never really support a revolutionary regime in Central America. As a U.S. diplomat in Managua recently observed, "We could have done so much with that money just a few months ago, but we've wasted our best opportunities in this country."

Costa Rican political leader Rodrigo Madrigal Nieto suggests the creation of a mini-Marshall Plan for Central America. Current U.S. aid to the region now totals just over $100 million annually. Nieto's proposal would cost about $1 billion more a year. Given the high level of U.S. expenditures abroad, that increase is relatively modest. American election-year politics, however, preclude any move in this direction before 1981. Instead, the Carter administration promotes the newly founded Caribbean–Central American Action, a program headed by Governor Bob Graham of Florida and designed to enlist private support for the region. While the Action program might produce limited benefits for Costa Rica and perhaps Honduras, it is unlikely that private investors will respond generously to the current, unstable conditions in the other three republics. In the absence of any joint executive-congressional commitment, the confusion and resentment generated by U.S. efforts in Central America will likely continue.

The result is a chaotic American policy. U.S. programs in Central America are inconsistent, confused, and indecisive. Statements of policy and expressions of concern lack credibility. The repeated visits by Assistant Secretary of State for Inter-American Affairs William Bowdler are perceived more as frenetic searches for a way out of crises than as any indication of serious, long-range interest in the area's problems. Many Central American moderates feel that the United States takes their problems seriously only when they begin killing one another in the streets.

Washington's Dilemma

Recent events raise the critical but uncomfortable question of what the United States should do if a moderate response becomes impossible. That point was reached in Nicaragua in June 1979, but the State Department continued to advocate a moderate compromise until Somoza fled to Miami. The approach only exacerbated the problem of diminishing American credibility. A similar point may be rapidly approaching in El Salvador. By supporting the current junta as the only alternative to violent civil conflict, the Carter administration is identifying with social and economic policies well to the left of any previously espoused by the United States in that part of the world. Yet the Salvadorian far left continues to denounce U.S. policy.

Part of the American dilemma stems from lack of experience in mediating between moderate regimes and radical opposition. Whereas the United States has successfully resolved disputes between moderates and conservatives, as in the Dominican Republic in 1978, American intervention in conflicts such as the current one in El Salvador demands a new kind of diplomacy. Furthermore, as many Salvadorians repeatedly point out, foreign intervention in such conflicts usually accelerates the polarization process and ultimately drives both the home government and the outside power toward the right. Despite these difficulties, standing aside and letting events run their course is politically unacceptable to the Carter administration—especially given the possibility that the result might be an anti-American, Marxist regime.

In the past, the United States counted on Central American armies to defend American interests in that region. The history of U.S. military influence in Central America is long, and the ties are intimate. Paradoxically, in every Central American country except Costa Rica, which abolished its army over 30 years ago, the military has become a major problem for American policy making.

No army in Latin America had more officers and men trained in U.S. military schools, and none had a closer relationship with the United States than did Nicaragua's National Guard. Yet the guard became the corrupt instrument of the Somoza family. Its brutality drove thousands of Nicaraguans to join the Sandinistas, and its internal weaknesses ultimately led to its total destruction. Such an outcome surely challenges the rationale for American training and support of other nations' armed forces, especially now that El Salvador's security troops—once again, groomed by the United States—are threatened with a similar fate.

The U.S. government's proposals for supporting the Salvadorian junta include a request for increased military assistance, notably a $5.7 million package for improvements in training, transportation, and communications. This proposal invoked considerable criticism, including a letter to Carter from the late Archbishop Romero, who claimed that such assistance "instead of favoring greater justice and peace in El Salvador, undoubtedly will sharpen . . . the repression."

In Guatemala and Honduras, conditions within the armed forces pose similar challenges for U.S. policy makers. In both countries, hopes for peaceful reforms in human rights and political freedoms require the acquiescence, if not the active support, of the military. In each nation significant segments of the officer corps, especially at junior levels, are sympathetic to such changes. But the higher ranking officers seem allied with the oligarchy and, in Guatemala, committed to a policy of brutal repression that ultimately alienates the armed forces from the general population. Corruption is most visible in Honduras, where every area commander recently received a Rolex watch and a Mercedes Benz. Again, it is difficult to see how efforts by an external power can deal effectively with such problems.

U.S.-sponsored training programs could educate officers on how corruption and popular alienation eventually destroyed the pre-1959 Cuban army and the Nicaraguan National Guard, but in the immediate future there is little the United States can do beyond encouraging these forces to reform themselves. Until this happens, American support for these armies only associates the United States with repression and brutality.

From the standpoint of American policy, the essential question in Central America is whether the United States can live with and perhaps even support revolution in its own back yard. Although the United States accommodated nations such as Mexico, the traditional answer in Central America has been a firm no. The Carter administration indicates a willingness to change this response, but with qualifications: only if Cuban influence is limited; only if an unspecified amount of pluralism is allowed; and only if each Central American country refrains from involvement in its neighbor's politics.

An Avenue of Escape

Remaining unspecified is what the American response could or should be if those guidelines are ignored and if revolution—particularly revolution directed against unpopular, repressive, military regimes—spreads throughout the region. Being forced to choose between acceptance of control over much of Central America by hostile forces and open intervention by American troops is the ultimate nightmare of American policy makers. While either option entails disastrous political consequences, current international and domestic political trends may tip the balance toward intervention. It might be impossible to find any effective option between doing nothing and sending in the Marines.

A concerned State Department recently tried to defuse the issue. In his April 8, 1980, speech on Central America, Bowdler pointedly remarked that "we will not use military force in situations where only domestic groups are in contention." This, however, leaves open the possibility of U.S. military intervention in response to perceived involvement by Cuba or any other outside power.

One possible avenue of escape from this dilemma would be to seek major involvement by others, such as Venezuela, Mexico, Western Europe, and even Japan, in efforts to stabilize and develop Central America. The U.S. government has already moved in this direction. Testifying before the Senate Foreign Relations Committee last December, Deputy Secretary of State Warren Christopher declared: "We need to try to find out how the Latin Americans think we should address the problems of Central America and their own problems. We don't approach it on a U.S.-dominated or know-it-all basis. I think that is a fundamental change in our attitude toward Central and South America."

Unfortunately, U.S. consultations with other countries on Central American problems are no more credible than direct U.S. relations with that region. Seeing little evidence of long-range planning or of a meaningful financial commitment and having no interest in overt association with frantic U.S. efforts at crisis management, most nations avoid direct involvement in the face of Central America's mounting turmoil.

Mexico has joined with its northern neighbor in support of the new Nicaraguan government but has criticized the U.S. position in El Salvador, where Mexican sympathies seem to

lie with the left. Venezuela has been more directly involved
with Central America, but U.S. efforts to coordinate policies
with the administration of President Luis Herrera Campins
are complicated by Herrera's close ties with the area's Christian Democratic parties. The United States is already suspected of favoring small parties of this type and cannot afford
any closer links with a single minority political faction.

In Congress there is widespread consensus on the bank-
ruptcy of traditional policies toward Central America. Senator Edward Zorinsky (D.-Nebraska), chairman of the Subcommittee on Western Hemisphere Affairs of the Senate
Foreign Relations Committee declared that in dealing with
the area, "the fundamental mistake we make . . . is to back
governments or regimes which enjoy little or no popular support."

A similar stand was taken by Senator David Durenberger
(R.-Minnesota), who told the Senate Foreign Relations Committee that U.S. policy in Central America had "too long
been characterized by inattention, ignorance, a lack of concern, and a blind acceptance of the status quo." Durenberger
added that "we have frequently mistaken the support of governments for the friendship of populations while many people
in these regions have labored under the twin burdens of repression and poverty."

It is easier to recognize past mistakes than to correct
them. A turnaround in U.S. policy requires positive commitment rather than continual obsession with fears of domestic
political embarrassment and expanded Cuban influence. The
current attitude produces a policy that is perceived as a holding action, designed to slow the rate of change but incapable
of affecting the nature of that change. This type of policy
generates little enthusiasm and attracts few capable followers.

A Failure to Be Responsive

A recurrent fear expressed in discussions of contemporary Central America is a new variation of the old domino
theory. Many observers argue that failure to limit Cuban in-

fluence in Nicaragua, to prevent radical victories in El Salvador and Guatemala, and to deal effectively with the economic problems of Honduras and Costa Rica, would deal an irreparable blow to U.S. prestige throughout the hemisphere. Capital flight would increase, moderate political factions would collapse, and hard-liners on the right would resort to all-out repression to maintain their power.

Although exaggerated, such scenarios contain an element of truth. Central America is a small community, and events in any one nation often affect developments in another. Thus, the governments of Honduras, El Salvador, and Costa Rica are already concerned about the impact on their populations of radio broadcasts originating from Nicaragua.

Such interdependence works both ways. The key challenge for U.S. policy is to offer a viable, pluralistic alternative to radical violence as a means of altering existing social and political structures and promoting economic development. Ideally, such an alternative would then influence neighboring states.

At the moment, the best location for this kind of effort is Honduras. The April elections restored Honduran faith in the domestic political process and probably halted the precipitate decline in the military's public image. The Carter administration has already indicated through diplomatic channels its hopes that the new Constituent Assembly will not limit election voting rights to assembly members but rather will open political participation to include the general population and the leftist parties excluded from April's voting. The United States has also encouraged the government, the military, and the assembly to work for honest and prompt direct elections for a new president and congress. Recent statements by the military and the major parties in Honduras suggest that this scenario may actually occur.

A hopeful U.S. government has attached requests for a Honduran package to current emergency aid proposals for Nicaragua and El Salvador. Unfortunately, the Honduran proposal is no exception to the rule that Central America aid packages are small, poorly focused, and contingent upon approval by a slow-moving Congress. In the case of the Honduran development package there is no assurance of any significant funding beyond the upcoming fiscal year. Moreover, the proposed assistance does not address such fundamental problems as access to American markets, terms of trade and technology transfer, or guaranteed energy supplies. Once again, U.S. rhetoric seems to outstrip its ability or willingness to commit American resources.

An example of the type of program which could restore American credibility and promote positive development throughout Central America is the current national literacy campaign in Nicaragua. Financed and inspired by Cuba, Nicaragua is endeavoring to eliminate nearly 50 per cent illiteracy in less than a year. Major U.S. assistance would make possible a similar effort in Honduras. A literacy project would mobilize national energies, especially among the youth; support future education programs in health, sanitation, and agriculture; and give both Honduras and the United States a badly needed sense of accomplishment. A literacy campaign in Honduras would also provide opportunities for cooperation with other regional powers in Central American development efforts.

Central America's problems are critical, and the time left for dealing with them in a peaceful, democratic manner is extremely short. Despite the polarization of internal politics and the lack of credibility in U.S. policy, positive elements do exist. Guatemala should soon be more than self-sufficient in petroleum. Honduras and Nicaragua have significant areas of undeveloped land, and Costa Rica, with its democratic traditions and high level of literacy, can draw on valuable human resources. Important support for reform could come from the Roman Catholic Church, whose energies in Central America are already devoted to promoting justice and human development.

Many Central Americans share the sentiments of a Costa Rican congressional leader who stated sadly that "the United States does not really care about Central America." What has been lacking is a definite commitment by the United States to support political and financial alternatives to the violent revolutions of the far left or the brutal repression by the entrenched right. Any verbal commitment by the president and Congress to the future development of Central America must be coupled with significant amounts of long-term economic assistance. In the conclusion of his April 8 address, Bowdler recognized the urgency of responding to the current situation in Central America: "Central America is in a critical period of its history. Our support for peaceful change can increase the likelihood that more democratic and equitable societies will evolve out of the present crisis. Conversely, our failure to be responsive can only help the enemies of freedom."

Unfortunately, if history offers any guide, it is that the United States will probably fail to be responsive. Domestic politics, budget concerns, and preoccupation with big-power politics may well keep the United States from making any serious commitment to Central America. If, after a century and a half of involvement in Central America, the United States can still offer no positive commitment to nonviolence and democratic development in that region, then its hopes for peace and justice in more remote areas are slim indeed.

THE CRISIS IN EL SALVADOR[6]

Not since Vietnam has the domino theory enjoyed such currency in Washington. Less than a year after Nicaraguan President Anastasio Somoza was driven from Managua by the first Latin American revolution in two decades, neighboring El Salvador teeters on the brink of full-scale insurrection. In truth, El Salvador has hardly had a government over the past 12 months. The nation's nominal rulers have long since lost

[6] Reprint of article entitled "Oligarchs and Officers: The Crisis in El Salvador," by William M. LeoGrande, assistant professor of political science in the School of Government and Public Administration, the American University, and Carla Anne Robbins, fellow of the Institute for the Study of World Politics, New York. *Foreign Affairs.* 58:1084–1104. Summer '80. Reprinted by permission from *Foreign Affairs,* Summer 1980. Copyright 1980 by Council on Foreign Relations, Inc.

control of their own security forces and today stand isolated amidst a rising tide of political violence from both Right and Left.

In Washington, policymakers are searching desperately for a solution to El Salvador's complex political equation, but the answer remains as elusive as the opening to a Chinese box. The current crisis may have no exit short of civil war—a bloody denouement that would not only shred the social fabric of El Salvador but would also pose grave risks to regional peace. Current U.S. policy, while designed to avoid such a conflict, is not working. While the United States has successfully thwarted two rightist attempts to overthrow centrist governments, the Salvadorean junta today is no closer to finding a permanent solution to its political crisis than it was when it came into power six months ago. The junta's impotence stems from its isolation; it has yet to create for itself any significant base of political support. Such isolation has been a chronic problem for Salvadorean governments, and it is only by overcoming this historical dilemma that the current crisis can be permanently resolved.

II

El Salvador is burdened with the most rigid class structure and worst income inequality in all of Latin America. For over a century, the social and economic life of the nation has been dominated by a small landed elite known popularly as "the 14 families" (*Los catorce*), though their actual number is well over 14. The family clans comprising the oligarchy include only a few thousand people in this nation of nearly five million, but until recently they owned 60 percent of the farmland, the entire banking system, and most of the nation's industry. Among them, they received 50 percent of national income.

The tensions inherent in such a social structure are exacerbated in El Salvador by severe population pressure on the land. With over 400 people per square mile, population density is the highest in Latin America. Over 200,000 peasants are landless—a more severe imbalance of land and labor than in Mexico. Unlike most of its neighbors, El Salvador has no undeveloped territory for surplus agricultural labor to colonize; cultivation already extends up the slopes of even active volcanoes. Illegal emigration (to less populous Honduras) acted as a safety valve for the potentially explosive situation in the countryside until the 1969 "soccer war" closed the border. An expanding manufacturing sector offered another alternative to rural laborers in the decades after World War II, but the war with Honduras also pushed the economy into a recession from which it has never fully recovered.

The dominance of the oligarchy and the persistence of rural poverty produced an immense potential for class conflict. For decades, the oligarchy's primary political objective has been to prevent this latent conflict from erupting into class war. Despite its economic preeminence, the Salvadorean oligarchy has exercised political hegemony indirectly. The military has ruled El Salvador since 1931, and the history of the nation's governance has largely been a history of the twists and turns in the political alliance between oligarchs and officers.

This alliance was forged in 1932 when the armed forces took control of the government to suppress a massive peasant uprising. The insurrection, endorsed but by no means controlled by the Salvadorean Communist Party, was crushed at a cost of some 30,000 dead. The psychic scars left by this abortive revolution and its suppression disfigured the nation's political culture in ways that are still evident. For the oligarchy, the growth of even moderate opposition has always raised the specter of 1932. A strong current of belief persists among the oligarchs that the threat of revolution can only be effectively met as it was in the 1930s—by bloody suppression.

The military has shared the oligarchy's fear of revolution, though it has occasionally opted for reform rather than repression as a more reliable bulwark against the Left. The coup that has come to be known as the "revolution of 1948" brought to power a coalition of young military officers with a modernist vision. Motivated not only by the fear of radical revolt but also by their desire to see El Salvador develop economically, this modernizing military embarked upon a program of "controlled revolution": moderate reforms (none of which challenged the dominance of the oligarchy) blended with heavy doses of political repression for radical opponents. The oligarchy tolerated such reformism because it promised modernization without structural change, and because an authoritarian regime centered in the armed forces seemed to offer security against the Left.

This practical partnership between oligarchs and officers gave birth to an electoral system that was largely a charade. Moderate opponents could vent their views in periodic elections, but control of the government was reserved for the military's own political party, the Revolutionary Party of Democratic Unity (PRUD). Perpetual electoral victory for the PRUD was guaranteed by the military's power to count the ballots.

The developmentalist program of the military modernizers stimulated economic growth, but yielded no improvement in equity. With economic growth came demographic growth of the urban middle and working classes, both of which bridled at the military's monopoly on politics. At issue was whether the military and its oligarchic partners would allow the creation of a system of politics—i.e., an institutional process for reconciling the conflicting political demands of the nation's significant social groups. The oligarchs preferred the security of authoritarianism to the uncertainty of electoral competition.

The officers were less unanimous. In 1960, a rising tide of civil unrest disrupted the prevailing political consensus within the armed forces. Alarmed at the regime's unwillingness to open the political process and fearful that such rigidity could lead to revolution, progressive officers joined with civilian opposition leaders to depose the PRUD government. The new government promised to accelerate the pace of social reform, offering a program similar to what the Peruvian armed forces would propose eight years later. Such reforms were beyond the oligarchy's threshold of tolerance; it mobilized its conservative supporters within the armed forces, who toppled the new government by countercoup after only three months.

The political system built after the countercoup was a carbon copy of what had gone before. The PRUD was dissolved, but then resurrected as the Party of National Conciliation (PCN). Like its progenitor, the PCN was dedicated to modest reform and political liberalism within the confines of military rule. The PCN also reestablished the military's working partnership with the oligarchy; its program of social reform left unscathed the socioeconomic foundations of oligarchic power.

The deterioration of the Salvadorean economy in the wake of the 1969 war with Honduras set the stage for political turmoil in the 1970s. The proximate cause, however, was the same as it had been in 1960—the military's determination to maintain its monopoly in politics (by electoral fraud if necessary) rather than relinquish power to its civilian opponents. Despite its electoral facade, the Salvadorean polity in 1970 was no closer to having an open political process capable of producing the orderly resolution of political conflict than it had been a decade before.

By 1970, Christian Democrats (PDC) had become the principal focus of opposition. Indeed, the PDC's strength virtually preempted any growth on the far Left. In the late 1960s, when virtually every government in Latin America faced guerrilla challenges inspired by the Cuban revolution, in El Salvador there were none.

The opportune time for a "centrist solution" to El Salvador's socioeconomic ills came in 1972 when the Christian Democrats stood at the summit of their popular support. By all informed accounts, the PDC won the 1972 presidential election. The PCN was able to snatch victory from the jaws of electoral defeat only through blatant fraud and brutal suppression of the resulting protests. As if acting from the script written a decade earlier, the progressive wing of the armed forces joined with PDC leaders to attempt a coup. Unlike 1960, however, the attempt failed, leaving conservative officers in control of the military.

Even the pretense of political liberalism was jettisoned forthwith. The Christian Democrats became the principal target of government repression, which destroyed the party's effectiveness as an electoral opposition, and with it the viability of electoral opposition per se. Most of the PDC's leadership was driven into exile and most of its rank and file was driven to the Left. The PDC contested the presidency once more in 1977, but the result was a foregone conclusion.

The government's assault on the center also created the far Left. Three guerrilla organizations began operating during the 1970s and expanded as the center was demolished. The Popular Forces of Liberation (FPL) was founded in 1970 by radical university students and dissident Communist Party members. A year later, another group of dissident communists joined with radicals from the Christian Democrats to form the Revolutionary Army of the People (ERP), which split in 1975, leading to the creation of the Armed Forces of National Resistance (FARN).

The most impressive gains on the Left were made by the "popular organizations." Begun at mid-decade, these coalitions of peasant, worker, and student unions pressed demands for immediate social improvements by staging mass demonstrations and acts of civil disobedience. There are three major popular organizations: the Popular Revolutionary Bloc (BPR); the United Popular Action Front (FAPU); and the Popular Leagues of the 28th of February (LP-28), named for the day in 1977 when security forces killed over 100 demonstrators. Though their demands and tactics are similar, political differences among the popular organizations prevented them from mounting any joint actions until early 1980. Most of those differences centered upon the proper long-term strategy for bringing the Left to power, and also reflected rivalries among the armed groups with which the popular organizations are affiliated.

The growth of the Left terrified the oligarchy, which responded by financing death squads on the right (e.g., the White Warriors' Union, the White Hand, the FALANGE, and others). Local political activists, including peasant leaders, trade unionists and priests, were the principal targets of the death squads during the late 1970s. As in other nations, the paramilitary Right is widely suspected of having links to the government's security forces.

As the 1977 presidential election approached, the second reign of the military modernizers showed unmistakable signs of decay. The government's sporadic attempts to enact a modest agrarian reform law between 1973 and 1976 were blocked by the influence of the oligarchy and the Defense Minister, Humberto Romero. The moderate opposition, led by the Christian Democrats, was in retreat under the drumfire of repression, while both the armed and popular wings of the Left were gaining strength. The oligarchs, meanwhile, were funding their private paramilitary minions. In the face of this growing crisis, the PCN signaled its determination to hold fast rather than compromise by nominating the conservative General Romero for the presidency. He won, of course.

III

With Romero's election, the regime of the military modernizers became, in effect, a regime of military conservators. Despite popular demands for access to the political process, the authoritarian military regime refused to create a political order it could not control. By its refusal, it produced instead political disorder which no one could control. The rapid deterioration of El Salvador's moribund polity began in earnest after Romero's election.

As so often happens with regard to Latin America, the United States did not become very concerned about El Salvador until the crisis was well underway. A small nation of little strategic importance or economic interest, El Salvador has seldom attracted much attention in Washington. Bilateral relations have ordinarily been governed by regional policies which the United States fashioned in response to exigencies elsewhere. The result has not always been wholly sensible. When counterinsurgency was thought to be an antidote to Cuban-style revolution, and the United States lavished security assistance on Latin America, El Salvador received some

four million dollars between FY 1961 and FY 1970 even though
it had no revolutionaries to speak of. It did, however, have a
military government which inevitably perceived the flow of
arms as an endorsement.

Military assistance to El Salvador was interrupted when
Congress began introducing human rights concerns into the
allocation of U.S. foreign assistance. In early 1977, El Salvador joined Guatemala, Brazil and Argentina in rejecting further arms aid because critics in the United States found their
human rights records dismal. Previously authorized aid continued to flow to El Salvador, but no new authorizations were
made until 1979. Concomitantly, economic aid was cut by
half, from approximately $20 million to $10 million.

El Salvador first attracted high-level attention in the
Carter Administration in June 1977, when one of the right-
wing death squads, the White Warriors' Union, accused the
Salvadorean Catholic Church of promoting communism, and
threatened to kill all the Jesuits in the country. Since several
activist priests had already been assassinated, the threat was
not taken to be an idle one. Under pressure from U.S. church
groups and members of Congress, the Carter Administration
launched an intensive campaign to convince General Romero
that El Salvador's relations with the United States depended
upon preventing the prospective massacre. To underscore its
concern, the United States vetoed a $90 million Inter-Ameri-
can Development Bank loan to El Salvador.

The effort was an apparent success. The slaughter of the
Jesuits never materialized (though half a dozen more priests
were assassinated over the next two years); the activities of
the death squads subsided temporarily (reinforcing suspicions
that they were operating with official sanction); and the Romero government itself began to ease official repression. In
the hope of reinforcing what it took to be liberalization,
Washington granted approval for the loan in October.

Unfortunately, this change in policy, intended as an in-
centive, was interpreted as irresolution. Less than a month
later, the government responded to the assassination of indus-
trialist Raúl Molinas Canas by passing the draconian Law for

the Defense and Guarantee of Public Order. The Public Order Law effectively made it illegal to oppose the government in any fashion whatsoever. It instituted press censorship, banned public meetings, outlawed strikes, made it a crime to disseminate information that "tends to destroy the social order," and suspended normal judicial procedures for such offenses. Mere suspicion was specified as grounds for arrest. The day after this law's passage ended any pretense of democracy in El Salvador, U.S. Ambassador Frank J. Devine, speaking to the Salvadorean Chamber of Commerce, endorsed the right of governments to do whatever is necessary to maintain public order.

Far from restoring stability, the Public Order Law accelerated the spiral of political violence and institutional decay. The clandestine guerrilla organizations proved to be beyond the reach of the government's security apparatus or the paramilitary right, so the brunt of the repression fell upon the more accessible moderates. The remnants of the PDC and the social democratic National Revolutionary Movement (MNR) were silenced, leaving only the courageous Archbishop Oscar Romero (no relation to the President) as a public spokesman for the moderate Left. Even the church was vilified by government propaganda, and the death squads resumed their assassination of priests.

The radical Left met the wave of official violence with a counterwave. The armed groups stepped up the bombings, assassinations of government officials, and kidnappings of businessmen both foreign and domestic. The popular organizations began a campaign of occupying government offices and foreign embassies to demand the release of prisoners arrested under the Public Order Law.

Frustrated at its inability to control the growing popular opposition, the military government made one major attempt to demolish its largest foe, the Popular Revolutionary Bloc. Following a March 1978 street demonstration that ended in violence, the government unleashed the largest of the paramilitary rightist groups, ORDEN, on the peasants of San Pedro Perúlapan, a stronghold of Bloc support. (ORDEN [short for the

Democratic Nationalist Organization] was created in 1968 as
a civilian auxiliary to government security forces in the countryside, and grew quickly to a membership of between 50,000
and 100,000.) In San Pedro ORDEN conducted a reign of terror
akin to that unleashed by Somoza's National Guard in 1975.
The effect was also similar; it further radicalized the rural
population, widened the gulf between the government and its
moderate opponents, and attracted widespread international
condemnation. In late 1978 and early 1979, a series of human
rights reports from Amnesty International, the International
Commission of Jurists, the Organization of American States,
and the U.S. Department of State unanimously condemned
the Romero government for its systematic torture, murder
and persecution of political dissidents.

When the mediation efforts in neighboring Nicaragua
brought the political crisis there to a temporary stalemate in
early 1979, the Carter Administration turned its crisis diplomacy to the burgeoning conflict in El Salvador. Abandoning
its embarrassing silence on the effects of the Public Order
Law, Washington began urging Romero to reduce the level of
official violence. As a conciliatory gesture aimed more at
Washington than at the opposition, Romero agreed to lift the
law in late February. The effect was negligible; political violence from neither the government's security forces nor the
paramilitary Right abated.

The fall of Somoza in July conjured up images of Central
American dominoes in Washington and prompted a major review of U.S. policy toward the region. Advocates divided
roughly into two camps. Those seeking a restoration of military aid to El Salvador, Guatemala and Honduras argued that
the prospects for order would best be ensured by reinforcing
the existing military regimes, even at the expense of human
rights. The opposing view, which ultimately prevailed, held
that the *anciens régimes* of Central America had become ob-
solete and could not be sustained in the long run. Rather than
enlisting on the side of military dictatorships that faced eventual extinction, this view ran, the interests of the United
States would be better served by policies aimed at managing

the inevitable social and economic change. Implicitly, such management meant—as it had under the Alliance for Progress—a search for "openings to the center" and policies to promote the center while containing the Left.

Rent by escalating political violence, El Salvador moved quickly to the top of the policy agenda. The Carter Administration resolved not to repeat the mistakes it had made in Nicaragua, where it failed to break fully with Somoza and enlist wholeheartedly on the side of the moderate opposition until the eleventh hour—several hours too late. Washington pressured General Romero to move El Salvador's political conflicts back into the electoral arena where the Christian Democrats and the social-democratic MNR could retrieve the political initiative from the Left.

Romero responded with promises of reform, including a pledge that the 1980 congressional elections would be internationally supervised to ensure fairness. But he was adamant in his refusal to reschedule the presidential election, which was not due until 1982. Convinced that the tattered fabric of El Salvador's polity would not hold together until 1982, the United States was not satisfied. ·Neither was the opposition. Even the moderates refused to confer with the government on its promised reforms until the violence of the security forces was ended. Romero would not or could not end it.

By trying to accommodate the United States, Romero undercut his own support on the Right. As order unravelled, so did the partnership between the oligarchy and the armed forces. The government's obvious inability to contain the Left was, in effect, a failure to meet its part of the implicit political bargain struck between the oligarchy and the conservative PCN. Romero's willingness even to suggest a relaxation of repression while the Left was gaining ground signaled to the oligarchs that the government could no longer be trusted to provide for their security. Since the government was no longer reliable, the oligarchs took their defense into their own hands, and violence from the paramilitary Right escalated sharply. That the oligarchs still had allies within the military is confirmed by the fact that, despite Romero's promises, the

behavior of the security forces did not change. By the fall of
1979, El Salvador was descending into chaos.

IV

On October 15, 1979, the Romero government was ousted
in a bloodless coup led by two young and apparently
progressive colonels. Charging Romero with corruption, electoral fraud and human rights violations, the colonels committed their new government to a thorough reform of the nation's "antiquated economic, social and political structures."
The oligarchic system, they charged, had not offered the people even "the minimal conditions necessary to survive as
human beings."

The colonels moved quickly to establish a popular base by
inviting the moderate opposition into the government. Three
moderate civilians joined the colonels in a ruling junta, and
the cabinet was drawn almost entirely from the centrist political parties. In a dramatic break with the past, the junta also
called for support from the country's previously excluded militant Left, saying that the Left "must understand that the
government is no longer their enemy." To gain such support,
the junta promised an ambitious program of reforms drawn
largely from the Common Platform, a list of demands issued
in September by a coalition that included all the major centrist parties and one of the Left's popular organizations, the
Popular Leagues. The junta pledged to end the repression,
create a democratic political system, and institute a wide
range of economic policies aimed at improving the plight of
the poor. Most important, it promised agrarian reform.

The popular response to these proposals was mixed.
Though the moderate opposition parties joined the new government immediately, Archbishop Oscar Romero was more
cautious in his endorsement. Acknowledging the junta's good
will, he warned that the nation's new rulers could rally popular support only by demonstrating that their "beautiful promises are not dead letters."

On the Left, reaction to the coup was even more equivocal. Two of the armed groups greeted the new government with calls for insurrection; they refused to believe that the military would or could break with the past and displace the oligarchy. By the end of the first week, however, the government's attempts to create an opening to the Left began to have an effect. Encouraged by the junta's support of the Common Platform and its promises to bring Leftists into the government, the Popular Leagues and the Revolutionary Army of the People gave the government conditional endorsement. Though they never offered explicit support, the leftist FAPU and FARN were also impressed by the government's apparent commitment to real change. Finally, in early November the Popular Revolutionary Bloc and the Popular Forces of Liberation agreed to suspend their attacks on the government for 30 days to give it an opportunity to make good its promises.

The junta did not use the time well. The pledge to investigate human rights abuses led to no arrests; the pledge to reorganize the government's security apparatus led only to a cosmetic reshuffling of personnel; and the pledge to conduct an agrarian reform led nowhere. In fact, the government could not even rein in its own security forces. Though the colonels had condemned the Romero government's indiscriminate use of lethal force against civilians, the practices of the police and National Guard did not change noticeably after October.

As the weeks passed, it became clear that more than mere indecision lay behind the junta's failure to act. The issue of the "disappeared" was indicative of the new government's dilemma. Despite its initial promise to discover the whereabouts of some 300 political activists, two weeks after coming to power the junta claimed that it could not find any of the missing. The junta dared not look too closely at the excesses of the Romero regime for fear of what it might find; senior police and military officials were almost certainly culpable in the disappearances. Such a discovery would have shattered the fragile unity of the armed forces—something the progressive officers refused to risk. The same predicament confronted the progressives at every turn because the conservatives objected to every major reform.

This political stalemate revealed in bold relief the historic dilemma of Salvadorean politics. In a closed political system that had never allowed significant civilian participation, public policy was the exclusive preserve of the armed forces. Reforms were inevitably constrained by the government's need to preserve at least a rough political consensus within the officers' corps. The oligarchy, of course, defended its interests through its links with the conservatives in the military. Bound together with their conservative compatriots by institutional loyalty, progressive officers could alter the status quo only in ways the conservatives were willing to tolerate—a tolerance ordinarily defined by the conservatives' fear of the Left. This, of course, was why three decades of military modernizers had failed to produce any significant change in El Salvador's outmoded social structure. It was also why the October junta failed. On every important issue, the progressives caved in to conservative resistance rather than risk a split in the armed forces.

The government's paralysis destroyed any chance it may have had to build a popular base on the Left or the Center-Left. By December all three of the popular organizations and their armed wings had gone back on the offensive, and even the moderates within the government had become deeply discouraged. In a final effort to break the deadlock in the armed forces, two of the junta's three civilian members issued an ultimatum: either Defense Minister José Guillermo García (the leading conservative) would resign or they would. Forced to choose openly between their commitment to change and their loyalty to the armed forces, the progressive officers chose loyalty. Backed by a majority of senior officers and local garrison commanders, García stood fast.

On January 3, less than three months after its birth, the Center-Left government collapsed when two of the junta's three civilian members resigned along with the entire cabinet (except for García, of course). In presenting their resignations, the civilians blamed conservative resistance for the government's impotence and its inability to build a popular base of support. The most dramatic demonstration of disillusionment with the junta and the possibility of peaceful change came at a press conference called by the former Education Minister, Salvador Samayoa. Samayoa explained that he had resigned to "fight for total liberation." He then picked up an AK-47 machine gun and walked out of the room escorted by two masked gunmen.

Despite the government's failure to win the trust of the Left or to retain the cooperation of the Center-Left, the colonels pressed on. Within a week, the Christian Democrats rejoined the government, justifying their decision on the grounds that there was no other alternative to civil war. A new junta was formed and a new round of reform proposals was issued, including promises to nationalize the banks and expropriate the large landed estates.

Superficially, the new junta seems hardly distinguishable from its predecessor; in Washington, it has been portrayed as a centrist government of progressive officers and moderate civilians who are committed to significant social change. Indeed, the January junta has even carried out (albeit reluctantly and under intense U.S. pressure) some of the promises the October junta left unfulfilled. Yet the new government's strategy for resolving the current political crisis is profoundly different. The October junta sought to combine structural change with a political opening to the Left, which was guardedly willing to let the government prove its sincerity. The junta failed when it was unable to overcome the conservative officers' resistance to reform. The new junta's strategy has been to assuage the Right's fear of reform by combining it with repression of the Left. The goal of building a Center-Left social base for the government has been abandoned. Instead, the government has sought to consolidate, as best it can, a political consensus for reform within the armed forces—even if the means of doing so leave it utterly isolated from the civilian populace. In this sense, the new government in El Salvador is no different from the military modernizers of the past. The reforms it advocates may be more extensive, but

its approach to politics is a familiar one—an authoritarian regime centered in the armed forces and buttressed by repression of those who dare to challenge the military's hegemony.

Even the effectiveness of the junta's reform program is
problematic. Though the junta has nationalized the banks and
expropriated several hundred of the largest private estates, its
reforms have been accompanied by a state of siege and wave
of repression as intense as any undertaken by the Romero regime. In the countryside, conservatives in the security forces
used the repression to obviate the agrarian reform and to ter-
rorize the peasantry. In the cities, the security forces have
used the state of siege to wage war against the opposition. In
the first few months of 1980, the number of people killed in
political violence was nearly a thousand, the vast majority of
whom were killed either by the police or the paramilitary
Right.

The strategy of reform with repression has destroyed what
little chance the January junta might have had to build a popular base of support. The reforms have alienated the Right,
and the repression has alienated everyone else. The PDC, a
partner in the government, is deeply divided over the junta's
strategy for governing. In March, several leading Christian
Democrats, including junta member Hector Dada, resigned
from the government on the grounds that reform and repression were mutually exclusive. Before he was assassinated
on March 24, even Archbishop Romero had begun to suggest
that insurrection against the repressive regime was justified.

The conservatives in the armed forces may have been mo-
mentarily won over to the cause of reform, but the oligarchy
has not. The oligarchs and their supporters on the far Right
have denounced the government as Marxist, and the death
squads have launched a new campaign of political assassination. Their targets have been not only members of the Left,
but also leaders of the moderate opposition and of the government itself.

On the Left, the climate of repression has forged unprece-
dented unity. In January, all the major popular organizations
and armed groups created the Revolutionary Coordinator of

the Masses to plan joint strategy; in March, the political parties and trade unions of the Center-Left formed a coalition of their own, the Democratic Front; and, in April, the Left and Center-Left came together in a grand coalition when the Revolutionary Coordinator joined the Democratic Front.

The strategy of reform with repression has left the January junta desperately isolated and precariously dependent upon the support of the United States. When rightists in the armed forces sought to depose the government in late February and again in May, there was no significant social or political group in El Salvador which the government could rally to its defense. Only the United States preserved it.

V

El Salvador has become the first test case for the new regional policy formulated by the United States in the wake of the Nicaraguan revolution. Since the October coup, the policy of the United States has been to support the government of El Salvador in its attempts to carry out significant social reform and forge a viable political center. When the uncooperative General Romero was deposed, the sense of relief in Washington was almost palpable; the October junta seemed a perfect vehicle for reform without revolution—i.e., a centrist regime which was both anti-oligarchic and anti-communist.

The proximate objectives of the United States since October have been to encourage El Salvador's rulers to implement their promised reforms, to protect them from a rightist coup, and to avert an open civil war. The principal instrument for carrying out this policy has been economic and military assistance. In November 1979, the Administration sent the Salvadorean security forces a limited amount of riot control equipment along with six U.S. advisers to teach them how to use it. In the early spring of 1980, $6 million in additional military aid and $50 million in economic aid were reprogrammed for El Salvador, despite Archbishop Romero's personal appeal to President Carter, in which he warned that military aid would merely "sharpen the repression."

U.S. policy has been indiscriminate in its search for a

viable centrist government. The Carter Administration has
acknowledged no significant difference between the October
and January juntas, and therein lies the fallacy of U.S. policy.
The October junta tried, albeit unsuccessfully, to address
both the socioeconomic *and* political ills of the nation by
blending structural reform with a political opening to the
left. The January junta's program of reform with repression
ignores the most pressing political issues: the escalating violence, the growing polarization, and the ongoing isolation of
the government.

Confronted with these problems, U.S. policymakers contend that it is still possible to build a political center where
none now exists. Both the far Right and the far Left are, pur-
portedly, too fragmented to mount a successful assault on the
government. Thus, if the regime can be sustained by the
United States in the short run, its program of social reform
will eventually attract centrist support.

To this end, the policy of the United States is to encourage
the junta to move cautiously (so as to preserve its tenuous
hold on power) on three fronts: (1) to implement real social
reform, thereby building some measure of popular support no
matter how diffuse; (2) to rein in the Right, even if it means
removing some ultraconservatives from the security forces;
and (3) to enlist the support of the Center-Left opposition,
leaving the radical Left isolated on the political periphery.
The first two stages of this program are underway now, and
the Right's resistance constitutes the most immediate threat
to the government's survival. Two coup attempts have already been foiled by the skillful and tireless efforts of U.S.
Ambassador Robert White. [Ambassador White was later removed by the new Reagan Administration. See "Dominoes in
Central America," in Section II, below.—Ed.]

The third objective, however, rests upon the unrealistic
hope that the grand coalition which has been formed between the Left and the Center-Left can be broken up. In essence, this is an attempt to replay the final months of the Somoza regime, when the United States pursued an identical
policy to no avail. Behind its reformist rhetoric, policy toward

El Salvador is an attempt to prevent another Nicaragua. What Washington appears to be incapable of grasping is that in El Salvador, as in Nicaragua before it, the centrist forces which the United States regards as its natural allies have joined with the very forces which the United States perceives as its natural enemy—the radical Left. The centrists are no longer in the center.

Failure to comprehend this realignment produced policies that were irrelevant to the balance of political forces in Nicaragua. *That* is the mistake we ought not to repeat in El Salvador.

The strength of the Left is such that it cannot be contained short of extermination. It has become a veto group in Salvadorean politics—no centrist government can rule without its tacit support and no reform program can succeed in the long run without its participation. The recently unified Left and Center-Left opposition includes everyone but the government and the far Right.

If civil war is to be averted and real changes implemented, the junta must return to the strategy of October: end the repression and try once again to bring both the Center-Left *and* the radical Left into the government. Though the polarization of politics has worsened since January, the Left might again be willing to halt its attacks on the government if it can be convinced of the junta's sincerity. The principal obstacle to such a change in government policy is the same now as it was in October. No opening to the Left or even to the Center-Left can succeed until the repression is brought to an end, and the repression will not abate until the government gains effective control of its own security forces. It cannot do that unless the progressives in the armed forces can be induced to break with their conservative compatriots.

In the current stalemate of Salvadorean politics the impetus for such a change must come from the United States. Rather than giving unqualified support to reform with repression merely because the current government is vaguely centrist, the United States ought to use what leverage it has to induce the junta to open the political system. Without

pressure from the United States, the progressive officers will
not break with their conservative compatriots, end the political violence, or institute real reforms. The slide into civil war
will not be arrested.

Policymakers in Washington object that such a shift in
U.S. policy would provoke a coup from the Right. The junta's
social reforms have already strained the political consensus in
the officers' corps to the breaking point; an opening to the
Left would rupture it. The danger of a rightist coup is certainly real. The Right planned a coup in February and another in May but was dissuaded when the United States stated
unequivocally that it would oppose a rightist regime. A similar stance might once again deter a coup and give the junta
the freedom to pursue a reconciliation with the Left.

There is no gainsaying the complexities of implementing
such a policy. In a situation as volatile as El Salvador, the tone
and timing of initiatives can be as important as their sub-
stance. But the current U.S. policy is no less pragmatic than
this alternative. And, whatever the risks, an opening to the
Left offers a better prospect for avoiding civil war than does
the strategy of reform with repression. As political violence
continues and the opposition coalesces around an increasingly
radical program, the possibility of a rapprochement with the
Left is quickly slipping away.

If the United States hopes to induce the Salvadorean government to broaden its popular base at all, it must become
more sensitive to the nuances of using foreign assistance as an
instrument of policy. Though the current level of U.S. military assistance is not enough to alter the military balance between government and opposition or to provide the United
States with very much leverage, it nevertheless strengthens
the impression that the United States endorses the political
violence of the security forces. By ending military aid, the
United States could send a clear message to the armed forces
that it does not support attempts to impose military solutions
on political problems.

Economic assistance, on the other hand, not only provides
better leverage because of its greater quantity, but is also less

likely to be misinterpreted. It can be used both to redirect the junta toward a political opening and to help finance the requisite social reforms. Indeed, political violence has thrown the Salvadorean economy into such a crisis that economic assistance is virtually indispensable. Consequently, Washington's threat to withdraw aid has already been successfully used to induce the government to expropriate the large landed estates, and to deter the Right from expropriating the government.

It may be that no U.S. policy can avert civil war in El Salvador. The Carter Administration has pledged that the United States will not intervene directly in a battle between domestic forces. But in the frigid international atmosphere of the new cold war and a heated domestic presidential race against Ronald Reagan, the pressures for direct intervention will be intense—especially if the current U.S.-supported junta is in place when a civil war erupts.

U.S. intervention, whether in the form of massive military aid or U.S. troops, would be a diplomatic disaster both regionally and globally. In Latin America, it would immediately resurrect charges of U.S. imperialism and shatter our fragile relations with Nicaragua. It would make a mockery of our human rights policy, giving rightist regimes throughout the region an opportunity to repudiate as paternalistic and interventionist U.S. attempts to moderate repression and foster democracy. Furthermore, it would wreak havoc in our relations with most of the Third World; the diplomatic and moral advantage which the United States has reaped from events in Afghanistan would be completely lost. And though it has become fashionable to remonstrate against the evils of the "Vietnam syndrome," sending U.S. troops to El Salvador might prove to be much easier than bringing them home.

There is also the nightmare scenario of a civil war escalating into a regional war engulfing all of Central America. Indeed, the war has already become internationalized to an extent; both Guatemala and Cuba have sent arms to support their respective sides. If the nightmare becomes a reality it will probably be the doing of Guatemala. The rightist govern-

ment in Guatemala has a history of coming to the rescue of
the Right in El Salvador, and has recently warned ominously
of the need to halt the "communist tide" before it reaches
Guatemalan shores. Though the Guatemalan armed forces
have their hands full at home, they might well enter a civil
war in El Salvador if the Left appeared to be winning. The
revolutionary government in Nicaragua would be hard
pressed to stand idly by in the face of Guatemalan intervention, and there is even the remote possibility of a major
Cuban response.

Any serious internationalization of a civil war in El Salvador would produce almost irresistible domestic political
pressure for direct U.S. involvement. Yet the costs of intervention would be no less severe. It is therefore imperative
that the United States do everything in its power to prevent
direct intervention in El Salvador by any foreign power. Al-
lying itself with Mexico and Venezuela, which fear instability
in Central America even more than does the United States,
Washington should use all its moral and diplomatic weight to
rally regional opinion against external intervention. For
example, the threat of diplomatic and economic sanctions
against external combatants by the Organization of American
States might prove to be an effective deterrent.

VI

The possibilities for peaceful, evolutionary change in El
Salvador appear to have been exhausted. The current U.S.
policy of supporting reform with repression is exacerbating
the polarization of the polity rather than creating a viable
center. The only conceivable alternative—urging the regime
to create an opening to the Left—is admittedly a long shot. It
may well be that only a civil war can cut the Gordian knot of
Salvadorean politics. And civil war will bring with it all the
attendant dangers of internationalization and temptations for
U.S. intervention.

It is impossible to predict who would win a civil war in El
Salvador, but there can be no doubt that the bloodshed would

be horrific. The Right favors a solution akin to the massacre of 1932, and the Left is unlikely to be as generous in victory as the Sandinistas have been in Nicaragua. The United States could hardly maintain cordial relations with the government of victors, whoever they might be. In short, the outlook is dismal, both for the people of El Salvador and for the United States.

How can the United States prevent a reenactment of this tragedy in Guatemala and Honduras, the Central American dominoes still standing? In concept, the post-Somoza policy which the United States has adopted toward the region is a great improvement over the policies of the past. Washington has rejected as inadequate the short-term solution of uncritically propping up conservative regimes with economic and military assistance. In its place is a pledge to promote fundamental social and political change.

The success of this new policy, however, will not be determined by its good intentions. First, it will depend upon the ability of the United States to act before full crises develop and the possibilities for peaceful change evaporate. To date, Washington has been so preoccupied with putting out brushfires that it has hardly begun to address the problems which make Guatemala and Honduras candidates for future crises.

Moreover, the success of this new policy will depend upon the resolve of the United States to pursue its stated commitment to change consistently, even at the expense of short-term stability. History offers some valuable lessons in this regard. We would do well to recall that the Alliance for Progress encompassed similar goals, albeit on a more grandiose scale. Yet despite some gains in economic growth, the Alliance produced little basic social change and failed dismally in its efforts to promote democracy.

The Alliance died of schizophrenia. The United States never resolved the contradiction between the Alliance's developmental and security components, between reform and repression. When this contradiction produced authoritarian regimes rather than democracies, U.S. policymakers rationalized reality into a virtue, arguing that the problems of economic growth caused such severe political strains that modernizing nations could not "afford" democracy. The pluralist clash of interests was sacrificed to the peace of authoritarian order. Democracy, so the argument went, would follow in the wake of modernization—a sort of trickle-down politics.

The new policy of the United States toward Central America revives the hopes of the Alliance for Progress, but its application in El Salvador betrays the persistence of the Alliance's schizophrenia. The attraction of the current Salvadorean government is that it promises to square the circle by providing both basic social change and security against the Left. The reality now, as in the 1960s, is that it cannot do both. If El Salvador opts for real change, it can only be accomplished by allowing the Left to return from the political wilderness to which it has been relegated by decades of military rule.

Both Guatemala and Honduras will face similar choices in the near future. Moreover, as the search for democracy becomes a hemispheric concern, Brazil, Argentina and Chile will all confront the issue of how to accommodate the social and political demands of a Left opposition radicalized by years of suppression. The challenge for U.S. policy is not to let the emergence of such opposition elements weaken our commitment to social and political change. The first necessary condition for creating stability in Latin America is to create open democratic political systems that allow the Left to come in from the cold.

II. MILITARY RULE, PARTISAN WARFARE, AND OUTSIDE INTERESTS

EDITOR'S INTRODUCTION

The articles that follow point up the continuing threat, internal and international, posed by clashes between rightist and Communist elements. Proud, resentful of outside intervention yet often seeking it, Latin Americans find their chronically unstable governments vulnerable to the economic or military pressures of foreign powers.

The first selection, from *Newsweek*, summarizes the ground swell of insurgency in El Salvador and elsewhere in Central America—an irresistible force of have-nots guaranteeing further convulsion. Violence and anarchy in El Salvador, with their consequences for the United States, are also detailed by Richard Alan White, reporting in *America*. In South America, too, democracy has fared badly. A *U.S. News & World Report* survey reveals seven of the twelve nations ruled by the military, with little hope for free elections. (Differing views are offered by Martin C. Needler, whose article on the military withdrawal from power is reprinted in Section III.)

Professor Jorge I. Domínguez, in a *Daedalus* analysis of the "bargaining relationship among allies and adversaries" that constitutes hemispheric security, is less inclined than other observers to see developments in the Caribbean as necessarily endangering U.S. strategic interests. The brief excerpt that follows, reprinted from *Américas*, is a financial statement of U.S. economic interests and business investments in Latin America.

The next two articles address themselves to the image and role of the United States. In the first, Carl J. Migdail, writing in *U.S. News & World Report*, indicates that we are losing ground as Soviet and Cuban influence grows. In the second, an interview in *Multinational Monitor*, corporate organiza-

tion spokesman Henry Geyelin presents the views of the
American business community on private enterprise as a positive force in Latin American development.

Democracy versus dictatorship is the theme of the final
article in this section, a *World Press Review* extract from a
Venezuelan magazine that examines the array of influences
on nonaligned Latin America, from Soviet-Cuban intervention to Chinese Communist political advice to the right-wing
Chilean junta. Citing the example of Venezuela as a hopeful
sign, journalist Conrado Contreras urges all democratic countries to join in a campaign to restore liberty and human rights
in other Latin American nations.

DOMINOES IN CENTRAL AMERICA?[1]

It had begun as the funeral of Archbishop Oscar Arnulfo
Romero, the victim of a gunman—but it ended as one more
bloody step toward all-out civil war in El Salvador. More
than 50,000 mourners had jammed into the plaza in San Salvador last week when the first bomb exploded. Within min-
utes, the square was a bedlam of chattering automatic rifles,
blazing firebombs and stampeding survivors. Scores of
wounded and 31 dead lay crumpled in the rubble. The prospect of another Central American revolution alarmed Washington deeply, for the tindery countries of the region—once
dismissed as so many banana republics—have suddenly become strategically vital to the United States.

Central America has assumed special importance since
the U.S. setbacks in Iran and Afghanistan. To the north, Mexico's oil now looks more attractive and vulnerable than ever.
To the south, the Panama Canal still serves as a lifeline for
U.S. ships and foreign commerce. And as détente wanes, last
year's revolution in Nicaragua and this year's political vio-

[1] Reprint of article by Steven Strasser, a general editor of *Newsweek*, with Larry
Rohter in Central America and Jane Whitmore in Washington. *Newsweek*. 95:38–9+. Ap.
14, '80. Copyright 1980, by Newsweek, Inc. All Rights Reserved. Reprinted by Permission.

lence in El Salvador raise familiar fears of dominoes toppling under the pressure of Soviet-Cuban adventurism. "Change is coming in the region whether the U.S. likes it or not," says a senior U.S. diplomat in Central America. "The key question is: will the United States be able to live with that change—and guide it along moderate, democratic paths?"

The Carter Administration is now scrambling to build mutual respect between Washington and Central America. U.S. strategists cite the Panama Canal treaties as a major foreign-policy triumph. "My God, can you imagine how much more complicated Nicaragua would have been last year if we had had to worry about it spilling over into a Panama that was still resentful about the canal?" says a senior U.S. diplomat. The Administration has adopted a controversial, even-handed approach to regional convulsions, pressing for democratic reforms from right-wing generals in Guatemala and left-leaning Sandinistas in Nicaragua alike. Pragmatism is the essence of this live-and-let-live policy. "We give aid to Nicaragua with the recognition that it might turn out to be a Communist state," admits a State Department official. "If Nicaragua turns out to be a Yugoslavia or a Romania, at least it's a Communist state with some saving grace."

This equanimity in the face of Communism has won the Administration some powerful critics. Congressional opponents barely missed killing a modest Nicaraguan-aid bill two months ago, and last week a House subcommittee reluctantly approved military assistance for El Salvador's moderate junta after Administration briefers warned that Cuban aid was pouring in to the region's leftist rebels. Jimmy Carter's fence mending also has infuriated Central American right-wingers. "Our only hope is that the American people come to their senses by November and elect Ronald Reagan their next President," says a former Guatemalan ambassador to the U.S. "If not, we may soon see all of Central America fall into the hands of the Communists."

The immediate testing ground of U.S. policy is little El Salvador, whose slide into anarchy and violence has unsettled the entire region. Nicaragua, desperately trying to recover from its own revolution, fears an onslaught of thousands of Salvadoran refugees. Neighboring Honduras must contend with increasing Cuban arms shipments through its territory to Salvadoran guerrillas. Guatemalan hard-liners talk ominously about taking steps to stop the "red tide" before it reaches their own shores. And even the peaceable people of Costa Rica—a country so prosperous, democratic and tranquil that it fields no army—now feel threatened. "There is turmoil swirling around them," says a U.S. analyst. "They have always been the odd man out, an enclave of democracy in a sea of military governments. Now the old balance has changed, and Costa Rica's leaders are going through an agonizing appraisal of what this means to them."

Intervention: In an attempt to stop the momentum toward civil war in El Salvador, the U.S. has strongly backed the country's six-month-old military-civilian junta. But the junta's authority has been eroding gradually as extremists to the left and right contend for power. When right-wing colonels threatened a coup late last February, Washington intervened, warning that it would cut off all support to any new, noncentrist government. The Administration has proposed $49.8 million in U.S. economic aid for the junta and another $5.7 million in military credits for such items as trucks and riot-control equipment. The U.S. also has endorsed the junta's attempts at reform, including expropriation of large landholdings and nationalization of banks and foreign trade. "The issue has been one of cosmetic change or profound change," says Robert White, the . . . U.S. ambassador to El Salvador. "I think it is clear to everyone now that we favor the latter."

White, 53, an outspoken career diplomat with extensive experience in Central America, has made plenty of friends—and probably as many enemies—in El Salvador. On arrival in San Salvador last month, he stunned the capital's business leaders by warning them that their complaints about the junta's reforms were like "rearranging deck chairs on the Titantic the night it's going down." Later he offered a "working hypothesis" that right-wing groups had organized the murder of Archbishop Romero. (Last week, however, White blamed leftist agitators for touching off the bloodshed at Archbishop Romero's funeral.) He has been denounced by both sides—as "a mafioso at the service of the darkest forces" by a left-wing Salvadoran revolutionary leader, and as "a Communist and a traitor to his nation" by Guatemala's former Vice President Mario Sandoval Alarcón, who is a right-wing hard-liner. [Ambassador White was dismissed by the new Reagan Administration in February 1981 as a sign of a change in policy. He had opposed additional military aid to El Salvador, arguing that the defeat of the leftist guerrillas could be brought about only by social reforms.—Ed.]

'*The Gringos*': In Nicaragua, the shooting has stopped but the war for a new national identity goes on. The U.S. has sought to shape the outcome, in part by blunting memories of its long kinship with Anastasio Somoza, a West Point graduate (1946) who used to tell generals in the region, "You need something from the gringos—just leave it to me. I know how to deal with them." When U.S. Ambassador Lawrence Pezzullo arrived last year, his first act was to shun the elegant ambassadorial estate, a symbol to many Nicaraguans of the corrupt past. So far, limited freedom of press and religion have survived in Nicaragua, and the Sandinistas have not silenced the calls for political pluralism. Last month, Alfonso Robelo Callejas, a businessman who is the Sandinista junta's token conservative, officially inaugurated his Nicaraguan Democratic Movement as a political party and then called for "ideological pluralism, effective democracy . . . and electoral freedom."

Even the quieter republic of Panama has offered the U.S. cause for concern. The Panama Canal treaties removed the main sore point in relations. But after the deposed Shah of Iran took up temporary residence in Panama, Panamanian students poured into the streets to denounce strongman Omar Torrijos's ties with the U.S. (They chanted: "Torrijos, Somoza: *la misma cosa*"—the same thing.) U.S. strategists still view Panama as friendly and basically stable, but they are keeping an eye on its political trends.

Honduras presents a more disturbing threat: its convenience as a staging ground for revolution. The Sandinistas trained in its hills before moving on Nicaragua, and U.S. intelligence sources now believe that Cuban arms and supplies are filtering through the country to El Salvador and Guatemala. The Honduran regime of Gen. Policarpo Paz García is considered relatively benign. It has scheduled elections for a constitutional assembly later this month, and U.S. strategists will be monitoring them closely. "We're not saying Honduras is next on the domino list," says a U.S. official, "but we want to make sure Honduras stays a neutral area."

Schisms: A major part of the Carter Administration's strategy for Central America involves manipulating U.S. purse strings to encourage cooperation—and to punish the uncooperative. One problem is that Congress is reluctant to join the game. Through the years, Central Americans have been quick to exploit such schisms between the U.S. executive and legislative branches. El Salvador's business community is now lobbying Congress assiduously in an effort to force the Carter Administration to cut off aid to the reformist junta. And in Guatemala, a right-wing business organization called "Friends of the Country" has arranged for groups of conservative Congressional aides to tour the nation and talk with government leaders about Guatemala's war against the "Communist threat." "Of course we're aware that the State Department has one policy and the National Security Council another," says a former Guatemalan official. In Congress, he adds, "we know who our friends are."

Three years ago, the Carter Administration cut off all military aid and most economic aid to Guatemala in protest of the military regime's human-rights violations. The U.S. fear is that the repressive style of Gen. Romeo Lucas García's government eventually will make Guatemala ripe for the kind of leftist backlash experienced by Nicaragua and El Salvador. But so far the U.S. fund freeze has encouraged more resentment than reforms. More than 40 political killings were reported during March alone, and a mass grave containing 26 bodies was discovered at the bottom of a gorge 70 miles east of Guatemala City.

The main snag in the new U.S.-Nicaraguan relationship also involves money. The Sandinistas were deeply resentful when the U.S. House of Representatives approved $75 million in emergency aid for Nicaragua—60 per cent of it targeted to the private sector—only on condition that the Managua regime guarantee human rights. "We expect the same kind of treatment you gave to Somoza: loans without conditions," argues junta member and former guerrilla commander Daniel Ortega Saavedra. "We don't have the obligation to give guarantees to any American congressman." With the grant tied up for at least another month by the U.S. budget squeeze, U.S. diplomats in Central America also criticize the conditions and delays. "It's pathetic, really," says one. "If we can't even get this through, then we are simply not equipped to play the game against the Soviets and Cubans."

Congressional critics charge that the Administration is throwing away its money on Marxist regimes in Central America. In particular, they point out the heavy Soviet-Cuban competition in Nicaragua. Just days after Congress delayed aid to the Sandinistas, a delegation of Nicaraguan leaders showed up in Moscow to sign technical- and economic-assistance agreements. In addition, Cuba has poured 2,000 teachers, medics and technicians into Nicaragua, as well as hundreds of military advisers. Havana also recently welcomed a second group of 1,200 young Nicaraguans to Cuba's "Isle of Youth," where they will undergo training and indoctrination.

According to U.S. intelligence, Cuba has cautiously stepped up its activities throughout Central America within the last six months. Besides the comparatively open Cuban role in Nicaragua, Cuban supply shipments have been landing steadily by boat in Honduras, along the secluded northern coast and down the Coco River. In addition, Cuban aircraft have been landing at remote haciendas in the interior. In El Salvador, as well, the Cuban role is becoming clearer. Says Ambassador White: "Cuba trains—and has been training for some time—revolutionary leaders of El Salvador. There are reports of arms transfers coming into this country through various ways, including Honduras."

Some U.S. analysts in Washington see a Cuban grand design for Central America: first, the fall of El Salvador by early next year; two years later, Guatemala; finally, Honduras, which in the meantime remains a "stepping stone" to other targets for subversion. But U.S. envoys in Central America cast some doubt on that prognosis. For one thing, arms trafficking is an old story in the region, and Cuba is only one of the traffickers. Furthermore, impoverished Cuba is not universally regarded as an ideal revolutionary model. "You cannot attribute everything that is happening in Central America to a conspiracy organized by Cuba or the far left," says a veteran diplomat.

Marines: An element of the old establishment in Central America yearns for the simpler days of U.S. diplomacy—such as 1954, when the Central Intelligence Agency helped overthrow a reformist regime in Guatemala, or 1965, when U.S. Marines landed to prevent a possible leftist take-over in the Dominican Republic. Yankee interventionism probably wouldn't work today. "I am sure the Russians would love to see you intervene in El Salvador so that they would look a little less dirty after what they have done in Afghanistan," cautions a Latin American diplomat. At the same time, the U.S. must avoid the temptation to stand too aloof. "The forces of change in Central America are powerful and inevitable," says one senior U.S. diplomat in the region. "With or without the Cubans, the ground swell of the have-nots would be irresistible. We can compete and we can win—but only if we want to win." If we lose, the loss will be irreplaceable.

EL SALVADOR BETWEEN TWO FIRES[2]

"Make no mistake about it. This is a war of annihilation." With these words, the Minister of Defense and Public Secu-

[2] Reprint of article by Richard Alan White, senior fellow, Council on Hemispheric Affairs. *America.* 143:262–6. N. 1, '80. Reprinted with permission of America Press, Inc., 106 West 56th Street, New York, NY 10019. © 1980 All rights reserved.

rity of El Salvador ended the interview. Col. Guillermo García's admonition was underscored that day, when I spoke with members of the Salvadoran Commission on Human Rights. In their nation, they explained, which is deeply divided by civil war, there are fewer than two dozen known political prisoners. The answer to this puzzling mystery is as simple as it is brutal: The Salvadoran armed forces do not take prisoners.

In this small Central American country, neighbor to Nicaragua, pitched battles are taking place between the various security forces and the revolutionaries; there is also the utterly predictable statistic that between 40 and 50 people will be killed each day in El Salvador, and the vast majority will be murdered by those ostensibly entrusted with upholding law and order. Approximately one half of the victims are killed in and around the capital city of San Salvador. Every morning, brutally tortured corpses—clad only in underwear, their thumbs characteristically tied behind their backs—lie in the streets.

The recent increase in torture and assassination by government agents and their paramilitary allies is part of an all-out effort to "eliminate the subversives," as Gen. Alberto Medrano, right-wing leader, explained. Just like the Army and the National Guard, the police too, leave the barracks only in three-vehicle convoys to carry out raids against suspected guerrilla hideouts.

In a double-speak public relations program to encourage citizens to inform upon their neighbors, Colonel García proudly pointed out that the armed forces have been running this advertisement since mid-July in the daily newspapers: "Salvadorans: Denounce Violence. This is the opportunity for us to defend our sacred right to live in peace. In the name of the Fatherland, denounce all suspicious or abnormal situations that could lead to violence. Your information should be given to the armed forces at the telephone number 26-8484 (You do not have to identify yourself, just denounce)."

Opposing the military is the Democratic Revolutionary Front (F.D.R.), a coalition comprised of the liberal and leftist sectors of the society. Its membership includes labor unions and professional associations, the more militant "popular organizations," such as the Christian Federation of Salvadoran Farmworkers and the United Front of Revolutionary Students. In addition to these nonviolent organizations, the F.D.R. also has four guerrilla groups that are waging an armed struggle agsinst the Salvadoran armed forces. Although precise statistics are not available, reliable estimates place the membership of the F.D.R. at between 200,000 and 400,-000 active members, with perhaps 20,000 armed guerrillas.

There is no doubt that the guerrillas carry out selected assassinations of right-wing leaders, increasingly attack military garrisons and convoys and commit their share of atrocities. Yet, to place El Salvador's massive daily killing in perspective, reliable sources agree that, conservatively, the armed forces and the right-wing paramilitary kill ten people for every one murdered by the revolutionaries. It is the nature of life in El Salvador that such grim calculations constitute a moral index, that once again the language of "body counts" returns to disguise the truth of a country in which the social contract itself is dying.

With growing frequency, the armed forces, especially the National Guard, simply run amok. Entire villages are attacked and pillaged. The April massacre at the Honduran border on the Sumpul River is one such example. According to the Honduran Council of Bishops, Salvadoran soldiers slaughtered hundreds of unarmed peasants as they attempted to escape across the river into Honduras. During the mid-August strike, using helicopter gunships and a massive number of troops, they unleashed a wave of terror that even caught the U.S. Embassy's supposedly bullet-proof vehicle in the crossfire. Nine bullets penetrated the van, wounding one of the U.S. diplomats on the heel. In the midst of the carnage, the people struggle to maintain some hold on daily routine. As the vice rector of the Catholic University in San Salvador, the Rev. Luis de Sebastian, S.J., told me: "The human capacity to resist violence is amazing, simply amazing. Our house was sprayed by machine gun bullets, so we built a wall."

Still, anarchy grows. For example, there is no longer any traffic control in the country. Salvadorans rarely stop at red lights, because of fear that they will be accosted by left- or right-wing groups, or for that matter, simply by criminals who regularly seize vehicles for political or criminal purposes. The police do not respond to calls to calm family arguments or assist in traffic accidents. One Sunday afternoon, I witnessed a Volkswagen van run over a motorcyclist just one block from the central plaza in San Salvador. The driver of the van sped away, leaving the rider badly injured and unconscious on the street. After calling the authorities and convincing the driver of a passing pickup truck to take the unconscious cyclist to the hospital, I waited for half an hour for the police to arrive. They never came. I had to leave the motorcycle on the sidewalk, undoubtedly to be stolen.

To what extent is the United States involved in the violence here? It is generally agreed that the United States ambassador, Robert E. White, is the single most powerful person in El Salvador. Moreover, we are sending $72 million in foreign aid this year, which includes $5.7 million in "nonlethal" military assistance. The latter is comprised, in large measure, of communication and transportation equipment, which although itself nonlethal, enables the Salvadoran armed forces to wage their on-the-record "war of annihilation" more effectively.

As in Vietnam, the present chaos in El Salvador has a long history. The story begins nearly a half century ago, when the Salvadoran army in 1932 massacred tens of thousands of peasants who organized to demand better wages and living conditions. Since then, the so-called "Fourteen Families," who dominate the nation's coffee and cotton economy (now numbering closer to 150 families), have maintained a nepotistic alliance with the armed forces and have encouraged their military allies to stifle any movement toward a liberalized society. Nevertheless, during the past decades, the "popular organizations" such as the Peasant Leagues and the Union of Rural Workers have proved very successful in galvanizing impoverished farmers and rural laborers.

Through the right-wing "anti-Communist" Democratic National Organization (ORDEN), vigilante tactics have been perfected to intimidate and control the workers. The founder of ORDEN, Gen. José Alberto Medrano (Ret.), explained to me that the organization was founded in 1961 "in order to indoctrinate the peasants, making them the backbone of the ideological campaign supporting the free-world system against the inroads of international Communism." ORDEN has waged a bloody campaign together with the Salvadoran armed forces, attacking the popular organizations of "Communist subversion," raping the women, executing the leaders, pillaging and burning their homes.

As this old system of unmonitored military force became increasingly counter-productive and served to further radicalize the population, the United States, hoping to forestall drastic structural changes in El Salvador, backed the bloodless military coup of Oct. 15, 1979, which overthrew the dictatorship of Gen. Carlos Humberto Romero. The five-member military-civilian junta, consisting of both progressive as well as hard-line officers and members of the Social Democratic Party, lasted only three months. The three civilian members resigned in protest of the escalating repression being carried out by the military and right-wing paramilitary organizations and the Government's inability to curb the excesses of its own security forces.

The second junta, formed at the beginning of . . . [1980], in which the more conservative Christian Democratic members replaced the Social Democratic members, itself experienced several months later a mass resignation for the same reason as its predecessor. Today the new Christian Democratic members represent but a fraction of their own constituency. Moreover, the "progressive" military member, Col. Arnoldo Adolfo Majano, the most liberal representative of the armed forces, has seen his authority truncated, and a hard-liner now occupies the position on the junta that once was his.

As military repression grew more severe, the junta began its economic reform effort. It nationalized the banks and all exports were brought under the control of the Government.

But its greatest hope lay in the agrarian reform program. In the first phase, all large estates over 1,250 acres were taken over by the Government. Former owners were compensated 25 percent in cash and 75 percent in Government bonds. Peasant cooperatives were formed by the workers of the estates, under an arrangement by which they would eventually take control and pay off the debt to the Government through a 30-year mortgage.

This strategy has proven rather ineffective because a great number of the estates have fallen into the hands of the right-wing ORDEN peasants, who have killed or frightened off the peasants belonging to the popular organizations. Moreover, the flight of previous owners and administrators has left the new cooperatives without vital technical and managerial personnel. Finally, the cooperatives lack adequate credit to purchase seed, fertilizer, insecticides and machinery.

The next phase of agrarian reform, "the land to the tiller" concept that could turn over lands between 375 and 1,250 acres from the absentee landlords to the people who work for them, is equally shaky. The ORDEN peasants and the armed forces have leveled such massive violence against the organized peasants that great numbers of them have been forced to abandon their homes and seek refuge in the mountains. These people will receive very little, if any, fruits of the agrarian reform program, which the U.S. agricultural specialist, Dr. Roy Prostermann, has designed for El Salvador.

Dr. Prostermann's past record in Southeast Asia does little to inspire confidence. He was the architect of the land-reform-effort in South Vietnam, which he claims was not successful because the United States failed to commit sufficient resources toward its success. As in Vietnam, it is simply too little, too late and under the wrong conditions.

In another chilling analogy to the tactic used in South Vietnam, the concept of the "strategic hamlet" is being employed by the Salvadoran armed forces in many parts of the countryside. Typically, a valley area will have one or two larger towns, with populations of several thousand, surrounded by smaller villages that are located in the nearby for-

est and mountains. Because of the attacks from the ORDEN
peasants, who according to the founder, Gen. Medrano, "flesh
out and provide the main body for the army in their battles
against the popular organizations," the "subversives" have
fled from their farms to seek shelter in the nearby impregna-
ble high mountain villages.

The Arcatao Valley, in the province of Chalatenango,
serves as an example of the rural chaos. The town of Arcatao,
which previously had a population of 3,000 inhabitants, sits in
the middle of the valley in the shadow of the mountains that
form the border with Honduras. In late July, I arrived in Arcatao with two workers from the Agrarian Reform Institute.
What we found was the Salvadoran version of the "strategic
hamlet." All but a dozen of the original 400 families had
abandoned their homes. Many had fled to the shelter of the
refugee centers in the provincial capital, or to the larger centers in San Salvador. Approximately one third had chosen to
escape the right-wing violence by fleeing to the high mountain villages, which offer some protection because of their relative inaccessibility.

I spent the afternoon talking with the National Guard
commander and the many ORDEN peasants who had been
forced to leave their homes in the surrounding villages and
move to the abandoned houses and military protection of Arcatao. These refugees explained that they had been driven
from their homes by the "subversives." In fact, I spoke with
several peasants who told me about a recent attack just five
blocks from the center of town and the military garrison, on
June 25, which left four dead, including two children. Judging
from the bullet holes that pockmarked the buildings and the
several wounded refugees that I interviewed, there is little
doubt that there was, in fact, a brutal attack. According to the
victims, it was the "subversives" who committed this atroc-
ity. When I asked how many "subversives" were in the
mountains, they said about 1,000. When I asked how many of
these were guerrillas, the answer was unanimous: "All of
them."

To get the other side of story, we borrowed three mules,

sombreros and a white flag, and set off up the mountain trail to find the guerrillas. Nearly two hours later, as we were approaching the summit of the mountain, a voice from the thick jungle-like underbrush ordered us to stop and dismount. As we stood in a small clearing, about a dozen teen-age boys, armed with shotguns, small caliber rifles and pistols, emerged from the foliage and silently surrounded us. We had found the "subversives."

Looking down on the town of Arcatao, where we could see the National Guard commander observing us through binoculars, we began talking with these young men. They explained that they were not guerrillas at all, but that they and the others in the camp were actually refugees from the violence perpetrated against them by the military and ORDEN. As night fell, we were invited into the village-camp of Las Cañadas, which rests at the very summit of the mountain, only a few hundred yards from the border with Honduras. What we found were not guerrillas but hundreds of undernourished and sick peasants. Fully half of these people were under the age of 10, and another 150 were women and old people. The remaining adult men with whom we spoke were all heads of their families, who were with them in the makeshift refugee camp.

That evening and the following morning I spent several hours taping interviews. The testimony of Amilcar Catalan is typical of the many other families there:

Q.—When did you arrive here?

A.—I arrived here five months ago. I did not come here because I belonged to any political organization. We came because the repression against us amounted to persecution.

Q.—What do you mean by repression?

A.—Repression means that they killed anybody that looked at them the wrong way.

Q.—Who are "they?"

A.—The National Guard and ORDEN. The day we left, 12 of them came to our family home. They made a brother of mine, Emilio, put his hands over his head and took him off and shot him. For these reasons, we had to leave our home in

Arcatao, because they were going to kill us all. This is what they said. We were threatened with death, so we could not stay.

Q.—Why did they do this to you and your family?

A.—Our family are woodcutters. We joined the Union of Rural Workers. This is our crime—we are poor and woodcutters—and that is why we are persecuted. If we stay in Arcatao, they will kill us. At least in this place we can continue surviving. It is for this reason that we left our homes, to save our lives.

The population of Las Cañadas has swelled from its original 80 inhabitants to more than 400 people during the last year. Now all are suffering from malnutrition, and many have contracted serious illnesses which include typhoid, yellow fever, dysentery, parasites and gangrenous infections.

An interview with another refugee sums up the situation in Las Cañadas.

Q.—How is life here?

A.—We have arrived at a point at which we do not know what to do. The food that we brought up here has run out. You can see the sickness.

Q.—Don't you grow corn?

A.—We had to leave our fields. It is too high up here to grow corn and they won't let us work our fields down below. As soon as we try, they begin shooting at us.

Q.—What happened to your house?

A.—They burned it after I left.

Q.—Why did they burn it? As vengeance?

A.—I do not know what vengeance it would be. I have not committed a crime. Perhaps it is because we, the poor people, are a nuisance to the millionaires.

Many have dug caves into the side of the mountain, which serve both as domiciles and, in the case of an air or artillery bombardment from the armed forces, as air attack shelters. Because of the 1969 war between El Salvador and Honduras, there is a three-kilometer demilitarized zone on either side of the border. Yet regardless of formal restrictions, this is no neutral zone for the refugees. As one man explained to me:

"The military and ORDEN do not let us come down to the town even to buy a pill. Neither does the Honduran Army let us go down to the towns over there to buy medicines, like we used to. They are in direct communication with the army and are trying to eliminate us. If one were to go down to one of the towns in Honduras, like before, they would be killed. This has happened. We are living between two fires."

Punctuated by the sounds of automatic weapons and mortar fire that was echoing across the valley from the army assault against the village refugee camp of El Portillo, he went on to explain that they live under the constant threat of a Salvadoran military attack, as well as harassment by the Honduran Army, which regularly patrols the zone in contravention of the peace agreement. These fears are not paranoid but founded in reality. The previous day a ranking officer from the main provincial army garrison in Chalatenango told me that they "had plans to move in and wipe out that nest of vipers." Red Cross reports concerning the fighting in various parts of the country specifically mention the use of helicopter gunships to bomb and strafe the villages. That afternoon, 14 women who were gathering wood just across the border were captured by the Honduran patrol. Fortunately, according to one of the women I interviewed, although they were beaten and three were raped, they were allowed to return to the relative safety of Las Cañadas.

When I repeatedly raised the question of the June 25th attack on Arcatao, these people insisted that they had had nothing to do with it. They did suggest, however, that it was possible that the killings were carried out by one of the bandit gangs, or even by one of the several guerrilla groups that do operate in the valley region.

But the refugees of Las Cañadas emphasized that they never leave their mountain refuge, and moreover, that they do not possess adequate arms to carry out raids in Arcatao. When I brought up the obvious point that the teen-age boys who first met us were armed, it was explained that these small arms were their principal deterrent against further attacks by ORDEN and the National Guard. After spending a day and a night with these frightened and suspicious people, I believe them.

This is not to say that the refugees of Las Cañadas or the approximately 1,000 other people spread out in a half-dozen similar settlements across the valley are neutral. Just as the armed ORDEN peasant refugees are sympathetic to the National Guard and rely in large part upon them for protection, the peasants who have sought refuge in the high mountain camps are sympathetic to the revolutionary guerrillas. In part, the reason for their sympathy is self-preservation. The guerrillas control the entire valley region outside of the town of Arcatao, and by accepting their presence, a *fait accompli* over which the mountain refugees have little choice, they are in turn provided some protection from their mortal enemies, the ORDEN and the armed forces. What is certain is that these refugees are much worse off than their ORDEN counterparts. Forced to live like hunted animals, they have had to relinquish their basic human rights.

A similar situation existed in the Torola valley in the province of Morazán. But in mid-July, the revolutionaries defeated the National Guard garrison stationed there, forcing the military to retreat to the larger town of Perquín. Along with the retreating soldiers came several thousand ORDEN peasants who had lived in the strategic hamlets of Torola and San Fernando under the Guard's protection.

To assist these refugees, the Salvadoran army, with the help of the U.S. Military Group stationed at the Embassy, has begun a large-scale "civic action program." Just as in the early years of Vietnam, the United States is now sending medicines and perhaps other material aid, as well as military advisers from the U.S. army base in Panama to assist and train the Salvadoran armed forces in "civic action."

It would be an error to think that the purpose of the U.S. military advisers and material was to simply provide humanitarian aid for suffering refugees. In fact, relieving the plight of the refugees is of secondary importance. The principal purpose of the civic action program—as I read in the official document authorizing the program—is primarily military. According to this U.S. army cable, the purpose of the civic action program is to undermine and eliminate the popular support that the refugees provide to the insurrectionary forces.

As the Salvadoran military moved into the Torola valley in force, it encountered massive resistance. Battles raged between as many as 1,000 rebels and even greater numbers of Government forces. Using artillery and mortars to bomb the subversive camps, the armed forces have displaced many more people, swelling the number of refugees from 3,000 to more than 8,000 people. Needless to say, most of the more recent refugees are sympathetic to the guerrillas and are not considered "friendlies."

The resulting dynamic is an old story. Through the strategic hamlet strategy, tens of thousands of peasants are being displaced. Then these people, through civic action programs, are made dependent upon the very government that has uprooted them for food and health care. In turn, these new demands upon a beleaguered and corrupt government creates the necessity for even greater assistance from the United States.

Although the situation in El Salvador is far more complex than any one article can communicate, the parallels with the process through which we became embroiled in the Vietnam War are manifest: 1) indirect participation through economic and military foreign aid to a military dictatorship; 2) imposition of reforms conceived in the United States that fall short of satisfying the demands of a politically aware population; 3) condoning of the strategic hamlet concept of counter-guerrilla warfare, a strategy that was proven counterproductive in Southeast Asia; and 4) direct participation in an indigenous rebellion against an unjust social, economic and political system by sending material aid and military advisers to train an armed force that is slaughtering its own people.

The Salvadoran military government today is so discredited that even the U.S. Embassy privately admits that it no longer represents any significant portion of the population. Washington's contention that the violence has been committed by the extreme left and the extreme right, catching the large politically moderate sector in the middle, is simply without evidence. The Salvadoran Government is no longer politically credible. Consequently, this has left United States policy makers without real options. As one senior U.S. diplomat explained, off the record, "We are just hanging on here, hoping that something will break in our favor."

Even after lengthy discussions with U.S. policy makers and diplomats, it is difficult to pin down the rationale for our continuing support of the Salvadoran dictatorship. Once more, we seem to be acting out of cold war, knee jerk reaction, fearful that, as in Nicaragua, we will "lose" yet another country in Central America, to some form of socialist coalition. But the anger that many Salvadorans already harbor because of our assistance to the dictatorship there will pale beside the contempt in which the United States will be held if it continues supporting the ever-increasing needs of yet another decaying regime under attack.

MILITARY'S TIGHT GRIP ON SOUTH AMERICA[3]

Reprinted from *U.S. News & World Report*.

Nearly two decades after the U.S. created the Alliance for Progress with the purpose of building democracy in South America, military men still dominate more than half the nations on the troubled continent.

Massive U.S. aid has done little to nudge the region toward democratic reforms. Instead, countries into which Washington has poured billions of dollars are the very ones where democracy has most trouble taking root.

Seven of South America's 12 nations are ruled by their armed forces—Argentina, Bolivia, Brazil, Chile, Paraguay, Suriname and Uruguay.

Only Venezuela and Colombia have had freely elected governments for most of the past 20 years—and unrest may incite military intervention in Colombia. Peru, Ecuador and

[3] Reprint of article in *U.S. News & World Report*. 89:51–3. Ag. 18, '80.

Guyana also are run by civilians, although Guyana is governed largely as a one-man state.

A few hopeful signs have appeared. But in South America—where great wealth goes hand in hand with abject poverty—democratic gains in one nation often are offset by losses in another.

Peru, for instance, returned to a civilian government on July 28 [1980] after 12 years under military rule. Yet only 11 days earlier, a right-wing military junta had seized power in neighboring Bolivia to prevent a leftist politician from being elected President.

Permanent civilian rule stands small chance of returning anytime soon to the countries that now are governed by the military. In each, the entrenched leaders are men in uniform, and free elections are not even a glimmer on the horizon.

Why has democracy had such a hard time in South America? Many experts believe it is because freely elected governments too often have promised far more than they could possibly deliver. "It is left to the generals and admirals to straighten out the messes that civilians often create," says one authority.

Here is a country-by-country report by Joseph Benham, who covers Latin American affairs for the magazine.

Argentina: President Jorge Rafael Videla

"We have elections here, too," jokes an Argentine political analyst. "But there are only three voters."

The voters: A trio of military men who in 1976 toppled the corrupt regime of President María Estela Martínez de Perón, widow and Vice President of the dictator Juan Perón. Since then, Argentina's President has been Army Gen. Jorge Rafael Videla, 55, whose administration has won high marks from the U.S. for curbing Marxist terrorism and improving the country's economy.

Still a sore spot with Washington, however, is Videla's poor record on human rights and charges that he jailed without trial hundreds of opponents.

No Argentine expects free elections before 1987, if then.

One problem: Few civilian politicians of any stature have been allowed to emerge since the death of Juan Perón, whose widow still is being held under house arrest.

[Videla's designated successor, Gen. Roberto Eduardo Viola, was selected by the junta for a three-year term and was inaugurated in March 1981.—Ed.]

Bolivia: General Luis García Meza

After going through four civilian Presidents in little more than a year, Bolivia once again is under the control of an Army general.

Gen. Luis García Meza's predecessor, caretaker President Lidia Gueiler, lasted only a few months before she was unceremoniously dumped. Ironically, she had been installed in an effort to pacify the military commanders who objected to a more leftist choice.

Her ouster followed elections that were to return to the top job ex-President Hernán Siles Zuazo—a moderate by Washington standards, but far too left for the taste of the generals.

Says García, 54: "There will be no electoral adventures in our country."

Upheaval is not unusual in a land that has remained South America's poorest nation despite vast mineral wealth. Bolivia has averaged more than one revolution or coup a year since it won independence in 1825.

Brazil: President João Baptista Figueiredo

President João Baptista Figueiredo is a rarity in South American politics—an Army general who has moved his country toward democracy.

However, abolition of press censorship and granting academic and political freedom may be as far as he can go.

Student unrest and a series of sometimes violent strikes in key industries have stimulated talk that the country may be headed for a fresh round of stiffer authoritarian rule.

Figueiredo, 62, is the fifth Army general to head the country since the military seized control in 1964. But hardline critics argue that a government that is tolerant of its opposition will be too weak to come to grips with Brazil's serious economic troubles.

Relations between the U.S. and Brazil have been marred by the human-rights issue. Yet Figueiredo now seems intent on improving the record, and a visit to Washington is likely after the U.S. presidential elections are held.

Chile: President Augusto Pinochet Ugarte

Chileans call them the "Chicago Boys"—a group of U.S.-trained economists who have made the country the darling of the international financial community.

At the same time, their efforts have helped to assure the future of Gen. Augusto Pinochet Ugarte, 64, Chile's dictator since the overthrow of Marxist President Salvador Allende in 1973.

Inflation, once roaring along at 1,000 percent annually, has been cut to less than 40 percent. Chile again is attracting sizable foreign investment. Hundreds of nationalized firms have been returned to private hands, and money now is being spent on new industries.

Bolstered by the country's improving economy, Pinochet is showing signs of wanting to stay in power through most of the 1980s, if not longer. Despite his regime's harsh treatment of opponents, he enjoys considerable support among both military and civilian circles in Chile.

"Up to one third of the people actively support this government," says one Chilean political analyst. "Another third is traumatized by what the Marxists did to them. That adds up to a clear majority for Pinochet."

Relations with Washington are frigid because of the regime's brutality toward its foes and because of the assassination in Washington in 1976 of former Chilean Foreign Minister Orlando Letelier by Chilean secret agents.

Colombia: President Julio César Turbay Ayala

Painful memories of *la violencia*, the civil war in which at least 200,000 people were killed during the 1940s and 1950s, still linger in Colombia.

That fact, with the nation's huge problems, has made the military reluctant to challenge—at least so far—President Julio César Turbay Ayala, 64.

The situation could change if he cannot eliminate Colombia's two major problems—well-armed terrorist gangs operating throughout the country and a sorely troubled economy.

The best-known extremist organization is the so-called M-19 group that occupied the Dominican Republic Embassy in Bogotá for 61 days ... [in 1980] and held more than a dozen diplomats hostage, including the U.S. ambassador. Turbay's careful handling of that crisis moved his government even closer to the U.S.

The two nations already were cooperating closely in an effort to stem drug traffic. Narcotics have surpassed coffee as Colombia's principal export, with resulting widespread corruption.

Ecuador: President Jaime Roldós Aguilera

This impoverished country of 8 million people has a civilian President once again—but whether he will remain in office is anyone's guess.

President Jaime Roldós Aguilera, 39, was elected in 1979 after seven years of military rule. Since then, Roldós, a friend of the U.S., has spent most of his time squabbling with opponents and factions of his own party.

Ecuador's maverick Congress has already given the President a vote of no confidence, denying him extraordinary powers he says he must have to deal with economic and social problems.

For its part, the military shows no intention of moving in. But it is watching carefully to determine if the civilians can get their house in order.

[President Roldós Aguilera was killed in a plane crash in May 1981. After his death Vice President Osvaldo Hurtado Larrea immediately assumed the presidency.—Ed.]

Guyana: Prime Minister Forbes Burnham

Contrary to U.S. wishes, this former British colony has been turned into a one-party state, with Forbes Burnham apparently Prime Minister for life.

Since he took office in 1964, elections have been postponed more often than not. And those that have been held have been accompanied by charges of fraud and intimidation.

Guyana is best known in the U.S. as the nation where Jim Jones and his People's Temple cult came to ruin after the mass murder-suicide of its disciples shocked the world in 1978. Last year, the President blocked opponents' demands for an investigation of his government's close ties with the cult.

Even without a military takeover, critics say that democracy stands little chance while Burnham, 57, is in power. His foreign policy is oriented more toward the U.S., however, and less to Guyana's old friend Cuba.

Peru: President Fernando Belaunde Terry

Think of any social, economic or political problem that may beset a country, and it is one that Peru's new leader must solve if civilian rule is to survive here in the rugged Andes.

President Fernando Belaunde Terry, 66, is no stranger to the task. Returned in July to the Presidency by a landslide in free elections, he is the same man who was overthrown by the armed forces in October, 1968.

The country did not thrive under the generals, who never came close to resolving the nation's many woes. Social unrest was fueled by high inflation and starvation wages of $80 a month for the average Peruvian. Additionally, prolonged drought had crippled agricultural production.

Whether lasting civilian rule can be established depends largely on whether the new President can make good on promises to raise food production, to create a million new jobs and to attract new investments from overseas.

Partly out of wishful thinking, Washington is betting Belaunde Terry will succeed. The U.S. realizes that his success, or failure, could have major impact on the growth of democracy elsewhere in South America.

Paraguay: President Alfredo Stroessner

President since 1954, Gen. Alfredo Stroessner is assured of keeping his job as long as he is physically able.

Stroessner's combination of a hard line toward opponents and paternalism toward his friends is expected to keep him in office indefinitely.

Dissenters want the 67-year-old general out. But hopes for change rest on unconfirmed reports of his ill health rather than on a direct challenge.

Like most South American rulers, Stroessner's biggest headache is the economy. Inflation approached 29 percent in 1979—low for South America but much higher than well-managed Paraguay is accustomed to suffer.

Suriname: Prime Minister Henk Chin-A-Sen

Add the name of the former Dutch colony of Suriname to the list of countries bossed by the armed forces.

The Army toppled the government of Prime Minister Henk Arron in a coup last February and in his place installed Henk Chin-A-Sen, 46.

The new government finds favor in Washington as well as in Suriname's Army barracks. After initial misgivings about the coup, the U.S. now views the soldiers as populists who want to end political corruption and accelerate economic development. Badly in need of outside investment, the country has moved closer to the Caribbean Development Bank, the U.S. and the Netherlands, while rejecting offers of aid from both Cuba and North Korea—an encouraging sign, in Washington's view.

Uruguay: President Aparicio Méndez

Uruguay has a civilian leader, but his strings are pulled by the armed forces.

The military shut down Congress in 1973 and ordered President Juan María Bordaberry to get Uruguay moving again after decades of inflation and corruption. But in 1976, Bordaberry also got the ax, and his successor, Dr. Aparicio Méndez, 75, likewise serves at the pleasure of the military.

There always is talk here of returning to a limited form of democracy. But with inflation topping 83 percent last year, no one seriously expects it.

Like the Argentine military, the generals want to be respected by the United States. They give lip service to the idea of constitutional government. But with economic problems unsolved, they are reluctant to give civilians another chance at unfettered rule.

Venezuela: President Luis Herrera Campins

As a land that is rich and politically stable—at least by South American standards—Venezuela holds a unique position in this part of the world.

President Luis Herrera Campins, 55, is the envy of all the continent. His chief problem: Finding noninflationary ways to spend the country's 60-million-dollar-a-day oil bonanza.

Leftists are weak in Venezuela and pose no threat. Former President Carlos Andrés Pérez, Herrera Campins's immediate predecessor, still is a potent political force but creates no worry. Pérez is preoccupied defending himself against charges that he stole millions of dollars while in office.

Washington and Caracas maintain close ties even though they differ on oil prices—Venezuela is a member of the Organization of Petroleum Exporting Countries. Venezuela has strengthened that close relationship by acting as a steadying influence on countries in Central America and the Caribbean.

Copyright 1980 U.S. News & World Report, Inc.

THE UNITED STATES AND ITS REGIONAL SECURITY INTERESTS[4]

International security is not a fixed commodity but an evolving bargaining relationship among allies and adversaries. For the United States, international security means shaping an external environment where the political, social, and economic values embodied in its institutions and practices can survive and flourish, and where its territorial integrity is preserved. Military force is one instrument to achieve these ends. In this paper I will discuss seven topics regarding U.S. security in the Western Hemisphere, paying special attention to its military and political aspects. Two of these are relations with adversaries, such as the Soviet Union and Cuba, but five others are relations between the United States and its hemispheric allies (other than Canada). These are the sharing of security burdens, conflicts among Latin American states, internal security, international economic security, and conflicts with the United States. Indeed, this listing suggests two of the main themes of this essay: the problematic nature of U.S. security relations with generally, but not always, friendly neighbors to the south, and the rising primacy of economic conflict between Latin America and the United States.

Burden Sharing

Latin American countries generally have been unwilling and unable to share the burdens of hemispheric alliance maintenance. This is not unique to U.S. relations with its southern neighbors—the United States has comparable concerns in its relations with Western Europe and Japan—but it

[4] Reprint of "The United States and Its Regional Security Interests: The Caribbean, Central, and South America," article by Jorge I. Domínguez, professor of government, Harvard University, and author of books on Latin America and on human rights. *Daedalus.* 109:115–31. Fall '80. Copyright 1980 by *Daedalus,* Journal of the American Academy of Arts and Sciences, Fall 1980, Boston, MA. Reprinted by permission.

has considerable importance for the assessment of hemispheric security relations.

Security relations have been formalized in the Inter-American Treaty of Reciprocal Assistance, signed in Rio de Janeiro in 1947. The Rio Pact, as it is commonly known, has been supplemented over the years by bilateral treaties whereby the United States has provided military assistance to most Latin American countries. Another key document is the Charter of the Organization of American States (OAS), which includes responsibility for the maintenance of the peace in the hemisphere. There has never been a combined permanent military organization, as has characterized NATO, nor even some of the more explicit military arrangements of other U.S. alliances. An institution such as the Inter-American Defense Board is quite weak. It serves primarily to exchange information, provide advice, and establish contacts among participating military officers. It has no major operational significance and no forces under its direct command. Although its members appeared to pull together in reaction to guerrilla movements and subversion in the 1960s, that sense of shared mission and analysis weakened in the following decade. One of its principal accomplishments was the foundation in 1962 of the Inter-American War College.

In only two instances has an inter-American military force been established to serve in the Western Hemisphere. The first occurred during the 1962 missile crisis, the only time the Pact has been invoked to repel an action by the Soviet Union—the Pact's ostensible target at its founding. The Organ of Consultation recommended to allied members that they "take all measures, individually and collectively, including the use of armed force." A combined quarantine force was established under a U.S. commander that included two Argentine destroyers and, more "symbolically," a Dominican gunboat, although the force, of course, was overwhelmingly composed of U.S. units.

The second occurred in 1965, when the Tenth Meeting of Consultation of Ministers of Foreign Affairs of the OAS dealt with the Dominican civil war. It authorized the establishment of a temporary Inter-American Peace-Keeping Force. The United States had landed troops in the Dominican Republic, and the force was an effort to transform that unilateral decision into a collective endeavor. The United States again provided the bulk of the forces and resources. However, this time the commander-in-chief was a Brazilian general, with a U.S. lieutenant general as second-in-command for the combined forces. At its peak the force contained only about two thousand Latin American troops, mostly Brazilians. Costa Rica, El Salvador, Honduras, Nicaragua, and Paraguay also participated in the force. Although Argentina, Colombia, and Venezuela had been expected to contribute troops, domestic opposition prevented it. A Gallup poll asked 850 people in Buenos Aires whether Argentina should participate with its own armed forces in an inter-American military force established by the OAS; 54 percent said *no* and only 26 percent said *yes.* The U.S. Information Agency found strong opposition to sending troops to join the force in Buenos Aires, Caracas, Mexico, and Santiago. Only in Rio de Janeiro was there a plurality in favor. The OAS just barely approved the force after lengthy and divisive debate.

The 1965 events may have impaired permanently the possibility of a collective inter-American military force, regardless of U.S. participation in it. The U.S. proposal in Spring 1979 that the OAS consider sending a peace force to Nicaragua to expedite a transition from a Somoza to a post-Somoza regime was strongly rejected by most OAS members. As Assistant Secretary of State Viron P. Vaky noted in testimony before Congress, "This reflected how deeply the American states were sensitized by the Dominican intervention of 1965, and how deeply they fear physical intervention."

There are, however, some joint military exercises that have primarily political rather than military value. There is very little military integration (the exercises often simply identify the military weaknesses of the Latin American participants). Since the early 1960s the United States and some South American navies—especially those of Argentina, Brazil, and Chile—have participated in Operation UNITAS. The United States has supported the annual joint Central American military exercise, CONDECA, which has, at best, a doubtful future in the 1980s. The ideological distance between Nicaragua and Guatemala, for example, would seem to preclude military cooperation between them. The United States and some Latin American countries also participate in the joint surveillance exercise HALCON VISTA.

Of these, only UNITAS has some collective security value: Argentina and Brazil have aircraft carriers; Argentina, Brazil, Chile, and Peru have cruisers. But in a serious war with a major power, all these ships would require escort vessels, as they are vulnerable to submarine attack. In fact, these forces can only barely protect the home waters; their offensive capabilities are limited to quick "hit-and-run" attacks.

Another measure of the unwillingness and inability of these countries to bear collective security burdens is their military expenditures. In the late 1970s Mexico, Colombia, Costa Rica, Barbados, Surinam, Panama, and Trinidad-Tobago spent less than 1 percent of their gross national product on military expenditures. Brazil, Chile, and Venezuela remained under 2 percent of GNP for military expenditures; Argentina was just above. Only Peru was somewhat above 5 percent.

The countries of the Western Hemisphere have supported the United States politically in major crises with the Soviet Union. There was virtually unanimous condemnation of the Soviet invasion of Afghanistan (with only Cuba and Grenada opposed and Nicaragua abstaining). However, there are even limits to that support. Argentina did not join the U.S. grain embargo of the Soviet Union. This is not, however, Argentine greediness. A tacit understanding between the Soviet Union, Cuba, and Argentina has spared Argentina's military government from castigation by the communist countries and parties for human rights violations. The Argentine government has tamed the Argentine Communist party. And Argentina's military government has been less internationally isolated than Chile's. Argentina and Brazil will probably remain the Soviet Union's major Latin American trading partners after Cuba.

This lack of burden sharing is explained best by judgments

about hemispheric security. Many Latin Americans believe that they would not be directly involved in a war between the United States and the Soviet Union; if they are engaged, it will be impossible for them to make a major contribution because they lack the resources. Moreover, they believe that the United States, to defend its own global position and to honor the Rio Pact, would defend them in the unlikely event of a Soviet conventional or strategic attack on them.

The U.S. government shares this perception. There is no expectation of a conventional attack on the region or that these countries can either defend themselves or participate in hemispheric defense against a modern outside force if attacked. There are no U.S. forces or bases in South America because they are neither needed nor wanted. U.S. forces and bases that may be used in the region are located in the United States; very limited forces are stationed in the Antilles, and their principal mission there is to monitor Soviet and Cuban activity and to contribute to the defense of the sea-lanes. It is only in the Caribbean that a modest case can be made for burden sharing.

The Panama Canal Zone ceased to exist on October 1, 1979, when the Panama Canal treaties entered into force and most of the former Zone was turned over to Panama. The United States will continue to operate the canal with Panamanian participation until 2000. The United States has retained the use of the land and facilities necessary for the defense of the canal until that time. The canal exemplifies how security is not a fixed commodity. The canal has always had, and retains, military and economic significance. It contributes to U.S. and world commerce. But modern warfare has reduced irreversibly the canal's importance to U.S. security. The canal's military value will be inconsequential in a strategic nuclear war as it will also be in a conventional war, for no U.S. aircraft carriers on active or foreseeable duty can transit the canal because they are too large. Because the United States has a multi-ocean navy, the main ship movements are between forward areas and home ports. There is ordinarily no major movement of fleets or task forces between oceans.

There was never a need to move a vessel on an emergency basis during the Vietnam war, when the canal was of critical importance.

The canal treaties do not impair, and may enhance, the defense of the canal. The treaties have no effect on the canal's vulnerability to strategic nuclear attack. Moreover, the key to the defense of the canal from an external conventional threat is the ability of the U.S. Navy to control the international waters around Panama, which has remained unaffected by the treaties. But the treaties may improve the canal's security in three ways. First, Panama's rising economic stake in the canal and its eventual take-over after 2000 commit it to prevent disruptions. The likelihood that a Panamanian government will support or even tolerate terrorist attacks has virtually vanished. Second, a neutral canal is less likely to come under attack than a canal operated by the United States. Third, an attack on a Panamanian owned-and-operated canal would complicate the aggressor's relations with Latin American and other Third World countries. While the latter two are marginal effects, they serve to enhance the canal's security.

The canal treaties have led to security burden sharing between the United States and Panama. Panama shares the burden because it was the precondition to ownership of the Zone and the canal. But, however reluctant Panama may have been to entangle itself with u.s. security, that it shares the burden is now a fact. Panama's increasing stake in the canal provides for the common defense that serves all of the canal's users, including the United States.

Apart from the u.s. forces that will remain in Panama to protect the canal until they are withdrawn in 2000, u.s. forces and bases remain in Puerto Rico and Guantánamo [Cuba]. Neither is a case of burden sharing: one is a u.s. possession, and the other exists over the loud opposition of the Cuban government. There are also small air force and navy facilities in the Bahamas and the Eastern Caribbean island chain for missile and satellite launches and for underwater surveillance. These are examples of burden sharing primarily between the United States and the United Kingdom. As the Ba-

hamas and an increasing number of Eastern Caribbean mini-
states have become independent, or are about to, agreements
governing these facilities need to be renegotiated, although
none is of crucial military significance.

With the exception of Panama and the colonial inheri-
tances of some English-speaking Caribbean islands, formal
security burden sharing in the hemisphere is virtually nonexistent, because Latin American countries and the United States
agree that there are no external threats that require it and no
regional capability that could make a difference in the unlikely event of an attack. The United States consciously provides a security "free ride" to its southern neighbors, and the
latter accept it, at least implicitly. This suggests also that the
Rio Pact and associated agreements that formalize the free
ride may have enduring value in unintended ways. Instead of
providing for collective external defense, military burdens
are, by world standards, kept low, releasing funds for other
purposes. Again by world standards, the proliferation of modern weaponry has been modest, thus contributing indirectly
to hemispheric arms control. Finally, there are some real security interests in the defense of the sea-lanes in the Caribbean, including the defense of the canal, but existing political
agreements and military resources are adequate to the task.

The Soviet Union and Cuba

Soviet and Cuban activities that affect the security of the
Caribbean and Central and South America are consistent
with this judgment. Relations between the United States and
the Soviet Union in the Western Hemisphere are another example of how security is not a fixed but an evolving bargaining relationship. U.S.-USSR relations were governed for a long
time by the presumption that the Soviet Union would be politically inactive in this hemisphere. Even trivial Soviet involvement, as in the case of Guatemala in the early 1950s, had
elicited U.S. covert support for the successful overthrow of the
Guatemalan government. The Cuban revolution changed
that assumption. U.S.-USSR relations over Cuba, evolving since

1960, are governed by three understandings that limit Soviet operations in Cuba. No one security arrangement has been permanent. The only lasting feature has been the necessary renegotiation of the terms of these understandings.

The first and most important understanding dates from 1962. The Soviet Union withdrew its strategic weapons from Cuba in exchange for the expectation that the United States would not invade Cuba to overthrow its government. The second, in 1970, noted the U.S. expectation that the Soviet navy would not use Cuban ports as a base for strategic operations. The third, in 1979, included a Soviet promise not to introduce combat troops into Cuba in the future and the Soviet assertion that its present military personnel in Cuba had principally a training purpose.

Soviet use of Cuban facilities in the Western Hemisphere has, in fact, been limited. Although the USSR has been making slow qualitative changes in the type of submarine calling at Cuban ports, as well as changes in ports of call, to test the limits of the 1970 understanding, no part of Cuba now serves as an operational base from which the Soviet Union could attack the United States. Soviet military personnel in Cuba are too few to pose a credible threat to the United States and, by and large, are neither organized nor equipped for that purpose.

From 1969 (when these began) to 1978, there were nineteen Soviet naval and naval air deployments to Cuba, eleven of which also entered the Gulf of Mexico. While the average of the first seventeen deployments had been thirty-eight days, the two in 1978 lasted sixty-five and eighty-two days; there were eleven Soviet naval air deployments to Cuba in 1978 alone. The main purposes of these activities have been political. They demonstrate Soviet support for Cuba and Soviet interests in the region. They monitor U.S. responses to the Soviet presence. They demonstrate a Soviet ability to conduct naval operations in the American "Mediterranean."

There are also some modest military advantages gained by the USSR: the Soviet Union secures open-ocean training opportunities; Soviet and Cuban intelligence monitoring abilities are improved; and there have been marginal increases in the time on-station for diesel-powered submarines (some bearing strategic ballistic missiles) that have called on Cuban ports and in the reaction time of Soviet forces that can use Cuba.

U.S. air defenses were correspondingly limited, and in fact were reduced, in southern United States in the 1960s and 1970s, because the perception of threat from the south had declined. The small increases ordered by President Carter in 1979 serve also primarily for political purposes, although they counter slightly these Soviet military advantages. The president established a Caribbean Joint Task Force, with headquarters at Key West, to coordinate military maneuvers in the Caribbean and to monitor activities in and by Cuba. The president also expanded military maneuvers; soon thereafter U.S. forces conducted maneuvers in the Guantánamo base area. In all cases, however, the military significance of these Soviet and U.S. movements is quite modest.

The weaponry that the Soviet Union has provided Cuba is also, by and large, unsuitable and insufficient to pose a credible threat to the United States. The Cuban navy is essentially a coastal defense force, notwithstanding the delivery in 1978 of a *Foxtrot* class conventionally powered attack submarine. The Cuban air force's principal mission appears to be to support ground forces. The arrival of Mig-23 Flogger F aircraft by 1978 is consistent with this interpretation. The Cuban war experience earlier that year in support of Ethiopia against Somalia confirmed the need to equip the Cuban armed forces with more up-to-date type of ground support aircraft. While some Cuban aircraft could attack southern Florida, the combat radius of the bulk of the Cuban air force is limited. Cuba has been phasing out its older medium-range bombers. The Cuban army, including a large, competent combat-ready military reserve, has been committed mostly to Africa. The Cuban armed forces are needed for the defense of the governments of Angola and Ethiopia and for the maintenance of Ethiopia's territorial integrity.

The Soviet Union had also established diplomatic relations with many Latin American countries, including all the major ones (Argentina, Brazil, Colombia, Mexico, Peru, and Venezuela), by the mid-1970s. It developed close ties with Guyana and Jamaica. However, while political and trade relations between Latin American countries and the USSR clearly improved, the net impact of the Soviet Union on the region remained negligible and certainly far less than earlier dire forecasts. Although the USSR has become a major arms exporter in other parts of the world, the only Latin American country to have made substantial acquisitions of Soviet weaponry (other than Cuba) has been Peru.

Other Cuban policies in the Western Hemisphere also show the evolution of security relations. Cuba supported insurrections to overthrow enemy governments when it was virtually isolated in the hemisphere in the 1960s. That was partly justified on ideological grounds—it is the duty of revolutionaries to make and support revolutions—but it was also a strategy of international security. For example, Cuba's long-standing support to anti Somoza guerrillas in Nicaragua is explained in part by Somoza's support of the Bay of Pigs invasion and other efforts to overthrow Fidel Castro in the 1960s. By the 1970s Cuba broke out of its isolation. Collective inter-American sanctions, and some elements of U.S. bilateral sanctions against Cuba, have been removed, even if the U.S. trade embargo remains. Terrorist activities against the Cuban government have been better controlled by the United States. Cuba responded favorably to these changes. Both countries have delimited maritime jurisdictions and fishing rights, and they have a cooperative *modus vivendi* to control hijacking and drug traffic. The net result has been to improve Caribbean collective security. As it became conscious of the need to avoid provoking the United States militarily as one guarantee of the collective security of the Caribbean, Cuba emphasized government-to-government relations more. In May 1980, however, the Cuban air force in full daylight attacked a clearly marked large Bahamian coast guard vessel that had arrested two Cuban fishing boats in Bahamian waters, sinking it and killing four of its crew. On the following day the Cuban air force impeded Bahamian efforts to rescue the survivors.

Instead of providing an unqualified apology for a mistake, Cuba accused the Bahamian boat of serving U.S. interests—without specifying how—indicating that Cuba reserved the right to repeat such military responses in the future. The military attack had been without precedent. Given the frequency of fishing violations in the Caribbean, the Cuban policy could be seriously destabilizing. Cuba apologized only after the Bahamas threatened to charge Cuba with aggression before the U.N. Security Council.

Cuban overseas military forces have been posted primarily outside the Americas. There are no overseas front-line combat forces in the Western Hemisphere. Until 1979 there were no permanent Cuban military missions assisting governments in this hemisphere. The rise to power of revolutionary governments in the small island of Grenada and in Nicaragua in 1979 led to the crossing of another military threshold in the hemisphere. Cuba assisted in the training of their police and military forces for the first time ever. Along with the Bahamas incident and the slightly increased Soviet military activities in the Caribbean, these changes are cause for concern. Without being alarming, they do underline the need for U.S. policies to provide more options to Nicaragua and to other Central American and Caribbean countries.

President Fidel Castro has commented on the Nicaraguan situation. He told the Nicaraguan government to be prudent in its relations with the United States. It should "not be extremist, but realistic," and it should "go slow." He appealed to the United States to compete with Cuba in assisting Nicaragua, because that would serve the common objective of avoiding "another Vietnam." He has recognized that U.S. "imperialism has learned something, too" and, consequently, so should revolutionaries in their relations with the United States. As for the revolution in Grenada, it was unrelated to Cuba before it succeeded. And while Cuba has had a long relationship with the Sandinistas, the Nicaraguan revolution succeeded primarily for internal reasons. Cuban support was only one factor, albeit an important one, along with support from Costa Rica, Panama, and Venezuela, in Somoza's fall in 1979. Relations between the United States and Cuba in the

Caribbean have changed on the basis of a new and evolving mutual restraint. The United States has not landed its marines in Nicaragua, nor has Cuba. Even Cuba's increased aid to Nicaragua and Grenada has not sought to exclude the United States, while the United States has worked well with, and provided aid to, Nicaragua's revolutionary government. The ruling junta in Nicaragua continues to reflect a broad spectrum of political opinion; when two political moderates left the junta, two other moderates replaced them in May 1980. But the months ahead will reveal whether the United States and Nicaragua will continue to pursue moderate policies toward each other.

Cuba has also had aid programs with other countries in the Americas—Guyana, Jamaica, Panama, and, more modestly, Peru. Most of these countries initiated the request for Cuban support. Peru was an exception, because Cuban aid began as relief assistance after a major earthquake in the early 1970s. Notwithstanding Cuban aid, these countries have maintained great independence from many Cuban foreign policy views while sharing others; and relations between Cuba and Peru deteriorated sharply in early 1980 when thousands of Cubans took refuge in the Peruvian embassy in Havana. Only Grenada appears to have tailored its foreign policy very closely after Cuba's. Cuba's development of Grenada's airport should, in due course, ease transportation problems between Cuba and its armies in Africa. It will be important to watch whether Grenada comes to serve wider Soviet or Cuban purposes—including as a base of naval operations.

Although their military capabilities have improved, neither Cuba nor the Soviet Union can injure the United States from bases in the Western Hemisphere. Cuban foreign policy was rather cautious in the 1970s in order not to threaten the slowly improving security relations with the United States in the Caribbean. It is too early to tell whether the May 1980 incident with the Bahamas opens a new phase. The military disputes between Cuba and the United States that worsened in the 1970s occurred in Africa and the Middle East, not in the Caribbean or Central America. The real fears, justifiably prevalent in the 1960s, of Cuban activities in the Americas have been reduced because Cuban subversive activities are fewer—limited primarily to El Salvador and Guatemala—and because the u.s. government has learned not to attribute the spread of revolutions (a contemporary feature of Central American life), in the absence of credible evidence, to Cuban subversion. The Soviet Union and Cuba, therefore, do not pose a conventional threat, and pose a declining unconventional threat, to the United States or other countries of the region. To the extent that a conventional threat is potential, the United States has sufficient force to meet it.

In recent years, however, Cuba has become not only a factor in the international politics of the Western Hemisphere, but also a major contender for political and military influence in Africa and elsewhere. It may be useful, therefore, to look briefly at this wider context of Cuban foreign policy to understand Cuba's opportunities and limitations in the politics of the Western Hemisphere.

Since the Cuban revolutionary government came to power in January 1959, its leadership has pursued global foreign policies. Globalism responded to twin needs of the Cuban government. u.s. policies toward Cuba sought to enlist worldwide support to isolate the Cuban government; thus, the survival of that government required a global response to a global challenge. Equally important was the evolution of an ideology, a way to see the world, that led Cuba to become increasingly involved in affairs beyond its shores to advance its own interests and its revolutionary vision of the world. In the 1960s, when few noncommunist governments were willing to have normal diplomatic and economic relations with Cuba, Cuban foreign policy toward much of Latin America and Africa emphasized support for insurgents who sought to overthrow established governments. Partly because these efforts failed, and partly because a rising number of governments came gradually to establish relations with Cuba, the character of Cuban foreign policy looked rather different in the 1970s. Government-to-government relations came to predominate.

As the Cuban economy recovered in the early 1970s from its virtual collapse twice in the 1960s, and as the Cuban armed forces became increasingly professionalized so that they could engage in serious combat, the country was ready for the next stage in the evolution of its foreign policy. The changing international climate also played an important role. The United States appeared far less willing to become involved in overseas wars in distant places where the links to the security of the United States were unclear. Moreover, the specific circumstances of the two most important instances of Cuban military intervention overseas helped also to protect Cuba from retaliation by the United States. In Angola, Cuba could claim that it was protecting a black African country from a South African invasion, consistent with the preferences of most African countries. Support for South Africa in its incursion deep into Angola would have been very costly politically for the United States. In the Horn of Africa, Cuba came to the aid of Ethiopia to defeat an overt and massive invasion by Somalia. Cuban defense of Ethiopia's territorial integrity turned out to advance its own interests, while at the same time it was consistent with the policies of the Organization of African Unity and even with u.s. policies.

Cuba's overseas military commitments, relative to its population, are higher than those of the United States at the peak of the Vietnam war. Cuba has begun to incur some of the international and internal costs that come from such massive overseas activities. By sending its best personnel overseas, Cuba deprives its domestic society and economy of their services, with a consequent decline in production, productivity, and general efficiency. By early 1979, in the wake of two major overseas wars and a continuing large overseas presence, these "opportunity costs" began to be felt as the Cuban economy—disturbed, too, by the spread of plagues that injured the tobacco and sugar crops—nosedived. Cuba's current economic recession is the third worst in the history of revolutionary rule. That, in turn, has set the stage for substantial political discontent, reflected in part in the exile of over a hundred thousand Cubans in the first half of 1980.

Internationally, Cuba's close alliance with the Soviet

Union has been, of course, essential for the conduct and implementation of Cuban policies. The revolutionary government in Cuba could not have survived the crises of the past
two decades without Soviet support, nor could it have implemented its foreign military policies without Soviet assistance.
The Soviet Union gives massive aid to the Cuban economy
and provides weaponry to Cuba free of charge. The relationship between the two countries overseas, however, is best
thought of as a tight alliance. It is not a simple case of a pup-
pet responding to its master's will. The available evidence
suggests that Cuba, for example, may have taken the lead in
persuading the Soviet Union to participate in the civil war in
Angola in 1975 on the side of the eventual victors, the Popular
Movement for the Liberation of Angola (MPLA). And while
the Soviet stakes were certainly much higher in the case of
the war in the Horn of Africa in 1978, Cuba, too, had become
interested on its own in the affairs of that subregion.

More recently, however, Soviet policy has added to
Cuban foreign policy problems. In 1979 Fidel Castro became
the chairman of the so-called Non-Aligned Movement. He
sought to persuade many of the movement's members that
there was a natural alliance between them and the Soviet
Union. The Soviet invasion of Afghanistan changed all that.
Cuba has not been able to excercise the influence that it had
hoped to have with the movement, nor, because of this, was it
able to obtain the U.N. Security Council seat that it coveted.
Cuba's successor as chairman of the Non-Aligned Movement,
Iraq, has taken the lead in condemning Soviet actions in
Afghanistan.

Cuba remains willing and able to use its military might
overseas and especially in Africa. But the recent complica-
tions it has found in international relations, and in its internal
affairs, make it less likely that it would undertake large new
international initiatives in Africa or in the Americas. The
leadership will, however, probably try to persevere in the
fulfillment of its overseas commitments, notwithstanding the
problems that have emerged. And if Cuba does undertake
new military commitments, these may be more likely in

Africa where Cuban troops are already present and engaged. Thus it is less likely that Cuba would become massively and militarily engaged in the Western Hemisphere precisely because of the press of its commitments in Africa and at home, and because the dangers of retaliation are so much greater from the United States if Cuba were to take military action in the Americas. This judgment, then, is not very reassuring about international stability in Africa, but it provides somewhat greater assurance, albeit unintended, about the future evolution of relations between the United States, Cuba, and other Latin American countries. These are likely to be marked by much political competition but not by war.

The United States must continue to resist the temptation to exaggerate or overdramatize the admittedly real, but modest, advances made by the Soviet Union and Cuba in Central America and the Caribbean, most of which occurred independently of Cuban and Soviet actions and none of which threatens the United States. This subregion has seen U.S. interventions in the past—as in the Dominican Republic in 1965—when the United States, without sufficient justification, projected its global fears of the Soviet Union and China into its own geographic background. In the 1980s the United States should continue both to avoid such unwarranted linkages and to reject the use of the Caribbean as a staging area merely to demonstrate general U.S. strength or resolve.

Latin American National Security

Other security dimensions arise from conceptions of national security held in Latin American countries. Because their governments do not expect either to have to defend themselves, or be able to do so, from a strategic or conventional major power attack, they have not developed military establishments for that purpose. Instead, their armed forces respond to possible conventional warfare with neighboring countries and to internal subversion. The existence of serious political conflicts among Latin American countries, in turn, makes it more difficult for their governments to think of each other as allies or to be willing to bear collective security burdens with a Latin American neighbor that is perceived as a security threat.

From the time of the independence of most Latin American countries early in the nineteenth century, there have been many serious conflicts, and several wars, among them. However, there has not been a war in South America since Peru defeated Ecuador in 1941, notwithstanding many continuing conflicts. There is no assurance that prevailing antagonisms will remain peaceful indefinitely, but the record of conflict resolution is striking. I have identified elsewhere over two dozen border or territorial disputes in South America since 1960. Most have been settled in some way when the stronger state yields to the weaker state on territory in exchange for a larger package of other concessions from the weaker state, such as political influence and trade and investment contracts. This "hegemonial yielding" denotes diplomatic calculation and an ability to redefine stakes from narrow territorial issues to more complex packages where all can gain. However, because war is "unthinkable" in South America, troops have been mobilized quite often as a conflict ritual to press adversaries. But a cushion that reduces further the likelihood of war is the substantial control and discipline exercised by military commands at the border.

The military posture of the major South American states is consistent with this argument. They modernized weapons inventories in the late 1960s and early 1970s. However, their real combat readiness remains low, and their ability to sustain a war effort remains quite modest. They have very limited offensive capabilities for interstate warfare; much of their newly gained military mobility serves internal security needs better. The average percent change per year of their military expenditures, never high by world standards, slowed down from 1968–73 to 1973–78, when South America ranked at the bottom of the world's regions on this indicator. This force posture facilitates conflict ritual but not war itself.

The major South American states also sought to diversify their sources of weaponry and other military materials at about the same time that the United States unilaterally implemented an arms control policy in the region to prevent transfers of weapons that might be used for offensive interstate warfare. However laudable U.S. intentions, the policy simply made it easier for others to supply these weapons. From 1967 to 1976 the U.S. share of the value of arms transfers to Latin America fell to one third; it declined to one fifth among Latin America's major purchasers, or among estimated orders.

While the United States may have lost some opportunities for exercising political leverage, it is not at all clear that U.S. arms transfers programs have been unambiguously beneficial for U.S. policies in the past, nor that the diversification of Latin American arms suppliers has much affected the foreign policies of these countries. While Peruvian acquisitions of Soviet weapons coincided with the deterioration of relations between the United States and Peru in the late 1960s and early 1970s, the causes of that problem had little to do with Soviet influence, and are best explained by economic disputes between the United States and Peru. The only area where U.S. arms transfers may have been an important factor for political influence, as noted below, is Central America. A casualty of the diversification of suppliers is, of course, any hoped-for arms standardization within the alliance. An elusive policy at best in the past, arms standardization has always been a source of political conflict and mistrust. It is now dead.

No Latin American country has developed nuclear weapons and appropriate delivery systems or stated an intention to do so. There have been persisting efforts within Latin America to prevent the spread of nuclear weapons, principally through the Treaty of Tlatelolco, which seeks to establish a nuclear weapons-free region. Only two Latin American countries, Argentina and Brazil, are likely to have the capabilities to develop such weapons if they chose to do so. While they have not fully adhered to pertinent international treaties, there is at present no determined policy to develop nuclear weapons and delivery systems for them. Their programs have emphasized nuclear energy development, with

Argentina in the lead. Their long-standing dispute over the use of La Plata river system waters for hydroelectric development was resolved in 1979. That outcome—reached in time-honored fashion, with the stronger country, Brazil, yielding—may reduce political tensions while making it easier to develop nonnuclear energy resources.

In Central America the situation is far more troublesome. The most recent war occurred between Honduras and El Salvador in 1969; relations between the two countries have remained fragile. In this region, war is thinkable. The stronger countries are more likely to initiate conflicts and to win. Conflicts in Central America—unlike in South America—are often related to internal political or other weaknesses. Shooting accidents at the border occur more often because military command control is weaker. Two factors have attenuated conflict in Central America in the past. One has been the willingness and ability of the United States to help maintain the shaky peace. The other has been the constructive role played by the Organization of American States. Conflict has long been a part of Central American history, but it is compounded by the greater ideological heterogeneity that was evident as the 1980s opened, and by the erosion of u.s. influence. Central America in the late 1970s ranked at the bottom of the world's regions in weapons imports; however, small amounts can go a long way in these countries. Their average percent change per year in military expenditures doubled from the periods 1968–73 to 1973–78.

It is not inconceivable, however, that conflicts arising from Central America's newly found ideological heterogeneity could be contained. The major external actors in the region—the United States and Cuba—have common security interests in avoiding interstate war between their clients. The United States eschewed military intervention most dramatically in Nicaragua in 1978–79, and Cuba is already heavily committed militarily in Africa and has economic and political troubles at home. Both generally support the preservation of borders and of territorial integrity. Neither is at present actively trying to subvert each other's regional clients, although

Cuban support for insurgents in El Salvador and Guatemala has been rising.

Latin American definitions of national security, however, have moved beyond the usual interstate concerns. In the 1960s the armed forces began to perceive severe threats from internal insurrection and external subversion. Training and equipment-acquisitions programs were initiated to meet these perceived threats, with the United States providing considerable assistance. These policies succeeded too well. The need to combat such threats was at times turned into a general fear of social change. National security became not just an issue but an ideology to justify authoritarian rule. Although U.S. policies should not be held responsible for the rise of all these Leviathans (indeed, they may have moderated some excesses), they contributed to the development of an international ideological policy milieu that facilitated the emergence of repressive regimes in Brazil, Argentina, Uruguay, and Chile, and that confirmed the authoritarian proclivities of petty tyrannies in the northern Central American countries, Haiti, and Paraguay.

Except for the victory of the Cuban revolution in 1959, no other Latin American regime became a Soviet or Cuban ally from 1945 to 1979. That outcome was certainly surprising, given the expected security threats to the region from all quarters in the late 1950s and early 1960s. The United States intervened overtly in the Dominican Republic in 1965 to prevent a "second Cuba" (that is, the emergence of a communist regime allied with the USSR), although the real threat of that was unlikely; and covertly to the same end in Guatemala (1954), in Cuba (1961), and in Chile at various times. The success of two revolutionary movements in 1979 in Grenada and Nicaragua has reopened this question. U.S. policy has been more receptive to working with the revolutionary government in Nicaragua than the historical record would suggest. This government has been more moderate than its Cuban counterpart in the early 1960s, at home and in foreign policy. In 1979-80, for example, the Nicaraguan government disagreed with the Soviet Union and Cuba on the Soviet inter-

vention in Afghanistan and on the Kampuchean civil war.
The United States, by and large, has ignored Grenada, except
indirectly, by trying to improve u.s. relations and increase
economic aid programs to other Caribbean countries. It is
possible, then, that in the 1980s the United States might be
more able to coexist with these new revolutionary governments in the Caribbean and Central America than it has been
since the 1940s, and that these regimes—especially Nicaragua—will pursue a more independent foreign policy than
Cuba or Somoza's Nicaragua.

The United States as a Threat to Latin America?

In 1963, during the most active years of the Alliance for
Progress, a poll showed that 73 percent of residents sampled
in Mexico City and 70 percent of those sampled in Caracas
indicated that they had good opinions of the United States.
Residents of these cities were consistently more favorably
disposed toward the United States in the 1960s than residents
of Buenos Aires, Rio de Janeiro, or Santiago. Almost a decade
later those proportions had fallen to 54 and 64 percent, in
Mexico City and Caracas. Elites in both Mexico City and
Caracas were even less likely to have a good opinion of the
United States. During the same period of time, less than half
of Caracas residents sampled thought that the basic interests
of Venezuela were in agreement with those of the United
States. That was less agreement than for twelve out of thirteen other countries sampled throughout the world at that
time: people in Nairobi, Beirut, Manila, or Kuala Lampur, for
example, thought that their countries' interests were closer to
those of the United States.

To focus more clearly on Caracas, whose citizens in the
early 1970s still had a good opinion of the United States,
42 percent of its general public thought the United States
posed an economic or military threat to Venezuela, but only
37 percent feared the same from the Soviet Union. Most of
the fear about u.s. aggression focused on economic issues,
whereas in the case of the ussr, it was fear of military ag-

gression. Data on university-educated residents are even more striking: 60 percent feared U.S. aggression, while only 35 percent feared Soviet aggression. The elites, too, were more likely to fear economic aggression from the United States and military aggression from the USSR, but 24 percent of the elites feared U.S. military aggression, while only 21 percent feared Soviet military aggression. Only Canadian elites (out of fourteen countries surveyed) feared U.S. aggression more, almost entirely on economic grounds, and only Japanese elites feared U.S. military aggression as much.

On the U.S. side, a survey conducted in 1978 by the Chicago Council on Foreign Relations asked questions about eleven hypothetical international crises. The mass public was more likely to favor committing troops in the only Latin American case included in the list (Panama closing the canal) than in any other conceivable scenario. Elites interviewed were more likely to favor committing troops in the cases of Soviet invasions of Western Europe (including West Berlin) and Japan, but sending U.S. troops to Panama still outranked invasions of South Korea, Israel, Taiwan, or Yugoslavia. Although the Panama Canal was an emotional issue when this survey was taken, these data and the long record of U.S. interventions in Middle America provide some bases for a Latin American perception that the United States is the "enemy."

The argument has come full circle. Not only is burden sharing limited, and the use of the term "alliance" somewhat metaphorical, but according to a substantial share of Latin American elite and mass publics, the country to be contained is the United States. Policies of Latin American governments have been increasingly consistent with this view. Some have already been mentioned, such as the diversification of arms suppliers away from the United States. Latin American countries have sought to increase their economic security in their relations with the industrialized world, and especially with the United States. They are active members of the so-called U.N. Group of 77, the caucus of less developed countries within its Conference on Trade and Development (UNCTAD).

They have formed the Latin American Economic System, known by its Spanish initials SELA, that includes Cuba but excludes the United States. Venezuela was the key founder of the Organization of Petroleum Exporting Countries (OPEC). Mexico led in efforts to formulate the key United Nations documents on the so-called New International Economic Order. Ecuador, Peru, and Chile led a long and eventually successful struggle to obtain recognition of their 200-mile maritime jurisdiction zones, often over the bitter opposition of the United States that at times included the imposition of economic sanctions and limited cases of violence between U.S. fishermen and these countries' navies. Latin American governments have partly redesigned inter-American agreements to include notions of collective economic security, most of which are aimed at delegitimizing past actions of the United States.

This focus on economic issues builds on the Latin American perception that the more traditional security interests in the hemisphere do not warrant comparably high attention. The Soviet Union has never become a credible threat to them. Although, as the 1980s opened, Cuban relations with Venezuela and Peru had deteriorated considerably, the latter two no longer feared Cuban aggression. Venezuela was very concerned about Cuban policies in the Antilles and Central America, however, and its government was consciously positioning itself as Cuba's rival for influence in the subregion. Still, Cuba is perceived to be much less threatening than it was in the 1960s, and Cuban relations with some of its neighbors, such as Mexico, continue to improve. While interstate war is a concern, especially in Central America, economic security affects daily affairs far more. The armed forces of major Latin American countries now include economic considerations in their notions of national security. Thus state enterprises have spread in major economic sectors throughout the region regardless of ideology: from Chile to Venezuela, from Brazil to Peru, the commanding heights of the economy are in the hands of the state, with enterprises often directed by retired or active military officers. As the United States established a regional *modus vivendi* with the Soviet Union and Cuba and returned the Chamizal territory [once part of El Paso, Texas] to Mexico in the 1960s, the cays of Roncador, Quitasueño, and Serrana [off the coast of Nicaragua] to Colombia in the early 1970s, and the Canal Zone to Panama in the late 1970s, military and territorial issues have declined in importance in U.S. policies toward the hemisphere, permitting this new primacy of economic issues.

The major Latin American countries have restructured their economies. They increasingly export manufactured products, at times provoking conflicts with the United States. They are growing as bases of multinational enterprises. Argentina and Brazil are exporting weaponry. Brazil and Mexico are more active and engaged in private capital markets than most other Third World countries. Mexico and the Caribbean basin are also the major sources of migration to the United States, legal and illegal, and are likely to remain so for the balance of the century. Latin American countries, especially the larger ones, are becoming essential international actors; their interests must be taken into account if a world order compatible with U.S. interests and values is to be maintained.

The stakes of the United States in the hemisphere have been transformed. It is not that economic and social issues have appeared for the first time. Strategic raw materials have long been of concern for U.S. policy toward the hemisphere; petroleum security concerns have shaped relations between the United States and Venezuela for many years. Three other things, however, are new.

The first is the evolution or resolution of many U.S. military and territorial concerns so that they no longer matter as much as they once did. U.S. economic security policies have also been marked by learning and moderation. Cuba's uncompensated takeover of U.S. firms in 1960 was a prelude to overt and covert acts of war that failed. Peru's uncompensated seizure of U.S. firms late in that decade led to very troubled relations but no acts of war, and eventually to mutually satisfactory settlements. In 1965 the United States sent

troops to the Dominican Republic when just the sniff of
Marxism-Leninism was in the air. Relations between the
United States and the Nicaraguan revolutionary government
have so far been strikingly different. The internal consensus
that supported the Venezuelan government's decision to nationalize its petroleum industry in the mid-1970s, while
maintaining good relations with the United States, contrasts
sharply with the internal and international divisiveness of
much more modest nationalizations by the Brazilian government in the early 1960s.

A second change is the new clout of several of these major
Latin American states. Some have entered the international
economic arena as new industrial countries. The structure of
their trade has changed. The structure of foreign investment,
especially in Brazil, Mexico, Argentina, Colombia, and Venezuela, has moved sharply away from nonmanufacturing toward
manufacturing sectors. They are also active in international
politics beyond the hemisphere. Within the hemisphere, Brazil plays a newly influential role with its smaller neighbors, as
does Venezuela in the Caribbean and Mexico in Central
America. Andean Pact countries have acted in concert outside their subregion, coordinating policies toward Nicaragua,
for example.

The third change is the challenge posed by Latin American economies and societies to the weaker components
within the United States. Many of their new exports compete
with declining U.S. industries. Many migrants from these
countries threaten the jobs of the least skilled and most poorly
organized U.S. citizens, themselves often of Mexican or Carib-
bean-basin descent.

Security policies of the United States toward Latin
America suffer from the paradox of successful relations. Much
has been accomplished. To the surprise of many, these countries to the south have not come under Soviet or Cuban domination. To the regret of many, myself included, this has often
been accomplished through the establishment of authoritarian Leviathans. Many specific disputes have also been resolved (Panama Canal, Chamizal, and other territorial ques-

tions) or contained successfully (relations between the United States, the Soviet Union, and Cuba). The success of these policies has made it possible to focus more on issues with much higher economic content that have led to new conflicts. Even some old economic questions have been resolved. The United States and Latin America are much less likely to fight in the future about the expropriation of natural resource firms and utilities because so many of these have been nationalized already!

The paradox of success has another feature. Many U.S. policies, ranging from the Rio Pact to economic assistance, had sought to strengthen Latin American states. That has occurred, although the U.S. impact on this positive outcome was only marginal. The newly strengthened Latin American states have redefined their own security concerns and have come to challenge the United States in important ways. But they have also cast their lot more firmly with an international order, compatible with U.S. interests, through deepening their international links in trade, investment, and capital markets. The spread of these links toward Europe and Japan reduces the concentration of conflict that had characterized the older relationship between the United States and Latin America.

U.S. security interests in the hemisphere require the incorporation of its southern neighbors in an evolving relationship (including the United States, Western Europe, the older British Commonwealth—Canada, Australia, and New Zealand—Japan, and the newly industrial East Asian countries) based on these newer, deeper, and wider ties that are threatened more by some internal U.S. policies (trade protectionism, tougher immigration policies, "consumer hawkishness" toward Venezuelan or Mexican petroleum) than by Cuba, the Soviet Union, or other traditional adversaries.

The United States and Latin America are not enemies, and perceptions to that effect are gross exaggerations. But their interests are not simply harmonious or easily reconciled. Given these transformations of stakes, the success of many past policies, and the passing of old conflicts, new threats to

U.S. security interests in this hemisphere are often posed by factors arising out of internal policies in the United States and Latin American countries. There are still some traditional security concerns, but resources available are adequate for the task of dealing with their declining relative importance. The future security of the hemisphere will depend increasingly on a reconstitution of an internal U.S. policy consistent with its own liberal social and economic values and on a reshaping of Latin American policies, especially in the larger countries, to make them consistent with the collective political and economic security of allied Western European, North American, and western Pacific Ocean countries.

Security conceived as a bargaining relationship has been radically altered from 1945 to 1980 in this hemisphere. It has moved from military-territorial to economic issues, from extrahemispheric threats to intra- and multihemispheric concerns, and from an identifiable enemy abroad to a more generalized and less focused conflict. Only further attention to this different agenda, with many more and more complex conflicts, will lead to a new bargaining relationship between the United States and Latin America that could evolve toward success again in the 1980s.

U.S. STAKE IN LATIN AMERICA[5]

The Council of the Americas, an important association of U.S. companies, recently computed the U.S. economic stake in Latin America.

On the question of employment, the Council noted that one out of six domestic jobs depends on exports, and that each billion dollars' worth of exports creates an estimated forty thousand jobs and adds $2 billion to the GNP and $400 million to tax revenues. Last year Latin America purchased

[5] Excerpted from "Hemisphere Trends." *Américas*. 33:12. Ja. '81. Reprinted from *Américas*, monthly magazine published by the General Secretariat of the Organization of American States in English, Spanish, and Portuguese.

roughly $29 billion of U.S. exports, or one sixth of total U.S. exports.

As to direct private investment, the United States has $35 billion in Latin America and the Caribbean, or 80 per cent of U.S. private investment in the developing world. The U.S. share of foreign investment in the region, however, has dropped from 38 per cent in 1950 to 18 per cent today.

The U.S. policy of excluding aid to nations with a GNP greater than $1,000 per capita, the Council adds, has dramatically decreased U.S. assistance to the region. Current U.S. development assistance to Latin America on a bilateral basis is around $250 million, a large drop from the 1974 figure of about $1 billion. Similarly, military assistance fell from $142.5 million in 1976 to about $30 million last year.

WHY LATINS ARE LOSING RESPECT FOR THE U.S.[6]

Reprinted from *U.S. News & World Report*.

An anti-American tide is sweeping over the Caribbean and Latin America, raising fears that within the decade the U.S. may be confronted by a phalanx of hostile nations on its doorstep.

From Mexico to Argentina, once boundless respect for the U.S. is crumbling. Latins accuse the U.S.—despite its great wealth—of failing to handle complex economic problems at home and of lacking the will after its defeat in Vietnam to use its military muscle to achieve strategic goals.

In the words of one expert on the region: "To many Latins, the image of the U.S. as the powerful 'colossus of the north' has given way to an image of the U.S. as an impotent paper tiger."

More ominously, as America's stock has plummeted in the

[6] Reprint of article by Carl J. Migdail, diplomatic editor. *U.S. News & World Report*. 89:37. S. 15, '80.

Hemisphere, the influence of the Soviet Union and Communist Cuba has expanded. Even the military governments of such staunchly anti-Communist nations as Argentina and Brazil are building closer ties to Moscow as a hedge in the face of faltering American leadership.

The Latins' criticism of U.S. policies comes from both the left and the right. Radicals who insist that poverty and injustice can be cured only by instant change reject U.S. efforts to promote more-measured less-drastic reform. America's support of compromises is seen as collaboration with the enemy.

For their part, military strong men regard America's championing of human rights and economic-social changes as opening doors to Communist takeovers.

Buffeted by both sides, the U.S. has suffered a series of diplomatic and strategic setbacks.

☐ Communist Cuba's President Fidel Castro, a political pariah only a decade ago, not only has re-established relations with countries that once shunned him, but he has become a bulwark of support for leftist regimes in Jamaica, Grenada and Nicaragua. Young power-seeking leaders on other islands and in Central America form their own Castro-admiration society.

☐ Mexican President José López Portillo frustrated over American coolness to his bid for special U.S.-Mexico ties, now is trying to diversify trade of his oil-rich nation away from the U.S., its most logical partner.

☐ In Nicaragua the U.S. failed last year in its efforts to end the civil war by replacing the Somoza dictatorship with a middle-of-the road government. Now it is faced with preventing the Marxist-oriented Sandinistas from moving closer to Russia and Cuba.

☐ The White House hoped that the Panama Canal treaties, hailed as a major breakthrough, would improve ties with Latin America. It was a false hope. Latin nations welcome an end to U.S. "colonialism" but continue to press grievances against Washington.

☐ In South America, Brazil and Argentina, in a stunning reversal of their historic rivalry, are trying to forge an alliance that would replace America's traditional leadership role.

What's behind the headlong decline in the U.S. position in Latin America? Analysts point to two chief reasons:

First, America's failure to cope with tiny Communist Cuba shattered the legend of U.S. invincibility. The Cuban issue led to constant tensions between America and Latin nations and opened the door to increased Soviet influence.

Second, Washington has proved unable to convert the traditional U.S.-dominated community of American states into a still close, but more-equal association of hemispheric neighbors.

Although many Latin countries desired to maintain a special relationship with America, U.S. officials in the late 1960s proclaimed an end to the era of "paternalism" and, with a new policy of "globalism," pushed the region toward the rest of the world.

Led by then Secretary of State Henry Kissinger, officials decided that President Kennedy's Alliance for Progress—an effort to lead Latin America into the 20th century—was a failure. Alliance shortcomings, it was felt, demonstrated "incapacity of the U.S. to act as an international social engineer."

Ironically, many Latin experts had concluded just the opposite—that despite its faults, the alliance showed that the U.S. could produce significant economic and social improvement.

But with America, in effect, bowing out, a resentful Latin America rushed to join the nonaligned movement and to demand a new international economic order. Ties with Cuba were reestablished and diplomatic relations opened with the Soviet Union.

Summit call? Some experts believe that it is not too late. What is needed, they feel, is a major U.S. effort to build a new inter-American consensus.

They recommend that the U.S. call for a hemispheric summit meeting where chiefs of state could devise ways to halt chaos in the region and reverse the slide in U.S.-Latin relations.

Washington, they say, must also take note of the increasing numbers of Soviet-backed Cuban advisers in the region by firmly warning nations of the Caribbean and Central America that, although the U.S. respects their independence, it will protect itself against any and all threats to American security.

These Latin experts insist that the U.S. must stop dragging its heels. If Washington falters, they warn, Moscow and Havana will reap the rewards.

Copyright 1980 by U.S. News & World Report Inc.

MULTINATIONALS, DEVELOPMENT AND DEMOCRACY[7]

On February 14 [1980], *Multinational Monitor* held a frank and free-wheeling conversation with Henry Geyelin, president of the Council of the Americas. Geyelin is a leading spokesman for the U.S. business community on the role of U.S. corporations in Latin America.

The power and influence of the Council—and Henry Geyelin—is substantial. The organization's corporate members account for over 85 percent of U.S. investment in Latin America, and its board of trustees includes leading officials from some of the United States' largest multinationals. Exxon, Arco, General Motors, Alcoa, Morgan Guaranty, Del Monte, United Brands, Dow Chemical, and a host of other giant firms are represented on the Council's board.

The Council's stated goal is to "further understanding and acceptance of the role of private enterprise as a positive force for the development of the Americas." Its functions, however, often assume a highly political character. Geyelin frequently travels abroad, communicating the opinions of corporate America to leaders like Omar Torrijos [of Panama] and Augusto Pinochet [of Chile]. His influence was perhaps best illustrated late in 1977, when President Carter asked that the Council sponsor a luncheon to mark the signing of the Panama Canal treaties. Seventeen Latin America chiefs of state attended, including Videla of Argentina, Stroessner of Para-

[7] Reprint of interview with Henry Geyelin, president, Council of the Americas, and a leading spokesman for the U.S. business community. *Multinational Monitor.* vol 1, no 2:12–16. Mr. '80. Copyright 1980, Corporate Accountability Research Group. Reprinted by permission.

guay, and Romero of El Salvador. Walter Mondale, Zbigniew
Brzezinski, and leading corporate executives also participated. Under the direction of Henry Geyelin, some of the
Western Hemisphere's most powerful figures gathered under
one roof to "exchange views."

Joining Geyelin in the conversation was Samuel Hayden,
managing director of the Council. The *Monitor* here presents
highlights from an edited transcript of the interview.

Multinationals and Brazilian Development

*Multinational Monitor: Let's consider foreign investment
and development. Brazil, perhaps more than any other country in Latin America, is closely associated with a large-scale
U.S. multinational presence. Foreign corporations control 80
percent of the country's pharmaceutical sector, and almost
100 percent of its auto industry. Since the 1964 coup, U.S. investment has increased by over 500 percent. At the same time,
while Brazil now has the second highest per capita GNP in
South America, its Physical Quality of Life Index (PQLI), a
measure designed by the Overseas Development Council to
gauge the economic well-being of a population, is the second
lowest in South America. How do you explain this divergence
between growth and economic well-being?*

Henry Geyelin: You know, when you look at Brazil, and
you look at the population, you have to ask what part of it is
totally outside the economy, and what part is in the economy.
I think you will find that those segments of the society that
are in the economy have prospered. It is certainly true that
up in the northeast, and in the Amazon area, where there isn't
even any contact between Indian tribes and civilization as we
know it, that brings down the level of per capita GNP. But in
Sao Paulo, you have got, I can't remember the figures, an increase of people in the middle class. There has been a spectacular growth and filtering down.

Samuel Hayden: The question in my mind is what's the
starting point for this discussion? I don't know what you are
driving at. You're driving at the link, I guess, between the

multinationals and development strategies in Brazil. I think it's pretty clear that the multinationals are not making the strategy.

Monitor: Our question is what is the relationship between the multinationals, the military government—which certainly cannot be considered representative of the people—and the segment of the population that benefits most directly from their operations.

Geyelin: The multinationals bring in the capacity for production, for the creation of wealth. And the amount of wealth that you create is then distributed according to wages, return on investment and expansion of the production facilities. And this process is going to go on for a long time. To just multiply wealth overnight is impossible.

Monitor: I think the more important question is, though, does the creation of wealth for a select segment of the economy, and I think you will agree that at this point only a small segment of the population is able to consume most of the wealth produced in Brazil, involve an erosion of the economic well-being of a majority of the people?

Geyelin: The rich grow richer and the poor grow poorer, is that what you're saying?

Monitor: Well, let's look at the Brazilian "miracle," that period of 10 percent annual GNP growth between 1967 and 1973. During the miracle, automobile production increased by 21 percent annually, and the production of luxury consumer goods rose by 25 percent a year. Multinationals enjoyed tremendous profits. GM's rate of return in 1971, for example, was 31.5 percent. At the same time, Brazil was the only country in South America where the rate of improvement in the Physical Quality of Life Index was actually negative. Doesn't it seem clear that large profits and the health of multinationals, along with rapid GNP growth, in no way benefitted Brazil's poor?

Geyelin: What is the percentage of people that have come into the economy who were outside the economy? I haven't got the figures and you're throwing a lot of figures at me. I have seen a terrific increase, I think it was something like 12-

15 percent per annum, of people who were outside the economy coming into the economy. From the lower middle class, to the middle class, to the upper middle class. There is an escalation of sucking in from the bottom going on all the time. Now that doesn't say also that the poor don't remain just as poor as before. But I don't know why you're talking here about multinationals. Multinationals are only in there at the sufferance of the Brazilian government and the Brazilian economy.

Marketing: A Need for Corporate Responsibility?

Monitor: Food processing has been an area where U.S. investment in Latin America has been accelerating over the last five years. Mexicans, for example, consume 14 billion bottles of soft drinks every year. Three-quarters of the market is controlled by foreign corporations, 42 percent by Coca Cola alone. In Brazil, Coke and Pepsi, through massive advertising, have displaced consumption of guarana, a natural fruit drink manufactured by local businessmen. How do you think massive advertising by corporations, to promote consumption of products like Coca-Cola, increases the well-being of Latin America's people?

Geyelin: Are you saying, in effect, that you should legislate against those people drinking what they want to drink? You know, if they drank it and threw up, they wouldn't drink it again, no matter how much advertising there was.

Monitor: That's not the question we are asking. David Rockefeller, founder of the Council of the Americas, gave a speech in the early seventies about the need for multinationals to be good corporate citizens in the countries where they operate. Should corporations exercise a certain amount of restraint as to where they will market a product, or is it up to a Mexican peasant child to have all the information and to be aware that drinking a soft drink is not nearly as nutritious as drinking a local fruit drink?

Geyelin: Oh, I see. You should go around and have somebody everywhere saying no, you can't buy Coca-Cola because the nutrition habits in your family are not good; your nutrition habits are good, so you can buy it. That's ridiculous.

Monitor: Isn't that an exaggeration? We're talking about selective marketing on broad terms. You don't find corporations advertising cigarettes in a magazine read by young teenagers. If a corporation has to make a decision to go out and create a demand for a product, is there a question of corporate responsibility involved in heavily marketing something like Coca-Cola in a low-income area, where it would seem unwise for the people to develop a pattern of heavy consumption? Is there a divergence in that situation between increasing sales for multinationals and the health and well-being of the population?

Geyelin: Absolutely not. I mean, it's giving them the choices. You say Coca-Cola has no nutritional value, well neither does tequila. Yet, you talk about the fact that Coca-Cola may have cut down on the consumption of a good orange juice or something. It may have also cut down on the consumption of something less nutritional, like a guy going out and getting drunk everyday—and I don't blame him—on tequila. How much does it cut into that market?

Hayden: Look, the operative thing is the definition of corporate responsibility. I think most companies would probably say that their working definition of corporate responsibility is, number one, legal and, number two, that the product they're putting out is safe. You are asking a pretty difficult question here. You are asking corporations to sacrifice themselves for some social development purpose.

Political Development and the Military Government

Monitor: Let's move from economic development to the question of political development and the growth of democratic structures. In 1968, Sal Marzullo, public affairs officer for the Council, prepared a pamphlet addressing this question. I'd like to read a passage from that pamphlet. "The military government is part of the historical tradition of Latin American development. The modern young officer group of Latin

America has been increasingly trained in the U.S., and has re-turned to its country with many forward-looking ideas. Very often, and unfortunately, it is the military alone that can guarantee stability and provide sufficient time so that signifi-cant social changes can be made within the society."

This passage seems to suggest a view that democracy is somehow unworkable in Latin America. Does this passage ac-curately reflect the sentiments of U.S. business? Do U.S. cor-porations prefer to do business with authoritarian regimes rather than democratically elected and representative govern-ments?

Geyelin: The answer is certainly no, absolutely no. It doesn't make any difference from a corporate viewpoint whether it is an authoritarian government or a popularly-elected government as far as doing business. All that you need is economic and social stability. I've always had a thesis my-self: Can the U.S. export its political system? Let's go back to the formation of our country. It all revolved around a thing called self-discipline. You must remember, everyone came over here because they wanted to break away from imposed discipline. They felt they had internal discipline, whether it was the Calvinists or fugitives from justice. And there was an innate self-discipline in this country. Now, taking that same basis, look at immigration to Latin America, and I pose this as a question. Where they lived under the *caudillo* system, under the church, all discipline was imposed from without and not maintained from within. If you start from two differ-ent bases of society how long can you expect to take the same moves at the same time within those societies to stabilize them?

Monitor: You suggest that authoritarianism and military government are somehow embedded in the cultural tradition of Latin America.

Geyelin: No, I didn't say that. I would tend to believe that a society which has never had to impose self-discipline, where all discipline was imposed from without, was less capable of running itself than one in which there was individual self-dis-cipline.

Chile, U.S. Business and Human Rights

Monitor: Well, Chile, for over a hundred years, enjoyed a very noble democratic tradition. The collapse of Chilean democracy with the 1973 overthrow of Allende really spurred on the debate over human rights and foreign policy. According to President Carter, in a speech given in Brazil, "the American business community supports completely a commitment of our nation to basic human rights." In contrast, Jack Carter, manager of Goodyear's $34 million operation in Chile, has publicly stated, "I don't think the [Goodyear] board spent more than five minutes talking about human rights when we made the decision to invest in Chile." In 1978, the Council of the Americas held 77 workshops, seminars and discussions on relations between the U.S. and Latin America. According to your Annual Report, only two of those 77 were devoted primarily to the question of human rights. Do U.S. corporations encourage or discourage human rights in the countries where they operate? Are they concerned about human rights?

Geyelin: Sure, there's no question. We are just as concerned as anybody else. I just . . .

Hayden: Business implicity believes that it contributes to human rights, and that its contribution is in the economic area—jobs, wages and salaries, technology transfer, etc. The human rights policy of the U.S. government only seems to concentrate on two parts of the definition of human rights—civil and political—and ignores the third part, economic.

Monitor: How do you explain Jack Carter's statement? Has concern been translated into positively encouraging greater human rights?

Geyelin: Now you are talking about implementations. A policy and its implementation are two different things.

Hayden: U.S. companies have some concerns about the way the government's human rights policy is being implemented. And that concern really relates to lost business opportunities. When the policy says Argentina is a gross violator of human rights, therefore certain types of goods are not going to be sold by the U.S. free enterprise system to Argentina, and then Argentina turns around and buys the same goods from the Soviet Union, is this what we want the policy to do? The net result is that it hasn't affected anything, and that's just an example. [According to the U.S. Department of Commerce, Argentina imported only $11 million in goods from the Soviet Union in 1978, while it exported nearly $400 million. One official commented that "the Soviets have nothing to sell to Argentina."—*Multinational Monitor*]

Monitor: Can you comment on how, in the case of Chile, U.S. banks have contributed to the growth of human rights?

Geyelin: You tell me how they have contributed to the violation of human rights.

Monitor: Okay. In fact, I'll let a number of U.S. Congressmen speak for me. Since 1976, the U.S., to protest human rights violations, has cut off all military, and almost all economic assistance to Chile. At the same time, private bank loans to Chile have soared. In 1975, they totalled about $100 million. By 1976, they had increased by over 500 percent. Today, multinational private banks control 90 percent of Chile's foreign debt.

Last August, 35 Congressmen argued that bank lending has reduced the impact of U.S. foreign policy. Senator Kennedy agreed. On the Senate floor, talking about private lending, he said, "Massive funding such as this may be what enabled five Latin American governments, whose U.S. assistance has been reduced in response to human rights violations, to reject all U.S. aid and continue their anti-democratic practices." How do you respond to charges such as those made by Senator Kennedy?

Hayden: I think the answer is only one basically: the companies are confused by the human rights policy. If the U.S. government flat out said: no loans to Chile, there wouldn't be any loans to Chile.

Geyelin: But I think you will find that for the most part, the loans have gone to revitalizing the economy, and bringing back economic well-being, which consequently lowers dissension and diffuses the human rights issue.

Monitor: You say bank loans have improved the human

rights situation? I'd like to quote from a report by the United Nations Economic and Social Council, which concluded "it is the inflow of foreign capital that has to a great extent permitted the viability of an economic policy that has had severe repercussions on the living conditions of the vast majority of Chileans . . . on their right to work, to food, to health, to housing and to education." Today, for example, the average caloric intake of a Chilean is about 1550 calories, compared to 1750 in 1970.

Geyelin: What was it in 1973?

Monitor: 1800.

Geyelin: And in 1974?

Monitor: In 1975, it was 1600. What we are witnessing is the progressive erosion of the health of Chileans.

Geyelin: No, what you will see now is a progressive improvement. I think you will find that the erosion was just during that god-awful period when inflation was so incredibly high. From 1978, you will see the curve is rising and rising rapidly. I'm interested in seeing the 1979 figures, they will be quite astounding.

Monitor: Proposed direct foreign investment since the coup has totalled about $4 billion. Over 90 percent has gone into mining, where workers have faced more repression than in any other sector of the economy. Late in 1978, when workers at La Chuquicamata, a mine now owned by Anaconda, protested government policies by refusing to eat in company mess halls, 1600 of them were arrested and 72 exiled to the Andes. Why have corporations concentrated so heavily in investments in mining? What has been the impact of foreign investment on the labor situation in Chile?

Geyelin: Let's go back to the beginning. The government said we can't run the mines as well as you can, we want to sell them back to you. Okay, it's a good business deal, I'll buy it back. And why did the government do it? Because they can't exploit the reserves as well as we can.

I don't know about the specific labor case you are talking about. I'm talking in the broad overall picture. I think you'll find that the government of Chile, and it is in no small part due to some of our council members' activities down there, including our own, removed the labor minister and brought another one in, and met almost all the demands put forth by the AIFLD and the AFL-CIO. [The American Institute for Free Labor Development was established in 1962 to promote a "democratic trade union movement in Latin America and the Caribbean." Critics have accused the organization of supporting CIA destabilizaton efforts in the region.—*Multinational Monitor*] And for this to be done by an authoritarian government is quite amazing to me. They now have a step-by-step process for bringing back the labor movement as it is run in this country.

Monitor: Yes. Today, for example, a labor union can elect to go on strike, but if the strike goes on for more than 30 days, management has the power to lock the workers out and hire replacements. If the strike extends for 60 days, workers are assumed to have dismissed themselves, and lose all social security benefits. Workers in "strategic industries" still don't enjoy the right to strike. Workers at La Chuquicamata, for example, cannot legally strike.

Geyelin: You can't legally strike here on the MTA [the New York Metropolitan Transit Authority] or the police force. You've got injunctions by the government all the time saying they can't strike.

Nicaragua: Foreign Investment and Political Change

Monitor: Let's consider the case of Nicaragua. In the final year of the popular insurrection against Somoza, U.S. multinational banks made loans to the government on increasingly short terms at increasingly high interest rates. These loans in effect prolonged the death and economic destruction in Nicaragua. They allowed Somoza to buy additional weaponry, and, as has been shown by an Economic Commission for Latin America study, they allowed Somoza and his family to facilitate a great deal of capital flight out of the country . . .

Geyelin: I think the mere fact that you are saying on

shorter terms at higher spreads demonstrates that the banks
realized the tenure of office was very short.

*Monitor: No, that's not the question. You've made the
point that bank loans to an authoritarian government help to
create wealth, help to increase stability, and contribute to the
development of the country. In this case, it would seem that
bank loans allowed Somoza to gain additional capital to continue his war effort. And now the responsibility of repaying
those loans falls on the new government, which is representative of the people. [According to the United Nations, while foreign loans totalling $600 million fell due on the Nicaraguan
government in 1979, the country's central bank held reserves
of only $3.5 million.] How did that contribute to the political
stability of Nicaragua, and don't you think a similar case can
be made for bank loans to Chile?*

Geyelin: If I were you, I would go down and get an interview with a couple of banks, major lenders, and find out
where those loans were going, before you jump that question.

*Monitor: For example, a Spanish bank, late in Somoza's
reign, made a $190 million loan to finance the purchase of
jeeps and trucks, hardly, I would say, wealth-producing
assets. They were directly linked to the war effort, Somoza's
battle against his own people. At the same time, the bank paid
a commission of $28 million to members of Somoza's family
and the government.*

Geyelin: Well, you better go and talk to the Spanish
banks. I have no idea what the loans were made for, so I really
can't answer that.

Hayden: You'll have to go and talk to the U.S. banks as
well. I literally don't know how the money was spent.

*Monitor: We are curious about the reaction of the U.S.
business community to the downfall of Somoza. Despite the
history of U.S. corporate involvement in Nicaragua, in a universally recognized situation where businessmen had to contribute to Somoza's personal enrichment, we now find the
Council of the Americas having arranged a visit to the U.S. by
three officials from the new government. What do you feel the
American business community has learned from events in
Nicaragua over the past year?*

Geyelin: I don't know that it's learned anything. It's had another proof of what you always know could happen. That's the reason why you take out insurance. I think the reaction of the U.S. business community has been very sophisticated and, I would say, enlightened, in an hour of disaster in Nicaragua. We said, okay, that's something which has come to pass, now what can we do to help insure the possibility of creating a new viable investment climate.

Monitor: To put the question in a more general context, isn't business inextricably tied up with politics, particularly in a country where a small oligarchy controls the government?

Geyelin: I think business is a totally apolitical animal. Corporations aren't in the business to remove or establish governments. They are only interested in markets and investment climates. What you do is go to your government and say "that's a son of a bitch there, what are you going to do about him? Are we keeping him in or out?"

Monitor: But in a country like Nicaragua, how can making a payment to the ruling family, or doing business with a family-owned firm, be removed from giving it the economic wherewithal to maintain its hold over the country?

Geyelin: That is a by-product of it. I grant you, in following the steps down, it results that way in particular instances, as it did with Trujillo in the Dominican Republic. But you can take it to the other extreme. I guess what we could do is send in the marines, take over the government, and set up a new one like we think it should be run. You are going back to marine morality.

Hayden: Look, in Chile, if the U.S. government thinks that the bank loans are really propping up a corrupt regime, that human rights are suffering, the U.S. government, which follows the human rights very carefully, should say this can't happen any more. It's the legal side. Diplomatic relations often determine what U.S. corporations do.

Monitor: Do corporations have any responsibility of their own, as corporate citizens, to consider questions of human rights and political authoritarianism in the countries where they operate, given that their operations per se have an impact on the political and human rights situation in that country?

Hayden: I think I know what you are saying. Morality truly begins at home, and it begins with individuals. And if individuals happen to be corporations, and if their operations tend to augment certain negative factors, shouldn't they back out, shouldn't they make the decision consciously themselves as ethical people? I think the answer is probably yes, they would do it. But you know, you've got to put it in context. You take a look at a company like General Motors. A company that has millions of dollars invested in a country, and has had it there for years and years, cannot make the decision to just turn around and walk away.

Monitor: Well, that leads us back to an earlier question. When a company invests in a country like Chile or Argentina, and the government introduces policies based on repression, based on the need to defuse the political forces at work before its rise to power, and the company gets itself into a situation where it can't pull out, doesn't it necessarily align itself with the economic elite and the government?

Hayden: Not necessarily, not necessarily.

Monitor: What does it do then?

Geyelin: It's doing its own thing.

Hayden: It's doing its business. Look, you asked what did U.S. companies learn from Nicaragua. They are learning, and this is my own interpretation, they are learning very slowly how to do political risk analysis. Their decisions are almost always made on economic terms. We've got share-holders and investors we are responsible to. We have to make the company grow. And how do we make it grow? We look for economic opportunities. It's economic survival.

Geyelin: That's something I'd like to come back to—the question of political risk. I think the long term political stability, instead of the short term (what's going to happen in the elections tomorrow) is going to be a more major concern. If we can come up with the proper analysis, and we are working on a matrix concept now . . .

Monitor: But once a business is in a country with an authoritarian government, doesn't that company have a stake in maintaining the stability of that government?

Geyelin: If I'm a lending officer at Chase Manhattan Bank, and I've got that much in deposits there, and I've got a spread of this much, and I've got to make this much money out of it, and it looks perfectly legal, and the government says it's okay, I'm going to make my money out of it. Companies are not political animals. They do their thing best and set a good example. When they are overseas, they become good corporate citizens.

'LIBERATING' LATIN AMERICA[8]

The longstanding promotion and protection of dictatorships in Central America may soon turn countries such as El Salvador and Guatemala into new Nicaraguas. While their starved and oppressed populations might welcome this, the U.S. would rather have their governments emulate the democracies of Costa Rica and Venezuela. If there is more violent change in Central America, it will result from local uprisings provoked by pro-American dictatorships—which, by barring social progress, insure that the ensuing change will be deep.

Soviet hegemonism is as much a threat to an independent, nonaligned Latin America as is the imperialism of the U.S., other Western powers, and, most recently, China. However, the presence of Soviet advisers near Guantánamo Bay does not imply that Moscow will try to extend its military influence to other parts of the region, or that future revolts in El Salvador or Guatemala will be caused by Soviet-Cuban intervention. Such revolts would adversely affect the U.S. and would thus be welcomed by the Soviet Union, but many Soviet objectives run against the interests of democratic Latin Americans: witness Moscow's discreet attempts to maintain good relations with the Argentine Government of Gen. Videla.

The goal of the Soviet Union and Cuba is the international

[8] Reprint of article in *World Press Review* by Conrado Contreras, writer for the weekly *Resumen* of Caracas, Venezuela, from which it was adapted. *World Press Review.* 27:50. Ja. '80. Copyright © 1980 by The Stanley Foundation. Reprinted by permission.

imposition of the Marxist-Leninist system which promises quick, major economic, social, and cultural advancement but bogs down once it has dealt with the most basic problems of underdevelopment. This system is controlled by a party elite—and requires the sacrifice of human rights. Such an objective—along with the establishment of Soviet military bases in the area—will be difficult to achieve in Latin America.

Because Latin America is not subject to military domination, as are Southeast Asia and parts of Africa, Moscow promotes détente between Latin American nations and Cuba—an objective which, ironically, also promotes greater political freedom and economic independence for the countries of Latin America.

Petrodollars have enabled Venezuela to play an important role in Latin American affairs. An unconstitutional change of government seems unlikely where influential business groups enjoy the favors of the State and even the ultra-leftist parties base their hopes for social change on open debate and the electoral process. Venezuela's radical parties may be the most sensible and realistic of the Latin American Left. Labor-management conflicts or strikes are unlikely.

The country's military Establishment, like all others in Latin America, shares the inefficiency and corruption of the other sectors of an underdeveloped democracy—an overgrown bureaucracy, great social inequalities, and frenetically consumerist values. But it guarantees basic liberties and, more importantly, offers the possibility of social change.

The best example of the military's inability to lead a country out of a judicial, social, and developmental dilemma is in Brazil. The architects of Brazil's "economic miracle"—which will leave the country's future civilian leaders with a pauperized population and a foreign debt that reached $40 billion in 1978—have justified Brazilians' "political sacrifice" by pointing to the growth rate. Although that rate reached 10 per cent in 1974, it has averaged only about 2 per cent a year since 1976. Added to this is a high level of corruption that, except in a few cases, has been kept secret by press censorship.

Many elements could inhibit the spread of Venezuelan-style democracy. China is giving political advice to Chile's President Pinochet, who is skillfully courting international support by denouncing imperialism and U.S. and Soviet hegemonism. Military governments such as Chile's and Argentina's spread militarism by sending their representatives on tours of the continent, operating secretly in democratic countries, and trying to establish close relations with the armies of those countries.

If Venezuelan democracy is a valid approach to tapping social restlessness, effecting political change, and fulfilling the aspirations of the majority, and if it is vital to restoring fundamental liberties in other Latin American nations, then all democratic countries must join in a relentless campaign for human rights. Dictatorships may respond with a similar campaign against democracy—but they have been doing that for years.

EDITOR'S INTRODUCTION

The excerpts in this concluding section center on the quest for democratic reform and social justice in Latin American lands whose governments have brutally suppressed basic human rights. Extremist regimes of both Left and Right come to power with promises of immediate law and order, relief from oppression, and eventual free elections; then, having ruled by measures aimed at crushing adversaries, they frequently find themselves in turn toppled by opposition forces their policies have nurtured. In the history of the area, the events in El Salvador in 1980–1981—however crucial their political, moral, and strategic implications for the United States—constitute only the latest outbreak as this volume goes to press.

In the first article, reprinted from *Armed Forces and Society*, Professor Martin C. Needler presents case studies of military withdrawals from power in South America, discussing the internal factors as well as the importance of the climate of opinion in the United States.

The next selection, extracted from the book *Cry of the People*, by Penny Lernoux, documents the religious war between Church and State, the issue being human rights. One aspect of the struggle is the persecution and martyrdom of bishops, priests, and lay citizens who have challenged right-wing dictatorships; another is the role of U.S. government and corporate agencies that have aided some of the organizations responsible for the persecution. Background on another instance of rightist repression is provided by Clifford Krauss in a *Nation* article reporting on the activism of Guatemala's Indian majority—a rising militancy triggered by the vastly unequal distribution of cultivable land.

A constructive development is outlined in an item from the magazine *Américas*—the establishment by the Organization of American States of the Inter-American Court of Human Rights, not yet operative and disparaged by cynics, but potentially a force for good.

Two *New Republic* articles follow: preinaugural editorial speculations on Reagan administration policies with respect to human rights, and a less hopeful prediction of coming events by Ronald Steel (who, like Professor Domínguez in the *Daedalus* selection in Section II, downgrades the strategic importance of Central America). Further prognostications—of tests that will require delicate Latin American diplomacy on the part of the new administration—are offered in a *U.S. News & World Report* article.

Professor James Petras, in an essay reprinted from the Socialist magazine *Monthly Review*, next examines U.S. interventionism, analyzing human rights foreign policy in the context of economic interests.

The concluding selections in this survey present further assessments of and guidelines for U.S. action. In an excerpt from *Foreign Affairs,* conservative writer William F. Buckley, Jr., proposes that the issue of human rights be removed from foreign policy decision-making and placed under the jurisdiction of a Commission on Human Rights, which would make public its factual reports but never issue policy recommendations.

A New York *Times* report by Richard Halloran follows, examining the dreaded possibility of a repetition of the Southeast Asia experience in Central America, with the giant United States bogged down in tiny El Salvador, as it was in Vietnam.

A more positive course of action for the Reagan administration is proffered in the last article in this volume, a reprint from *The Economist* that suggests means to combat the Marxist Left without supporting the repressive Right.

THE MILITARY WITHDRAWAL FROM POWER IN SOUTH AMERICA[1]

Latin America, of course, continues to have pride of place among the regions of the world affording material for the study of the coup d'état, for over a century an integral part of the political process in the region. A range of studies now exists which treat the phenomenon with a certain degree of rigor, and it may be that we have gone almost as far as we can go given the data base and the methods at our disposal.

But until now there seems to have been absolutely no systematic treatment of the problem of military withdrawal from power. This is clearly a critical area for study, particularly at the time of writing—late 1979—when a tendency to the transfer of power from military to civilian hands is visible in South America. What I propose to do at present is not to have the last word on the subject but rather the first word, that is, to open up discussion in this area.

Of the ten countries of South America, Colombia and Venezuela have for twenty years been governed by elected civilian administrations, their last previous military dictatorships having been overthrown in 1957 and 1958, respectively. Paraguay, on the other hand, is normally ruled by generals acquiring power by other than electoral means (the current incumbent has just celebrated his twenty-fifth year in power), so little can be learned about the voluntary relinquishment of power by the military in either case. Uruguay and Chile were democratic regimes of long standing but are now both ruled by military governments which seized power in 1973 and give no sign of being willing to give it up, if one discounts vague half-promises made from time to time to appease the United States government. The countries which have a recent history of military withdrawal from power, or which seem currently

[1] Reprint of article by Martin C. Needler, professor of political science and sociology and director of the Division of Inter-American Affairs, University of New Mexico. *Armed Forces and Society.* 6:614–24. Summer '80. Copyright 1980 by Inter-University Seminar on Armed Forces and Society. Reprinted by permission.

to be seriously planning such a withdrawal are Ecuador, Peru, Bolivia, Argentina, and Brazil.

In August 1979 the military junta ruling Ecuador handed over power to Jaime Roldós, a populist elected with an overwhelming two-thirds of the popular vote in the second round of presidential elections. Within the same week, the military rulers of Bolivia transferred power to Walter Guevara Arze, the president of the senate. Guevara was chosen provisional president of the country after none of the presidential candidates was able to secure a clear majority in either the popular vote or the congressional vote that followed. Presidential elections are scheduled for May 1980 in Peru, with the transfer of power taking place the following July. In 1973 an Argentine military government, headed by General Lanusse, relinquished power to the popularly elected Hector Cámpora. In Brazil a military government, headed at present by General João Baptista Figueiredo, is putting through a "democratic opening," which has meant a political amnesty, freedom of the press, and the free organization of opposition parties. Let us examine each case in detail.

Ecuador

The fifth nonconsecutive presidential term of José María Velasco Ibarra was brought to an end in 1971 when the armed forces, under General Guillermo Rodríguez Lara, seized power. The causes motivating the coup included the chaotic state of the country, a normal consequence of a Velasco Ibarra administration; the likelihood that if the scheduled presidential elections were held the person elected would be Asaad Bucaram, an unpolished, even uncouth, populist of ethnically dubious (that is, Lebanese) antecedents; and, most importantly, the attempt made by Velasco's defense minister and nephew to manipulate military appointments and retirements to enhance his and Velasco's personal power.

Rodríguez Lara made some statements about following the example set by the military government in power in Peru and pursuing economic development and social justice; but

his government proved essentially to be a traditional Ecua-
dorean one, muddling through from crisis to crisis without
clear direction. Nevertheless, the government's symbolic
movements in a nationalist and socialist direction, however
feeble, provoked protests. Businessmen involved in international trade protested government acts designed to favor the
growth of national industry, such as the maintenance of high
tariffs. Landowners protested what was in actuality hardly
more than a nominal attempt at agrarian reform. There was
also disquiet within the armed forces because Rodríguez Lara
seemed to be attempting to build his personal political position, instead of just functioning as a representative of the military institution. As is normally the case in Ecuador, plotting
against the government was catalyzed by economic difficulties. A reduction in oil production and exports led to a rapid
decline in government revenues and a balance of payment
deficit. The lack of legitimacy in the way the government had
come to power made it possible for a range of opposition
forces, concerned about general economic conditions, specific economic grievances, or institutional military interests,
to join with civilian politicans who were tired of being out of
power on a platform of removing Rodríguez Lara and returning the country to constitutional rule.

An unsuccessful coup in 1975 opened a period of political
and military turmoil which led in January 1976 to a successful
seizure of power by the three service commanders acting on
behalf of the military as a whole. The new government was of
the junta type, with the senior officer, the naval commander,
acting as nominal president. Drawing part of its legitimacy
from the demand to return power to civilian hands, the junta
did proceed with plans for elections. Some civilian political
forces were involved in the planning for a return to constitu-
tionality, but Bucaram was barred from running for the presidency by a decree that candidates had to be Ecuadorean-born
offspring of Ecuadorean-born parents. Even so, there were
forces within the provisional government that looked for ex-
cuses to drag out or bring a halt to the plan to relinquish
power, and it was not until Roldós won an overwhelming

victory in the second round of presidential elections that it became certain that the transfer of power would in fact take place. Most observers had assumed that the outcome of the voting would be indecisive and would provide an opportunity for the military to retain power, claiming that elections had not provided a clear resolution to the succession problem. Not only did Roldós' landslide victory remove this argument, but it guaranteed that a military continuation in power would have led to a popular uprising.

Bolivia

In Bolivia the return of power to civilian hands took place in the following manner. General Hugo Banzer had seized power in 1971, representing a conservative coalition based on business interests from Santa Cruz, a city in the eastern lowlands. Deftly maneuvering among military and civilian factions, using repression against the country's main organized labor force, its miners (as had governments before his), and manipulating Bolivia's long-standing claim to access to the Pacific (lost to Chile almost a hundred years before), Banzer managed to stay in power longer than any president of Bolivia in this century.

The fundamental fact about Bolivia's politics is that no existing force is capable, on its own, of dominating the country's political life and assuring stability to a government. Prior to 1952, the traditional oligarchy, based primarily on mining interests, played such a dominant role. For twelve years following the Revolution of 1952, the country's political center of gravity lay in the MNR, the National Revolutionary Movement, led by Víctor Paz Estenssoro, which held together in a loose coalition the country's peasants and miners, sectors of the urban middle class, and a much weakened military owing ostensible loyalty to the MNR. The unity of the movement, however, shattered as economic hard times and the requirements of international and United States aid ran counter to mineworkers' interests, as the military was strengthened (ostensibly to be used against guerrilla threats, but actually to be used against the miners), and as other leaders of the movement resented Paz's attempt to change the constitution and perpetuate himself in office. Since the splitting of the MNR, a variety of power factors—miners, peasants, students, business interests, and a factionalized army have formed transitory alliances, maneuvering to control the country, without being able to form any long-lasting coalition that would aggregate a clear preponderance of power.

Banzer had managed to create something of a preponderant alliance, but it decayed during his tenure in power. Confronted with the final erosion of his power base, Banzer agreed to hold elections, giving his reluctant support to a military candidate, General Juan Pereda Asbún. Pereda was an air force general and had less than wholehearted support from the army; there were also some factions that remained loyal to Banzer himself. In the election, an alliance of the left-wing forces—miners, students, and middle-class intellectuals—managed to secure enough peasant support to gain a majority for Hernán Siles Zuazo. Pereda refused to accept this result and staged a coup which removed Banzer from office and annulled the elections. Without wholehearted military support, however, and confronted with a majority of the voters who had opted for his opponent, Pereda stood on shaky ground. Plotting against him began, led by what was called "the generational group," a set of younger officers, academy trained, more professionally oriented, and reputedly tired of the continual factionalism and political meddling of the top echelons of the officer corps. Appreciating that it was the better part of valor to join the planned coup rather than attempt to oppose it, the army commander, General David Padilla, led the overthrow of Pereda with the promise that constitutional authority would be restored. In fact this occurred in August of 1979. Even though no candidate received a popular majority, and none of the candidates was able to put together a majority in the congress—an apparent deadlock which would have normally provided the setting for a military coup—the military stepped down from power after handing authority to the provisional president elected by the congress.

Peru

In Peru, the transfer of power to civilian hands is scheduled for July 1980, after almost twelve years of continuous military rule. The military seizure of power in 1968 had overthrown a mildly progressive president who had expropriated, in ambiguous circumstances, a United States owned oil company that had been a notoriously bad corporate citizen. The terms of expropriation were thought to be too favorable to the company. The military government taking power was led by General Juan Velasco Alvarado, who proved to be an unusual combination, the ranking officer on active duty who was also a shrewd politician and a radical populist. After a period of manipulating appointments and promotions to favor the more radical officers, Velasco managed to convert what was a small radical minority within the officer corps into a slight radical majority on the key policy-making bodies. He then put through fairly extensive reform measures, including agrarian reform, the nationalization of fishing and other industries, expropriation of the Lima press, profit sharing and worker's ownership in industry, and so on.

Resistance from the propertied classes was ineffectual, but Velasco was never able to organize a mass popular base behind the government, as most of the voters were strongly committed to old-line populist parties. Despite worsening health, Velasco held on to power until substantial economic deterioration set in, growing out of general world conditions, natural disasters that contributed to the decline of Peru's fisheries, and inordinate foreign indebtedness, assumed in large part to provide expensive modern armaments for the armed forces. The economic crisis and the unpopular measures taken to combat it provided the occasion for the removal of Velasco by Francisco Morales Bermúdez, a more moderate officer who stopped short of repudiating the Peruvian revolution and Velasco's achievements but instead referred to his own government as "the second phase of the revolution." Nothing the Morales government did seemed to improve the economic situation, and the military was divided not only over economic and other policy questions, but also over how far, if at all, to withdraw from political life. The political parties, encouraged by the Morales coup and by the government's helplessness in the face of economic problems, maintained the pressure for a return to constitutional government. A convention was called to draft a new constitution, and presidential elections were scheduled.

Argentina

Argentine politics had never managed to achieve the stability of a regularly functioning system at any time after the overthrow of Juan Perón in 1955. The military were caught in the paradoxical position of wishing to return power to democratically elected officials without allowing the Peronists to return to power, even though the Peronist vote represented upwards of a third of the electorate. After the Radical party had split, the Peronists were the largest single party. For ten years Argentina witnessed a bizarre game in which elections were held while the candidates of the leading party were prohibited from running and elected presidents served their terms only so long as it appeared that their policies were not contributing to the Peronists' return to power. The question of what strategy to take toward the Peronist problem split the military, and it split the political parties, too.

Finally, in 1966, General Juan Carlos Onganía seized power on the premise that his government would rule until it had restructured the economy and society to the point that the conditions that gave rise to Peronism would have been removed, and it would be possible to return the country to constitutional politics without the Peronists winning elections. This was never a feasible scenario. The Peronists remained in control of the labor unions, and the military were inclined to interpret normal industrial conflict as a Peronist attempt to seize power; yet it was difficult to see how the economy could be run without the collaboration of the unions. Onganía ran a right-wing or "liberal" economic policy which provoked union opposition and which he interpreted as a police problem; he was finally removed by the

Army Chief of Staff, General Lanusse, in 1970 when popular discontent had reached the stage of guerrilla insurrection in some provinces and terrorist bombings and kidnappings in the cities.

Onganía's successor as president, General Levingston, attempted a "nationalist" economic policy that succeeded only in adding runaway inflation to the economic problems bequeathed to him by Onganía. In 1971, Lanusse removed him and assumed the presidency himself. General Lanusse concluded that the key to the country's political and economic problems lay with Perón. The unions still called themselves Peronist, but so did the guerrillas, the urban terrorists, and a variety of reformers and socialists too. Perón alone was in a position to order the unions to moderate their demands and the terrorists to lay down their arms. The other part of Lanusse's strategy, to get Peronist support for his own presidential candidacy, failed, even though the candidacy of Perón himself was forbidden. In the ensuing elections, which took place in 1973, Hector Cámpora, a Peronist loyalist who leaned toward left-wing Peronism, was elected, although he resigned after a few months, under criticism from the right, to allow Perón himself to return to power. Perón served less than a year, but long enough to indicate to all except some diehard left Peronists that his sympathies were with the right wing of his movement. His successor, his widow and vice-president, Isabel, proved unequal to the daunting task of making economic or political sense out of the situation, and her regime became a morass of large-scale graft, economic incompetence, continued left-wing terrorism, and unrestrained right-wing counterterrorism. When the military again seized power in 1976, it was with a program of using unlimited respressive force to crush the guerrillas completely, and no new withdrawal from power is on the horizon.

Brazil

In Brazil the situation has been quite different. There the military government has operated, since shortly after the seizure of power in 1964, with a constitutional facade that includes the periodic election of a president, the norm of no presidential reelection, an officially sanctioned two-party system, and so on. President Ernesto Geisel (1974–78) and President Figueiredo (1979–   ) have tried to mitigate the severity of the repression that formed the key element in the system in its earlier days. They have eliminated the sanctioned official use of torture, have decreed amnesty for political prisoners and exiles, and so on. The system is moving—one hopes irreversibly—in the direction of reconstitutionalization. The dynamics of the Brazilian case are different from those of the others mentioned. There has always been regularized succession to supreme power. The president is elected formally by an electoral college, but the regime's nominee has already been chosen in a conclave of general officers. An officially sanctioned two-party system existed until late 1979, when legislation was passed legalizing other parties.

What has happened is that the process by which the regime's candidate for president is picked, even though it takes place within a restricted circle, nevertheless has many of the results of an open electoral process. Prospective candidates try to secure support by making promises, and candidates who lack support within that circle try to widen it in order to bring the influence of other elements to bear. A dynamic sets in of the gradual expansion of the number of influentials and the pledging of precandidates to proto-platforms, which has resulted in the steady widening of the political arena, the elimination of the worst excesses of the regime, and a movement in the direction of reconstitutionalization that has become known as the *abertura democrática*.

Discussion

What conclusions can be drawn from the foregoing? The first regularity that seems to emerge from the cases discussed is that the military government that returns power to civilian hands is not the same one that seized power from the constitutional government in the first place. That is, to use the terms current in Peru, the regime that transfers power back to constitutional hands is a "second phase" of the military regime. The reconstitutionalization of the regime requires two steps, the first of which is a coup within the military which removes from office the original conspirators and replaces them with a government pledged to, or at least open to, the relinquishment of power. In the Brazilian variant, this second phase has actually continued through more than one presidency.

Second, the factors motivating the phase two coup are not unlike those, or at least are drawn from the same list as those, motivating the phase one coup. Stated more generally, the reasons for returning power to civilian hands resemble those for taking it from those hands in the first place. This is not to say that the phase two assumption of power in a specific country will be based on the same motivations as the phase one seizure of power immediately preceding it, only that the motivations for phase two seizures are similar to those alleged in general for military seizures of power. To begin with, the state of the economy is critical. A military government that has presided over a period of economic deterioration, as in the Peruvian and Argentine cases, is more likely to be overthrown, just as is a civilian government under the same circumstances. Then, the undermining or weakening of the position of the military institution, always a key factor in motivating a military seizure of power, can provoke the overthrow of a military government, too. However, the specific form of such a threat to the military's position is different under military than under civilian governments. A military government, for example, may be seen as giving the armed forces a bad name by the way in which it rules. More common perhaps, in the cases cited above, is the feeling that the military presidents, who came to power as institutional representatives, were using the armed forces to build a personal power base independent of the military institution and for self-interested purposes that the institution itself did not share. That was certainly the case with Rodríguez Lara, Pereda Asbún, and Levingston.

Third, it should be noted that in second phase coups, just

as in those of the first phase, the conspiracy (or in Brazil the shift of direction) involves not just the military, but rather an alliance of military and civilian elements. This might well have been expected, since one of the objectives of the second phase coup is precisely to return power to civilian hands. What is striking, however, is that the civilian groups involved may in fact consist of the same individuals that collaborated in the planning of the first coup. This may lead to hurt and bewildered comments by leaders of the initial military government, who complain pathetically that the same people who urged them to take power then demanded their removal from power. The point they miss, of course, is that the civilian politicians who tried to promote the original coup did so not to put the military in power, but to prepare the way for their own assumption of power—even if that has to take place in two stages rather than one. One of the most striking examples of this kind of tactical behavior was that of Carlos Lacerda, a right-wing politician deeply involved in the plotting against the constitutional government of Brazil that was overthrown in 1964. He subsequently joined forces with the very politicians he had helped to overthrow and blacklist in a "Broad Front," campaigning for a return to civilian authority.

Fourth, one has to point out the critical importance of the international climate of opinion in promoting movement in the direction of reconstitutionalization. A large part of this climate of opinion is determined by the attitude of the United States government. Even when one considers only moral factors, it is clear that a proconstitutional position by the government of the United States encourages civilian opponents of military regimes and causes military officers themselves to question their continuance in power. Of course, not only moral factors are involved; a variety of material incentives, such as the giving or withholding of "aid," including military supplies, can be persuasive. In the case of the withdrawals from power discussed here, it is not without significance that four of the five, all except Argentina, took place or are taking place during a period in which the government of the United States placed considerable stress on democracy and the defense of human rights.

From this analysis, it becomes clear that the withdrawal from power by military regimes, while in one sense the diametric opposite of the military seizure of power, is in other respects part of the same class of events as the military seizure of power itself.

[For a brief summary of developments as of August 1980, see "Military's Tight Grip on South America," in Section II, above.—Ed.]

THE CHURCH, THE STATE, AND U.S. INVOLVEMENT[2]

The central issue in the ongoing religious war between Church and state in Latin America is human rights. One aspect of this struggle is the persecution of bishops, priests, and laity who have challenged a right-wing totalitarian ideology that has engulfed the area. The other, integral part of the story is the verified role of the U.S. Defense Department, the CIA, and corporate industry in the rise of this totalitarianism. Thus, on many occasions, Catholic bishops and priests, including U.S. citizens, have been tortured or murdered by organizations funded and trained by the U.S. Government, sometimes with the direct connivance of U.S. agencies. Because of this involvement, important sectors of the traditionally conservative Latin-American Catholic Church now oppose U.S. capitalism. . . .

El Salvador: Microcosm of Latin American Ills

The most densely populated, most undernourished country in Central America, with nearly five million people in an area the size of Massachusetts, El Salvador is a microcosm of Latin America's social and political ills. Ninety percent of the peasants have no land, and they comprise two thirds of the

[2] Excerpts from p xiii, p 62–7, and p 203–14 of *Cry of the People: United States Involvement in the Rise of Fascism, Torture, and Murder and the Persecution of the Catholic Church in Latin America*, by Penny Lernoux. Copyright © 1980 by Penny Lernoux. Reprinted by permission of Doubleday & Company, Inc. The author, an expert on the Latin American church, is *The Nation's* correspondent in Latin America.

population. Two percent of the people own 58 percent of the arable land. The average monthly income of the peasant families, 50 percent of them illiterate, is twelve dollars. Four fifths of the children are ill-nourished. Unemployment and underemployment total 45 percent.

Ever since commercial coffee growing came to the country in the nineteenth century, the large growers have been progressively squeezing the peasants off their communal lands. With no virgin land to exploit and an annual birth rate of 3.5 percent, El Salvador's desperate peasant population rose up—and was slaughtered—time and again; in 1932 President Maximiliano Hernández' government killed thirty thousand of them. The "green revolution's" agricultural advances hastened the land accumulation, and thousands more were driven from their tiny plots by large cotton, sugar, and coffee estates. "Coffee eats men!" became the anguished cry of the starving peasants.

In 1969 a "soccer war" erupted between El Salvador and neighboring Honduras. The pretext was a dispute on the playing field, but the real cause of the gunfire that killed two thousand was the invasion of Honduran territory by three hundred thousand land-hungry Salvadoran peasants, an exodus actively encouraged by the military regime to free farmland for such export crops as coffee and cotton. El Salvador's export earnings dramatically increased during the 1960s, but local food production and consumption plummeted, and the price in human suffering was enormous. Several thousand Salvadoran peasants were herded back over the border by Honduran troops in 1969, only to be met by more repression on their own side of the frontier. And though it lasted only two weeks, the "soccer war" permanently soured relations between the two countries, so disrupting the Central American Common Market that it has never recovered.

None of this mattered to the country's coffee oligarchy, supreme in its assurance of power and wealth. The "fourteen families," sons and grandsons of earlier dictators who had confiscated the communal lands of the peasants, continue to live in splendor, with mansions in San Salvador, lakeside chalets in the mountains, and colonial ranch houses on their haciendas, each with a permanent staff of six or seven servants. San Benito, the rich, new residential suburb of northern San Salvador, is a tropical Beverly Hills with acres of manicured lawn, orchid gardens, swimming pools, and marble palaces stuffed with crystal chandeliers, European art, and imported luxuries. At the other end of the social scale, in the southern part of the city where thousands of poor Salvadorans crowd the adobe tenement mazes, luxury means a pair of shoes or a small piece of white cheese to relieve the daily monotony of black beans and tortillas. Dirty, barefoot urchins beg through the narrow streets. The crush, the noise, and the smell are asphyxiating, said a rich Salvadoran, who cannot understand "how they live that way." He added that it is worse in the countryside because "the people are like pigs. This friend of mine, who says he has a social conscience, built some houses for his plantation workers. They were small but adequate and they had indoor plumbing, but would you believe, those people were so uneducated that they didn't even know how to use a toilet! What's the good of trying to help people like that?"

However they treat their peasants, San Salvador's rich can hardly be described as ungracious hosts: it is not uncommon for dinner guests at a San Benito mansion to receive such small party favors as diamond rings. Drinking, gambling, and whoring are favorite pastimes of the men, most of whom keep mistresses in apartments in the less-fashionable downtown area. Sports cars and an annual gambling tour of Europe also figure high on the list of pleasures. According to an American who married into one of the families, these rich playboys "are not all that bright," but neither are they stupid enough to share the good life with outsiders. Most marry within their own class, although a foreigner can occasionally penetrate this society if he is a white, Christian, European or American professional—marriage to a Jew or a slightly darker Salvadoran from the lower classes is taboo.

While many wealthy Salvadorans have been educated abroad, few will challenge the attitude of their fathers and grandfathers: "It's our land and we've got a gun to prove it." The idea that lucrative coffee-growing land should be converted to beans for local consumption is politically unacceptable; it raises the specter of agrarian reform. Besides, they say, it makes no economic sense, since El Salvador prospers more by importing foodstuffs with the foreign exchange it earns from export crops. What they really mean is that they prosper more: San Benito housewives can well afford the fresh vegetables and meat daily trucked in from Guatemala; most Salvadorans cannot.

A spurious republic with sham elections and a sham Constitution, El Salvador has always been governed by a privileged clique. (There have been only nine months of real democratic rule since 1931.) The current landowning-military coalition, known as the National Conciliation Party (PCN), dates from 1961, when a reform-minded junta was overthrown by military hard-liners with the blessing of the U.S. military mission. The PCN has maintained itself in power by repression and blatant fraud, so strewing the path of the opposition parties with obstacles that they gave up any attempt to participate in the 1976 municipal elections. Typical of the regime's heavy-handed tactics were threats by a paramilitary organization, the Falange, against the life of Mrs. Alicia Cañizales, who was running for mayor of the city of Sonsonate. Mrs. Cañizales dropped out of the race only when the Falange threatened to kill her children as well.

Under the enlightened leadership of San Salvador's elderly Archbishop Luis Chávez y González, the Church began gradually to take an interest in rural affairs—and was immediately attacked for its interference. Father José Inocencio Alas, the archdiocese's delegate in 1970 to El Salvador's first agrarian-reform congress, was kidnapped on his way to the congress by four men who seized him in front of San Salvador's cathedral. He was found the next day on a lonely road, his head shaved, and still suffering from the effects of the drugs and liquor his kidnappers had forced him to take. On January 2, 1972, Father Nicolás Rodríguez, the parish priest of Chalatenango, was arrested by agents of the National

Guard, which has both police and military functions. His brutally dismembered body was found a few days later on the outskirts of the city. Father Fabián Amaya, news commentator for the Catholic radio station YSAZ, received a series of death threats because he had disclosed, among other charges, the intimidation of workers and peasants during the 1972 presidential campaign. Despite strong pressure from the government, the hierarchy refused to silence Amaya or water down its charges of election fraud. What is more, a number of prominent bishops refused to attend President Arturo Armando Molina's inauguration; Bishop Pedro Arnoldo Aparicio telegraphed his refusal, saying he had "a more important appointment with the people." In reprisal for this obstinacy, the Catholic bookshop on the first floor of the YSAZ building was gutted by fire, the radio station on the second floor narrowly escaping the same fate.

These events were merely a warm-up for the nationwide repression that began in November 1974, at San Vicente in central El Salvador, the rural diocese of Bishop Aparicio, when police and Army troops arrested thirteen peasants who were involved in a rent dispute with the landowners. The soldiers raided the nearby homes, from which they stole food and money, and so badly mistreated a pregnant young woman that she miscarried. The arrested men were forced to walk naked several miles on the main road until they reached a local church, where they were ordered to lie on the floor while the soldiers kicked them and shouted profanities against the Catholic religion. The troops then moved into the fields, where they encountered six peasants returning from work. Four of the men died instantly when the soldiers opened fire. The two wounded peasants, José Morataya and Diego Hernández, were tracked to their huts, where the soldiers again shot them as they lay dying in their wives' arms.

"The whole neighborhood is in terror, and many of us are in hiding and don't dare return home," was the desperate message received by Bishop Aparicio. In response, he called for funeral services and the tolling of the church bells in all thirty-five parishes of the diocese of five hundred thousand

Catholics. The Bishops' Conference of El Salvador joined the prelate in denouncing such "deplorable actions which are symptoms of a decadent society, alienated from the Gospel." But the thirteen peasants were never seen again, and the violence continued. . . .

U.S. Capitalism and the Multinationals

When Nelson Rockefeller made his "goodwill" trip to Latin America in 1969, a collective groan went up from the U.S. business community there. "Who the hell in Washington thought that one up?" could be heard in offices and embassies from Buenos Aires to Quito. True, Mr. Rockefeller had diplomatic and business relations with the Latin Americans dating back to the Roosevelt years, but didn't Washington realize whom he represented? Standard Oil, that's who, and you know how the Latins feel about U.S. oil companies!

Sure enough, there were riots in La Paz, bombings in Montevideo, and an impressive display of Argentine terrorist technology, which demolished a string of Rockefeller-owned supermarkets within seconds of one another. "I don't see why we should have to pay the penalty for the oil industry's unpopularity," a U.S. bank manager beefed as he gazed at a sidewalk of shattered glass, all that remained of the bank's windows. Everyone was relieved when Mr. Rockefeller returned home to write for President Nixon a series of recommendations on hemispheric policy, the most important of which urged more military and police aid for the Latin Americans.

There is something quite comforting about an industry that everybody can stick pins into, and foreign oil serves that purpose in Latin America. The belief is that if an oil representative shows up anywhere south of the border to negotiate U.S. policy, all the good guys with refrigerators and drugs to sell will suffer from the backlash. What most U.S. businessmen fail to grasp is that, as far as the Latin Americans are concerned, a delegate from, say, Sears, Roebuck or Citibank is as unwelcome as someone smelling of U.S. oil. The Rockefeller mission was just an unusually tactless demonstration of what most Latin Americans take for granted: that U.S. foreign policy is run by corporate business.

Thanks largely to United States congressional investigations of the past eight years, that assumption has been amply justified; it can now be seen that many of the men who approved counterinsurgency training for the Latin-American military, assassination courses for the police, and CIA activities against democratically elected governments were also pillars of the U.S. business community. For example, the majority of those responsible for the decisions that helped scuttle Allende's government in Chile, including Treasury Secretary John Connally, CIA Director William Colby, Kissinger, and Nixon himself, were closely tied to corporate industry. (John McCone, a former CIA director, was a member of ITT's board of directors and a CIA consultant when ITT offered the CIA $1 million to fund the political campaigns of friendly candidates in the 1970 Chilean presidential elections. Though the CIA did not take the money, ITT channeled at least $350,000 into the elections; other U.S. companies contributed a similar amount. McCone knew that CIA funds had been used in 1964 to support the successful presidental campaign of the Christian Democrats' Eduardo Frei. CIA documents indicate that McCone informed Harold Geneen, ITT's board chairman, of these facts.) With few exceptions, the military coups of the past fifteen years in Latin America have been related in some way to U.S. business, the payoff after the coup—as in Brazil, Bolivia, and Chile—being special concessions to U.S. companies.

Although the United States never hesitated to use a big stick to protect its interests in Latin America, it was only after World War II that government and business became so interdependent as to be indistinguishable. The Dulles brothers' connection with United Fruit, though a particularly blatant example of the use of government power to benefit business interests, typifies an era in which corporate presidents and lawyers use their position in government to promote company goals. [John Foster Dulles was secretary of state in the Eisenhower Administration and Allen Welsh Dulles headed the CIA.—Ed.] This is not to suggest that all such people were, or are, guided solely by selfish motives—a good many executives-cum-bureaucrats genuinely believe that what is good for business is good for the United States, and therefore for Latin America. The trouble with this logic is that, just as the Defense Department's counterinsurgency courses became ends in themselves, corporate growth is used to justify every kind of villainy, including military dictatorship.

With such businessmen as the Dulles brothers in charge of foreign policy, it is easy to understand why Washington was persuaded that the only solution to Latin America's social and economic problems was the infusion of foreign capital and a sustained growth of the gross national products, and why these imperatives shaped the Alliance for Progress and other attempts at "development" that became so popular in the 1960s. As things turned out, foreign investment and aid only compounded the region's problems. GNP statistics may have looked good on paper, but in most cases economic growth was achieved at the expense of the people. Between 1958 and 1970, for example, the real wages of Brazilian workers declined by 64.5 percent. Whatever U.S. taxpayers may have believed, the Alliance for Progress was an excuse for business to gouge Uncle Sam as well as the Latin-American treasuries. Or as Senator Frank Church put it: "The present foreign aid program has been turned into a grotesque money tree, sheltering the foreign investments of our biggest corporations and furnishing aid and comfort to repressive governments all over the world."

President Kennedy chose Peter Grace, the archconservative chairman of W. R. Grace, to head a group of businessmen from twenty-five major corporations who were to evaluate the Alliance and recommend useful projects. They did their job so well that by 1964 David Rockefeller detected a "marked change in the attitude of those responsible for the Alliance" and could praise the State Department for recognizing that the Alliance "had had too much emphasis on social reform." AID [Agency for International Development] orders accounted for one third of all U.S. steel exports by 1969; the following year, AID-financed fertilizer exports ran to just under $100 million. According to AID officials, some $2 billion per year in U.S. exports were financed by the foreign aid program.

U.S. aid buttressed corporate interests in America in a host of ways. It was a marvelous stick to hold over recalcitrant governments. Bolivia, for instance, was gradually forced to abandon the reforms begun by its 1952 revolution as the country fell increasingly into debt to the United States. By 1967 AID could boast that "the adoption of reforms . . . in the nationalized tin mines, a revised mining code favorable to private investments . . . and a new investment code and a revised and more equitable royalties schedule designed to encourage private investment is largely attributable to AID assistance." AID could also take credit for undermining Bolivia's attempts to become self-sufficient in wheat and quinoa, a hardy grain grown since pre-Columbian times in the high Andes. Under the P.L. 480 (Food for Peace) program, which was a convenient way to dump surplus U.S. commodities on the world market, Bolivian wheat and quinoa were gradually replaced by cheaper U.S. flour. Of course, when the market for U.S. wheat improved, there were no more handouts, and wheat and flour now represent 43 percent of Bolivia's agricultural imports. That is exactly what the proponents of P.L. 480 had in mind. Said Senator Hubert Humphrey, one of its most enthusiastic supporters:

I have heard . . . that people may become dependent on us for food. I know that was not supposed to be good news. To me that was good news, because before people can do anything they have got to eat. And if you are looking for a way to get people to lean on you and to be dependent on you, in terms of their co-operation with you, it seems to me that food dependence would be terrific.

Local currency funds acquired from the sale of P.L. 480 commodities were earmarked for low-interest loans to U.S. firms or their subsidiaries, or for the purchase of arms by local governments ($693 million on military equipment between 1966 and 1971). These funds also proved a handy way to circumvent the limitations imposed by Congress. Because of human rights violations, Congress placed a $26 million ceiling on economic aid to Chile for fiscal year 1975 and cut off all military funding; yet the Chilean junta received the largest P.L. 480 allotment in Latin America, $65.2 million out of $80.2 million. When Allende was in office, P.L. 480 shipments to Chile were suspended, adding to the country's severe food shortages. The White House even turned down a government request to buy U.S. wheat for cash shortly before the 1973 coup, but within weeks of Allende's overthrow the Agriculture Department's Commodity Credit Corporation extended the junta credits of $54 million to buy wheat and corn.

In addition to low-interest loans to U.S. companies, AID funds paid for 50 percent of their pre-investment surveys, which often, and particularly in mining, saved these companies large sums. Senator Jacob Javits, one of the promoters of ADELA, a giant multinational Latin-American investment company, tried to defend such subsidies on the ground that "it enables AID to get smaller enterprises which are not in the field into this area of private investment." Among the "smaller enterprises" cited by Javits as beneficiaries of the program were United Fruit, Kaiser, Allied Chemical, American Metals Climax, and Standard Fruit. Once the investment was approved, the U.S. Government provided money for the country involved to build the necessary infrastructure, such as the highway and port facilities that serve International Nickel's giant concession in Guatemala. However, no local firm or government agency could obtain a loan that might enable it to compete with a U.S. subsidiary. Thus, while Washington had no qualms about advancing the Guatemalans $13.5 million for the nickel project, for years it refused to lend them money for a road to the Atlantic Coast that would have put United Fruit's inefficient International Railways out of business. Moreover, AID construction loans could be used only to employ U.S. companies, often at a cost higher than the Latin-American governments would have paid if there had been competitive bidding. Such was the case in Costa Rica, where AID refused to honor a loan for a water supply system after a local firm underbid its U.S. competitor, and in Colombia, where the World Bank insisted that the government specify that railroad rails, which it proposed to buy through international bidding, be of a size manufactured only by U.S. companies.

All AID loans were tied to U.S. products and, by 1969, 99 percent of AID-financed goods and services were being bought in the United States, often at prices 30 to 40 percent higher than the international rate. What this cost the U.S. and Latin-American taxpayers may be judged by the inflated prices U.S. drug companies charged AID under a program called Commercial Import Loans, or dollar loans made by AID to foreign governments, which in turn allocated them among U.S. subsidiaries to import products and equipment from the parent company. According to 1970 hearings by the Senate Subcommittee on Small Business, the drug subsidiaries took advantage of AID loopholes to inflate prices at the expense of U.S. tax money, the foreign consumer, and the foreign country's balance of payments. Comparing the prices AID was paying with those quoted on the European market, the subcommittee found that AID payments ranged from 3 to 113 times the European prices for equivalent products. AID's explanation was that "American suppliers are insulated from foreign competition," but as Senator Gaylord Nelson pointed out, that was no consolation to the poor Latin-American consumer, who "must pay 20 to 30 times as much as he would have to pay if [the drug] was coming from another country. AID later collected $1 million in refunds for overpricing and still had claims outstanding for some $2 million. The largest claims were against Wyeth ($218,573), Eli Lilly ($238,281), Abbott Laboratories ($371,903), Merck, Sharp & Dohme ($394,067), Roussel Corporation ($699,860), and Gedion-Richter Pharmaceuticals ($802,617).

AID also forced Latin-American governments to sign investment-guarantee agreements that protected U.S. companies against losses from inconvertibility (inability to convert local currency into dollars for remittance), expropriation, war, revolution, and insurrection, thereby involving the U.S.

Government in what initially were disputes between U.S. companies and Latin-American governments. Why the U.S. Government, or taxpayer, should be asked to bail out companies whose sharp practices were an open invitation to nationalization apparently never entered the discussion, nor did U.S. support of these companies' inflated claims for compensation. On the contrary, AID and the State Department threatened reprisals if the Latin-American governments did not sign the investment guarantees. Legislation was enacted requiring a cutoff date for aid if guarantees were not accepted, and when that did not work, the State Department began issuing guarantees without the Latin-American governments' consent. When Mexico steadfastly refused to sign, a group of seventeen companies led by Ford Motors told the State Department to step up the pressure, but Mexico, having wisely phased itself out of the Alliance for Progress, was not in the position of Bolivia or Brazil and could resist such pressure.

None of the high-sounding goals of the Alliance for Progress were achieved, including income redistribution or tax reform—and not just because the local elites opposed such reforms. Had the tax loopholes been closed and the labor force been given a greater share of national wealth, foreign companies could not possibly have developed lucrative new markets in Latin America. During the Alliance years, according to U.S. Department of Commerce statistics, three dollars went back to the United States for every dollar invested. Foreign subsidiaries compensated for the smallness of the consumer market—in Brazil, for example, it was only a fourth of the 110 million population—with enormous markups that gave these companies twice the margin of profit they earned in the United States. When the Alliance was finally buried at the end of the 1960s, about the only thing the Latin-American countries had to show for it was an enormous foreign debt—$19.3 billion, compared to $8.8 billion in 1961, when the program was launched.

Not only did the Latin-American people fail to benefit from the generosity of the U.S. taxpayer; AID—and CIA—money was also used to help destroy one of the few established outlets of popular opinion, the free trade unions. Not content with funneling Alliance funds into corporate industry, Peter Grace promoted the American Institute for Free Labor Development (AIFLD), a Trojan horse for the multinationals sponsored by the AFL-CIO. Created in 1962 with the financial support of AID, the State Department, W. R. Grace, ITT, Exxon, Shell, Kennecott, Anaconda, American Smelting and Refining, IBM, Koppers, Gillette, and 85 other large corporations with interests in Latin America, the AIFLD was organized, ostensibly, to combat the threat of Castroite influence in Latin-American labor unions; in reality it was a way for U.S. companies, working in cahoots with repressive governments, to replace independent unions with company ones. Explained Peter Grace, AIFLD's board chairman, the Institute "teaches workers to increase their company's business."

The AIFLD drew 92 percent of its annual $6 million budget from AID and the State Department and was also reported to have received sizable sums from the CIA. This money was used to train 300,000 union members at the AIFLD's Front Royal school in Virginia, where courses were, and are, heavily spiked with pro-United States, anti-communist propaganda. AIFLD money was also used to support the military coups in Guatemala, Brazil, and Chile, and the terrorism and racial violence directed against the leftist government of Cheddi Jagan in Guyana. AIFLD Executive Director William C. Doherty, Jr., who has been identified as a "CIA career agent," publicly boasted that AIFLD graduates "were so active [in the Brazilian coup] that they became intimately involved in some of the clandestine operations of the revolution before it took place. When U.S. Marines invaded the Dominican Republic, the AIFLD union was the only one to welcome them. Although the governments of Brazil, Chile, and the Dominican Republic arrested and murdered workers, and destroyed their unions and bargaining power, the AIFLD could not praise them enough, even going so far as to become their apologists at international labor gatherings. The AIFLD's National Workers' Confederation was the chief labor spokesman for Chile's junta.

Working through tame unions, the AIFLD collected detailed information about Latin-American labor leaders, the pretext being that such surveys were necessary for AID-financed workers' housing projects. Though precious few houses were built, and most that were proved too expensive for the average worker, the AIFLD was able to obtain a personal and political history of every union member, with addresses and photographs. Given the AIFLD's close CIA connection and the CIA's documented role in the Chilean, Uruguayan, and Brazilian coups, among others, it is all too probable that this information was passed on to the military regimes and their secret police.

The AIFLD also proved adept at smearing as communist such democratic labor movements as the Christian Democrats' Latin American Federation, in splitting the Dominican Republic's labor movement, and in providing such backers as United Brands and Standard Fruit with docile unions for their Honduran banana plantations. As AIFLD Director Doherty explained, "We welcome [the] co-operation [of management] not only financially but in terms of establishing our policies. . . . The co-operation between ourselves and the business community is getting warmer day by day." Thanks to such "good" business-labor relations, nineteenth-century sweatshops, complete with child labor, were reintroduced in the textile mills of Brazil, and hundreds of workers languished in the prisons of Chile. Still, it was in character—the AFL's foreign department got its start by supporting Nazi collaborators in the postwar unions of France. It was as a result of that work that the CIA agreed to finance its activities, according to Thomas Braden, director of the CIA's European operations from 1950 to 1954.

As the AIFLD's career in Latin America shows, the political costs of foreign aid and investment may be higher than the economic benefits they bring. Indeed, many of the arguments for corporate investment, while reasonable enough in theory, do not apply in a region like Latin America, where governments have neither the will nor the means to control or guide a transnational empire of companies that comprises the world's third-largest economy after the United States and the

Soviet Union. If the U.S. Internal Revenue Service, which employs some of the world's best technicians, is hard put to control these companies, what can be expected of poorly educated, grossly underpaid Latin-American bureaucrats without access to typewriters, much less computers? Thus some Latin Americans who a few years ago were enthusiastic promoters of capitalist development now question the arguments of big business. Said Argentine economist Raul Prebish, one of the fathers of the Alliance for Progress: "What is good for the consumer society is not necessarily good for development."

A key argument of these critics is that, whereas unemployment is among the most serious problems facing Latin America, foreign investment creates very few jobs. A company can hardly be blamed for wanting to reduce labor costs by increasing automation, yet automation is the last thing needed by a continent with 50 percent unemployment and underemployment. Petrochemical plants may reduce a country's imports and add a few points to the GNP, but they do not promote human development. On the contrary, capital-intensive investments have checked the post–World War II expansion of the labor base in Latin America. While industry's share of Latin America's GNP has grown from 11 to 23 percent during the past five decades, it employs exactly the same percentage of workers today that it did in 1925, a mere 14 percent of the labor force. In several countries, among them Chile and Peru, the percentage has actually declined. Some of this can be attributed to the population explosion, but the essential issue is the model of development: Do you make refrigerators and air conditioners or shirts and shoes? Do you build sophisticated hospitals or rural clinics, universities or primary schools? By choosing to encourage foreign investment in such technologically sophisticated industries as television sets or computers, a Latin-American country may actually be postponing any hope of real development.

Because they identify with the Americans and Europeans, Latin America's elites have chosen the industrialized world's model of development—for example, it is a matter of intense national pride with these people that their country has a steel industry, though there may be no economic or social justification for the expensive toy. The argument for promoting this model of development is the trickle-down theory—that as countries become richer, trade union organizations, rising food prices, and shortages of certain types of labor begin to improve the conditions of some of the poorest classes—small farmers, unskilled and semiskilled industrial workers, and so on. Such was the case in nineteenth-century England and in Japan. Of course, wealth takes a long time to trickle down— even in Japan it took at least a century—and it is doubtful that the Latin-American masses will wait that long. Indeed, it may never happen at all if, as in the Latin-American military regimes, trade unions are banned or severely limited, food prices and agricultural production are controlled by the rich themselves, and there is no possibility of political opposition or civic development. Certainly there has been very little trickle-down since World War I, when Latin America began to industrialize. The richest man in Latin America earns over $550,000 a week; the poorest, $90 a year; and the gap is still widening. Latin America's "burgeoning" middle class still accounts for only 20 percent of the population and, given the present growth of poverty, there is little likelihood that it will go higher in this century. Moreover, the price of foreign investment, quite apart from the issue of jobs, is now so high in political and economic terms that it can be seriously challenged on that ground alone.

BACKGROUND TO REPRESSION: GUATEMALA'S INDIAN WARS[3]

Last month, Amnesty International issued a report on Guatemala containing eyewitness evidence that the Government of Gen. Fernando Romeo Lucas García has engaged in a

[3] Reprint of magazine article by Clifford Krauss, roving foreign correspondent specializing in Central American affairs. *The Nation*. 232:304–7. Mr. 14, '81. © 1981 by The Nation Associates, Inc. Reprinted by permission.

deliberate policy of torture and repression of its opposition.
The Government has repeatedly denied that a single political
arrest has ever been made, but, in a rationalization familiar to
those who follow events in El Salvador, it claims that the mur-
ders, "disappearances" and torture that have taken place are
the work of right-wing "death squads."—The Editors

Under the cover of predawn darkness last July 28, a Guerrilla Army of the Poor (E.G.P.) commando team raided an
army outpost on a bluff overlooking the Ixil Indian town of
San Juan Cotzal. The integrated Ladino [Spanish-speaking]
and Indian force surprised the soldiers and killed several before retreating into the Guatemalan highlands. After the
army's *orejas* (ears) in the village told the commander of the
outpost that certain civilians knew of the impending raid but
had refused to warn the soldiers, flak-jacketed troops, many of
them Indians, forced open the doors of dozens of homes,
rounded up about sixty young males, executed them and
buried them in common graves.

Leftist rebellion and rightist reaction are nothing new to
Guatemala. Since Col. Jácobo Arbenz and his left-leaning regime fell to a Central Intelligence Agency-financed coup in
1954, more than 35,000 Guatemalans have died in political
violence. Guerrilla groups have come and gone—victims of
army counterinsurgency as well as their own ideological bick-
ering and strategic blunders. Rightist death squads have
changed their names a half-dozen times.

Nor is repression and exploitation of the Indian majority a
recent development. As soon as the Spanish swept through
Guatemala in 1524, thousands of Mayas were mobilized as
unpaid labor to produce cocoa, indigo, leather, gold and sil-
ver. Today the goods are different but the system largely remains: A half-million Indians are forced into what amounts to
debt peonage every year and compelled to migrate hundreds
of miles to toil at substandard wages on southern coastal
plantations.

What is new to Guatemala is the burgeoning activism of
thousands of Indians within the last year. That's bad news for
the Ladino elite, and the rightist regime that serves their interests has stepped up repression. Thirty Quiché peasants and

students occupied the Spanish Embassy in Guatemala City in January 1980, taking thirty-one hostages. They demanded an investigation into the alleged army killing of dozens of farmers around the town of Uspantan in Quiché. When police climbed onto the embassy roof and attempted to break in, a militant threw a Molotov cocktail. The entire building exploded in flames and twenty-nine militants, seven Spanish diplomats, a former Guatemalan Vice President, a foreign minister who had taken sanctuary in the embassy and a Guatemalan secretary were killed.

A less dramatic though potentially more important development soon followed. Exploiting widespread discontent over low wages, crowded housing, DDT poisoning and tropical disease among workers at the southern coastal plantations, the Guerrilla Army of the Poor had organized 75,000 Indian migrants through its labor wing, the Peasant Unity Committee (C.U.C.). Last February, the workers struck for seventeen days and won their first raise since 1972—a 186 percent hike that brought their minimum daily wage to $3.20. One hundred peasants suspected of taking part in the work action disappeared in June, presumably the victims of the death squads. Despite the loss of life, the C.U.C. strike was considered the most successful union action in years. The Government took notice and began broadcasting patriotic announcements in Indian languages defending the army and extolling the virtues of peace.

The strategy of the E.G.P. and the Revolutionary Organization of the People in Arms (O.R.P.A.), two of four guerrilla groups operating in Guatemala, has been to take power by exploiting Indian discontent. Active in Quiché since 1975, the E.G.P. has had growing success in recruiting Indians into its ranks by promising land reform and attacking the army's forced recruitment program. There is increasing evidence that Indian civilians in many towns are clandestinely helping the guerrillas by feeding and sheltering them. Over the past several months, O.R.P.A. has gained a foothold along a wide swath of mountain terrain in the western and central parts of the country by holding town meetings in local Indian tongues.

In war or peace, the plight of the Guatemalan Indians is bleak. Illiteracy in the countryside reaches 80 percent. Indian infant mortality exceeds 100 per 1,000 live births. Hunger, underemployment, mental retardation and alcoholism are endemic. To escape the misery of the fields, thousands of Indians reject their ancestral dress and migrate to the cities where they live in ragtag slums without running water.

The struggle for existence becomes acute in November throughout the highlands. In Santa Catarina Palopo, a town squeezed between steep mountains and the banks of moody Lake Atitlán, 1,500 Cakchiquel Indians barely eke out a subsistence ten months a year. When the rainy season ends in October, leaving the smell of rotting corn behind, families begin to run out of food and money. Out of desperation, about 400 Santa Catarina Palopo men join hundreds of thousands of their countrymen and migrate to cotton, coffee and sugar plantations on the sweltering southern coast. "My family doesn't have enough land," complained Manuel Gonzalez, a 28-year-old migrant of the town who clings to his Cakchiquel tongue and wears traditional striped culottes. Gonzalez must share an acre of exhausted soil with three generations of his family. "There is much pain on the coast and it is very hot. Sometimes it makes me mad but I have no choice but to go," Gonzalez added. Gonzalez hires out to contractors who offer him loans of between $5 and $15 to feed his family in exchange for a month or two of work on the plantations. His advance is taken out of his daily salary; when he returns to his farm in February he is often penniless or still in debt.

Small farmers have little choice but to go to the contractors: they do not qualify for Government credits and their land is too meager to support their families. A 3.3 percent annual population growth rate in the countryside has forced families to divide among themselves what little land they have. The overpopulation has driven peasants to climb Guatemala's steep mountains and volcanoes in search of arable land. Some of the high-altitude farmers suspend themselves from ropes to cultivate their precarious plots. The resulting deforestation of the mountains has caused severe erosion and floods that sweep down the mountainsides and carry away topsoil from the farms below.

One Government rural credit spokeswoman explained with a shrug that public efforts to aid the Indians had little impact because of "the low cultural level of the indigenous population." A more systematic analysis would demonstrate that Government policy is directly responsible for the forced migrations. After all, cheap Indian labor gives Guatemalan produce a competitive edge on the world market. "The politicians believe that if the Indians do better they will not work on the plantations. That is the sad truth," said a Government official responsible for Indian affairs. A list of the country's most powerful politicians and generals would duplicate a *Who's Who* of the Guatemalan landowning class. Jorge García Granados, private secretary and business partner of President Lucas García, is the second largest cotton planter in the country. Lucas García himself is a cattle rancher who owns at least 25,000 acres in the Transversal Strip region, where valuable oil deposits have been found. Over the last twenty years of strong economic growth, low business taxes and conservative monetary policies have succeeded in keeping inflation—and the Indian—down.

President Lucas García characterizes his Government as "center-left" and spends thousands of quetzales publicizing a $19 million program funded by the U.S. Agency for International Development to settle 5,000 landless families in the Transversal Strip and the projects of Bandesa, the public rural credit bank. But the Government's own statistics belie the promises officials have made in an attempt to avert a Sandinist-style revolution. Two percent of Guatemala's 7.2 million people own 70 percent of the nation's cultivable land. Some 200,000 peasant families own no land at all. Meanwhile, a few large landholders, who let as much as 30 percent of their land go unused, increased their acreage from 5.5 million to 6.7 million between 1964 and 1979.

Their right to let huge tracts of land lie fallow for decades while millions starve has a legal precedent. In 1954, the far-right National Liberation Movement (M.L.N.) forces of Col.

Carlos Castillo Armas overthrew Colonel Arbenz. Arbenz had been branded a Communist by Secretary of State John Foster Dulles when his program to distribute some unused land to peasants touched holdings of the United Fruit Company. After his takeover, Castillo Armas returned the "stolen" land, and then some, to the U.S. company and other landowners. Peasant leagues that supported Arbenz were crushed. The absolute inviolability of property rights remains a basic tenet of Government land policy to this day.

One of the worst massacres took place on the morning of May 29, 1978, when 700 Kekchi Indians gathered in the town square of Panzos, a village eighty miles northeast of Guatemala City, to give the mayor a petition demanding the return of lands taken from them by rich Ladinos. They were met by a large army detachment with automatic weapons at the ready. An Indian leader began shouting and swinging his machete at the soldiers, as if to beckon the unarmed peasants to attack them. The soldiers lost control of the situation and finally cleared the square in a frenzy of gunfire—leaving 114 men, women and children dead. E.G.P. guerrillas were quick to take revenge and blew up an army truck, killing seventeen soldiers.

The massacre, called "Guatemala's My Lai" by one local newspaper, climaxed two years of "disappearances" and evictions in the isolated northern province of Alta Verapaz. For centuries the indigenous Kekchi Indians lived there peacefully in communes, because the Ladinos had little use for property in an upland jungle region without roads. But a decade ago, oil and nickel deposits were discovered and the Government built a highway, which made the area attractive to cattle ranchers. Well-connected Ladino businessmen, generals and politicans found the National Property Registry only too happy to write them deeds to land that the Indians had occupied for centuries. The Indians could do nothing through the legal channels; they had no titles recognized by Ladino authorities. "The large landholders are not capitalists," explained a Government official active in Indian affairs. "They are rich people with a colonialist mentality. And

they always say the Indians are at fault for the country's
poverty."

That same attitude legitimizes the forced induction of
thousands of Indians into the army every year. Soldiers commonly surround the markets of villages and kidnap young
men, tie them up for days, force them repeatedly to insult
their Indian customs and train them to kill. The army recently began to recognize that the program was counterproductive and modified it. But there continue to be reports of
recruits who choose to commit suicide (particularly in the
southeastern Jutiapa army camp) rather than kill their brothers.

The guerrillas are fast becoming the only significant political force in the country committed to improving conditions
among Indians. Right-wing hit men, who function without
fear of Government reprisal, have systematically gunned
down moderate leaders who campaign for land reform and
gradual social change. Vice President Francisco Villagran
Kramer, the most influential liberal in the Government, resigned last September following several death threats.

Growing Indian and liberal support does not assure a final
leftist victory in a country with the strongest army in the area
and a considerable middle class that has a stake in the status
quo. In fact, in the last election, Lucas García only won by
defrauding an even more conservative candidate. And although there is growing evidence that the four guerrilla
groups in the country have begun a dialogue, sectarianism di-
vides them. The Rebel Armed Forces (F.A.R.), whose worker
and student members specialize in urban guerrilla warfare,
broke away from the thirty-one-year-old Communist Guatemalan Workers Party. (P.G.T.). O.R.P.A. and E.G.P., in turn,
split from the F.A.R. But even if the guerrillas were united,
their fight against the 18,000-man army would be decidedly
uphill. The guerrillas' armaments consist mainly of hunting
rifles and .45-caliber handguns. Even those who have automatic rifles are no match for soldiers armed with Israeli-made
Galil assault rifles and supported by 105-millimeter howit-
zers.

The Carter Administration, to its credit, did not contribute to the Guatemalan Army's buildup, but conservative pressures to abandon human rights will become decisive within the new Administration at a time when Guatemala is beginning to develop its impressive oil reserves. Just after oil engineers found that the rich Reforma Fields extended below the Mexican border into Guatemala, one U.S. diplomat commented, "It's foolish for our Government to distance itself from Guatemala. Washington is not fully cognizant of Guatemala's potential." Ronald Reagan has already pledged, during the campaign, not to "force" human rights on Guatemala's leaders. Roger Fontaine, one of Reagan's chief Latin America advisers, recently said that U.S. policy toward Guatemala should follow the model of "U.S. policy toward Greece at the end of the war."

But the Indians continue to tell the story of Tecun Uman, the last King of the Utatlan empire, who lost his life in a duel with Spanish conquistador Pedro de Alvarado 450 years ago. According to legend, Tecun Uman will rise from the dead and once more reign over his people with a just hand. In the meantime, Ladino leftists and a growing number of Indians are giving their lives to the cause of justice in Guatemala.

IN DEFENSE OF HUMAN RIGHTS[4]

The Americas, and the world, are feeling the effects of a movement that has grown from a slow, quiet beginning and now seems capable of reshaping the political world.

The protection of human rights—the goal of that movement—is a basic tenet of the Organization of American States, which adopted the *American Declaration of the Rights*

[4] Excerpted from "Hemisphere Trends," by Michael Morgan. *Américas.* 32:9–10. Ja. '80. Reprinted from *Américas,* monthly magazine published by the General Secretariat of the Organization of American States in English, Spanish, and Portuguese. The author, formerly a contributing editor of *Américas,* is now with the International Communications Agency, stationed in Peru.

and Duties of Man in Bogota in 1948, at the same international conference at which the OAS Charter was signed.

Since that time, the OAS has been moving gradually toward a multilateral, collective mechanism to protect the basic human rights of the individual. A Meeting of Foreign Ministers held in Santiago, Chile, in 1959 established the Inter-American Commission on Human Rights. The Commission was set up as an independent agency empowered to make recommendations to the governments in cases of human rights abuse. That was followed by the 1969 *Pact of San José*, or American Convention on Human Rights, signed in Costa Rica, which redefined the role of the Commission and set up an Inter-American Court of Human Rights.

The new Court, however, could not begin operation until a sufficient number of the American nations had ratified the *Pact*. The business of treaty ratification is a long, tedious process, and, because it is such a potentially controversial area, observers believed it would be many years before the Court was actually authorized to operate. Until mid-1977 only two nations had ratified the *Pact*. Yet in the late 1970's, with the sudden awareness of many in the international community of the need to back up moral outrage with specific enforcement, a rush of ratifications took place. In July 1978 Grenada became the eleventh nation to ratify the *Pact*, thereby fulfilling the minimum requirement to bring it into force and set the mechanism rolling for the election of members to the Commission and the Court.

Under the *Pact*, the Commission or a state party can bring a case to the Court if the Commission has failed to arrive at a friendly settlement between the victim and the state party concerned. The jurisdiction of the Court is optional under the *Pact*, and to date only Costa Rica has agreed to abide by the Court's verdict in all cases. The Court may award, in the case of established violations of human rights, fair compensation to the injured party.

Currently, the only nations subject to the Court's purview will be those that have ratified the *Pact of San José* (Bolivia, Colombia, Costa Rica, the Dominican Republic, Ecuador, El

Salvador, Grenada, Guatemala, Haiti, Honduras, Jamaica, Nicaragua, Panama, Peru, and Venezuela). Signatory nations that have not yet ratified the *Pact* are Barbados, Chile, Paraguay, the United States, and Uruguay. Those that have not yet signed it are Argentina, Brazil, Cuba, Commonwealth of Dominica, Mexico, Saint Lucia, Suriname, and Trinidad and Tobago.

Cynics have said that the Court will inevitably go the way of many such international enterprises, with national self-interest taking precedence. Perhaps they will be proved correct. But dramatic changes have happened over the last three years. The power of world public opinion has reached unparalleled heights, contributing directly to the fall of despotic governments in at least five countries throughout the world last year. Any government avoiding the verdict of a recognized international court will be running the risk of international censure.

In the end, it is a matter of educating all the people—both leaders and citizens—on what kinds of behavior of those in authority will not be permitted. The world is learning that torture, kidnapping, and repression are selfish acts of desperation, not valid means to an objective. And it is learning that in the jostling, competitive, conflicting pursuit of individual destinies no citizen or group of citizens should or can expect anything more than a fair compromise with their fellow citizens, and that each of us can go about our business, as long as we do not restrict the human rights—to liberty or bread—of others.

RIGHTS AND REAGAN[5]

In his first speech after losing the election, President Carter made a fervent defense of the human rights policies

[5] Reprint of article in *New Republic.* 183:5–6+. N. 29, '80. Copyright 1980 by The New Republic, Inc. Reprinted by permission.

that well may be the hallmark of his administration. Carter told the Organization of American States that human rights for Latin America was a "historic movement" that he was convinced would outlast his presidency. "For too long, the United States seemed wedded to the status quo—even when that meant poverty, social injustice, and even political repression," Carter said. "That attitude betrayed my country's dynamism and our faith and confidence in the future—and that, thank God, has been changed. Some claim that President Jimmy Carter elevated human rights and democracy on the inter-American agenda and that the agenda will change when I leave. They are wrong."

No one can know for sure until Ronald Reagan's new team is fully installed, but the preliminary signals being sent to the military dictatorships of Latin America suggest that President Carter is wrong, that the Reagan election means: relax, boys, the human rights heat is off. That seems the unmistakable message conveyed in person to the Latins by David Rockefeller of the Chase Manhattan Bank, who spent the week after the election traveling to Panama, Chile, Paraguay, Argentina, and Brazil. Rockefeller emphasized that he wasn't speaking for Reagan, but he is a man who clearly understands the drift of things. "In the campaign," he told a business audience in Argentina, "Mr. Reagan made it clear that he will deal with the world as it is. He is not going to try to change the world in his own image." The November 11 *New York Times* reported, with too little detail in a half-column story on Page A10, that government officials and businessmen in the countries Rockefeller visited turned out in droves to hear him criticize the Carter administration for basing American policy too much on human rights while failing to recognize the chaos and terrorism many of the countries face.

In his initial post-election press conference, president-elect Reagan gave human rights the same sort of "yes, we all believe in motherhood" treatment. "Yes, I think that all of us in this country are dedicated to the belief in human rights," he said. "But I think it must be a consistent policy. I don't think that you can turn away from some country because here and there they do not totally agree with our concept of human rights and then at the same time maintain relations with other countries, or try to develop them, where human rights are virtually nonexistent."

Reagan added: "I don't think that our record of turning away from countries that were basically friendly to us, because of some facet of human rights, and then finding that the result was that they have lost all human rights in that country—that isn't a practical way to go about that."

The Reagan team argues that the Carter administration made just this trade in Nicaragua, where the "moderately oppressive" regime of Anastasio Somoza was destabilized by US human rights pressures and then toppled by the Marxist-Leninist Sandinista movement which is now in the process of destroying freedom and cementing ties to Cuba and the Soviet Union. According to some leading Reagan advisers, Carter's policies have emboldened Cuba to step up its revolutionary activities throughout Central America so that local insurgencies in El Salvador, Guatemala, and Honduras may burst into a regional civil war. El Salvador seems near the point of collapse right now, and some Reagan advisers believe the new president may well be faced with the option of sending in the Marines. As things are shaping up, Central America may represent for Ronald Reagan the crisis area that the Persian Gulf has been for Jimmy Carter and Southeast Asia was for Richard Nixon and Lyndon Johnson.

We concur with the Reagan people that US policy in Nicaragua was ill conceived and horribly executed. But we do not believe that Nicaragua is now irretrievably in the communist camp and ought to be shunned or conspired against by the United States. And while we appreciate the grave danger to US strategic interests in Central America posed by Cuba, we do not believe it justifies a wholesale shutdown of US pressure for Latin governments to observe some human rights standards. The Carter administration may have thought it was called upon to turn every country into a liberal democracy, but its moralistic excesses do not justify reversion by Reagan to a policy of winking at torture and murder.

We believe it is possible to stand for human rights *and* to protect US national interests against communist assault, but it involves a policy different from that pursued by Carter and also different from that apparently contemplated by Reagan. The Carter administration thought it was necessary to get the United States "on the other side of history," believing that "our" side somehow inherently involved, as Carter said, "poverty, social injustice, and political repression" and was therefore destined to lose. There was a sense of guilt about the Carter human rights effort, an acceptance of the view that anti-US revolutions in Nicaragua and Iran were justified and that any new regimes they produced were preferable to those that the United States had "propped up" before.

All this is nonsense, of course. By any measure—political freedom, economic development, per capita income, infant mortality, incidence of political jailings and torture—"our side" of history is vastly preferable to its nearest socialist (or Islamic fundamentalist) alternative. South Korea is freer and richer by far than North Korea. People on Taiwan and Hong Kong are better off than people in the People's Republic. It is better in Thailand than in Vietnam and Cambodia, and was better in the shah's Iran than Khomeini's. All over the world, refugees stream constantly from the "other side" of history to ours. The pattern has been maintained this year in Latin America where, given a chance to leave, thousands of people risked their lives to flee Cuba. It is ironic that this demonstration of Cuba's utter failure as a society should coincide with new agitation in other Latin countries to adopt the model. Carter abetted this kind of movement by his failure to defend the capitalist democratic idea.

That is not a mistake the Reagan administration is likely to make. Rather, it is likely to make another: to sympathize with and assist despots and tyrants, simply because they have positioned themselves on our side of history. With few exceptions, the Reagan people tend to be friends, business associates, and ideological soul mates of Latin America's oligarchs and oppressors. The Reaganites are rightly offended by the notion that socialist repression is somehow preferable to fascist repression, but they are unable to see that they can combat the spread of this idea only by helping to end repression of any sort.

Criticizing Carter policy, Reaganites make the claim that when forced to choose between an Anastasio Somoza and a Cuban-backed Sandinista movement, the US cannot do anything in its own interest but back Somoza. That's true, if that's the choice. Many Reagan advisers claim that it is and that it's naive to think other alternatives are available in most Latin countries. But surely, consistent, patient, private US pressure on Somoza to reform his corrupt regime would have made it more viable and able to withstand leftist assault.

Reagan apparently intends to cut off financial aid to the Sandinista government. We believe that would be an error. We grant that Nicaragua is moving toward dictatorship, that it is building up an army twice the size of Somoza's, that there is increasing pressure on the press, and that political debate is being curtailed. However, most of our $75 million in aid is directed at the private sector, where democratic impulses are strong. If the ruling Sandinista directorate wants to convert the country into a Marxist dictatorship, it ought to bear the onus itself, and not be able to claim that the country was abandoned by an ideologically rightist US.

In El Salvador, where the moderate military-Christian Democratic junta is losing ground rapidly to extremists on the left and right, the Carter administration has furnished less economic help than it has to Nicaragua. It also has withheld full-scale military aid, leaving the regime to fight terrorists with rubber bullets and tear gas. If the junta is still in power on January 20, Reagan surely will step up aid and provide weapons. If that's still not enough to hold the center in place, the new Reagan administration will be faced with the choice of backing right-wing oligarchs with a history of repressing the Salvadoran population, intervening directly with US forces, or doing nothing, which might well result in a leftist takeover. One Nicaragua and one Cuba are enough in the region. The Reagan administration undoubtedly will back the rightists. Should this come to pass, the US—at the least—should insist that repression and alienation of the population be kept to a minimum, and exact a promise of immediate reform.

The crisis in El Salvador may spread to surrounding countries—even democratic Costa Rica is under increasing pressure from violent leftists—and so the United States may have to face the unpleasant prospect of backing rightists to forestall a regional disaster. But we do not have to drop our basic human rights principles elsewhere, or pay them only lip service.

Argentina, for example, is under no immediate threat of revolution. It was in 1976, when the military again seized power and instituted a reign of terror. Somewhere between 6,500 and 20,000 people disappeared between 1976 and 1979; since they have not resurfaced, it's probable they were murdered by the security police. Torture was widespread, political activity was curtailed, and press freedom was undermined. The Carter administration put Argentina under justifiable human rights pressure, but even at the height of the repression there, the regime had its American defenders— among them, Ronald Reagan and his vice president, George Bush.

As Reagan said in one of his radio broadcasts in late 1978, "There is an old Indian proverb, 'Before I criticize a man, I walk a mile in his moccasins.' Patricia Derian and her minions at Mr. Carter's human rights office apparently haven't heard of it. If they had, they might not be making such a mess of our relations with the planet's seventh largest country, Argentina, a nation with which we should be close friends."

This statement, particularly at the time it was made, bespeaks a dismal lack of sensitivity for human rights. One could say that at times and in places Carter's human rights policies have been excessive or naive, but not in 1978 in Argentina. Jacobo Timmerman, the courageous Argentine editor now in exile, says that, in fact, Carter's human rights policy "saved thousands and thousands of lives" in Argentina. We hope that Reagan will pursue similar policies and that when his first term is completed, the same may be said of him.

That may be said of Reagan if he can establish steady, resolute policies which encourage peaceful development in Latin America and discourage violent revolution and repression. It may be said if Reagan can make Latin America an area of urgent political and economic attention for the United States. It may be said if he can find a formula for moderate attempts to improve human rights in the area—not necessarily by trying to make despots into democrats overnight, but by inducing them, at the least, to respect the rights of their citizens to life and security.

ARE HUMAN RIGHTS PASSÉ?[6]

The word is out. Human rights has had its day. It is about as popular among the honchos of the incoming administration as an excess profits tax or a gun control law. All that tiresome stuff about censorship, repression, and torture. Who needs it? Hopelessly 1960s, as the Reaganites would say.

Some of the upwardly mobile members of Reagan's entourage—an assortment of hooky-playing professors, retired colonels, and former spooks—have been wandering around Central America lately, spreading the word that the president-elect has had it up to here with human rights. No more need to coddle Commies, they report. By Commies they appear to mean everyone to the left of the late Anastasio Somoza. And to back up their message they have put together a hit list of American ambassadors they intend to deep-six on January 20. A key criterion for inclusion among what the listmakers scornfully refer to as "social reformers" is a displayed softness toward human rights.

Right up at the top, naturally, are our beleaguered envoys in Nicaragua and El Salvador, Lawrence Pezzullo and Robert White. [For additional comments on Robert White, see "Dominoes in Central America?" in Section I, above.—Ed.]

[6] Reprint of article by Ronald Steel, contributing editor, *New Republic;* author of books and articles on American politics and foreign policy; and winner of the Bancroft Prize for the biography *Walter Lippmann and the American Century. New Republic.* 183:14+. D. 27, '80. Copyright 1980 by The New Republic, Inc. Reprinted by permission.

Their sin was to suggest that the way to preserve American interests in revolutionary societies was to work with reformers, even leftists, rather than automatically to side with the far right. Among the ideological purists now streaming into Washington this is considered soft-headed, if not vaguely treacherous.

The clearest signal of the new mood, however, was that flashed last month in Latin America by Mr. Finance Capitalism himself, David Rockefeller. Stopping in Buenos Aires, on a sortie that also took him to Paraguay, Chile, and Brazil, the chairman of the Chase Manhattan Bank told an enthusiastic assemblage of government and business leaders that the Reagan administration would not bug them on human rights. The incoming president would "deal with the world as it is," he declared pointedly. This in a city where government-condoned kidnapping and torture of suspected dissidents recently led a fact-finding committee of the Organization of American States to describe the situation as "state terrorism."

The message was hardly necessary, though Rockefeller understandably got carried away with enthusiasm for the kind of good business climate the Latin American juntas have provided. One can understand the exasperation of certain Latin regimes at the departing Carter administration. Its human rights policy, though often halting and hypocritically selective, nonetheless did manage to restrain some of the worst offenders and even saved a good many lives. Those efforts now apparently are going to be superseded by a new "realism" that calls for learning to love your friendly dictator.

The boys are already champing at the bit. In Haiti young "Baby Doc" Duvalier, son and heir of the late hatchet man, has just slammed the lid down on the press. Journalists critical of the regime—one of the hemisphere's nastiest and most venal—have been silenced and jailed after a brief period of greater press freedom induced by US pressure. Baby Doc and the military officers behind the throne got the message that it was all right to clamp down, and that they would have nothing to fear from the new administration in the way of an aid cut-off.

The message also has been spread to El Salvador, carried

personally by several members of Reagan's transition team. There the Carter administration's strategy of backing the military junta as a way of blocking either a right-wing or left-wing takeover has broken down almost completely. The far right, emboldened by the prospect of a friend in the White House, is moving to wipe out all opposition and seize full control of the junta. The kidnap-murder of six left-wing political leaders by a rightist death squad, some of whom wore the uniform of the Salvadoran National Guard, was designed to prevent a compromise truce between left-wing guerrillas and the junta. And the brazen assassination of three American nuns was a clear attempt to undercut Ambassador White's truce efforts and to test the limits of Washington's tolerance.

The combination of a lame duck US administration whose mandate is running out fast, and an incoming administration that would like the benefits of a rightist coup without the responsibility of officially blessing it, offers an irresistible opportunity to Salvadoran right-wing extremists. Rather than toppling the current junta, which for months has been moving steadily to the right, it may simply choose to capture it from within by expelling the few remaining centrist and liberal members. In either case its objective is to present Washington with a *fait accompli* by January 20, which the Reagan administration can accept in the name of realism.

Central America gives every sign of being the new stamping ground of the cold war fundamentalists now grouping around Reagan. These people, with their Manichean view of a world divided between the forces of light and darkness, are not only anti-communist, but anti-Marxist, anti-leftist, and even anti-liberal. Indeed they often seem to view liberalism as a way station on the road to communism. In so doing, of course, they not only give the Communists credit they do not deserve, but polarize politics. By defining the choice as that between right-wing repression and left-wing violence, they contribute to that condition. This in turn serves to justify their support of the far right, with which they are already ideologically atune.

This approach sometimes is justified in the name of realism, which is what it is not. It is not realism to equate liberals with Communists. That is simply to undermine the center and push reformers toward the extremes. Nor is it realism to maintain, as many fundamentalists do, that the United States has a vital interest in the political orientation of every government on the planet. That is simply paranoid globalism of the kind that should have been put to rest, but apparently was not, by the follies of the Vietnam War.

What the fundamentalists learned from Vietnam, however, was that there are some places where you can use force to get what you want (or at least try to), and other places where it is too dangerous. Intervention in Poland is not only dangerous, but likely would mean a full-scale entry into World War III. Nobody is advising that. The Persian Gulf, though indisputably a vital interest, is an area where—fantasies of the Rapid Deployment Force notwithstanding—no one has been able to figure out an effective use of American power.

Thus the inestimable beauty of the third world. For us, as for the Russians, it offers a perfect forum for manipulation and covert intervention. The view of third world countries as places where American "will" and "credibility" could be demonstrated was not invented by think-tank fundamentalists. Henry Kissinger practiced it for years in Vietnam, Cambodia, and Chile, and would have done so in Angola if Congress had let him. The incoming Congress probably would.

Central America is, in a sense, our Eastern Europe. It is the one area where the American presence, even if not exercised militarily, can determine the course of events. Carter's decision to let Somoza go, like Eisenhower's 20 years ago with Batista in Cuba, allowed the Sandinistas to topple a hated dictator. Both decisions were in line with fundamental American values. What happened later in Cuba in large part was due to Washington's mismanagement, and its inflation of a nuisance into an obsession. The Carter team, with considerable subtlety, has tried to learn from that lesson in Nicaragua, and with less success in El Salvador,

Those who claim to speak for Reagan are now trying to turn that policy around, to offer unqualified support to any Latin regime, however repressive, so long as it is on "our" side. Their rationale is an old one: better to stick with the far right than to take chances with a wobbly middle or an unfriendly left. John F. Kennedy expressed it perfectly in 1963 with regard to the Dominican Republic. "There are three possibilities in descending order of preference: a decent democratic regime, a continuation of the Trujillo regime, or a Castro regime. We ought to aim at the first, but we really can't renounce the second until we are sure that we can avoid the third."

As it turned out, the alternatives were not so stark. They rarely are. The US took a chance on a moderately democratic regime in Santo Domingo. It is still in power. This is what the Carter administration has been trying to do in Central America today. The results have been mixed. But Carter's choices in Central America have been limited. To back repressive regimes on the far right would merely polarize situations always in danger of splitting between two extremes. It would make Marxists the only effective alternative to the extreme right and ensure that change, when it came, would be virulently anti-American.

To this the Reaganites have an answer: in Central America the United States has the power to maintain its "friends" in power. Throughout this century every regime in the area has governed with Washington's blessing. They may have been brutal, repressive, and rapacious, but at least they were ours. We have the power to make sure there are compliant regimes in the area, it is said. Why should we settle for anything less?

The answer is clear enough. Such a policy, brutal and cynical as it is, could be justified only if American security were vitally involved. This is not the case and never has been. Central America's importance to this country is entirely symbolic. We have viewed it as a protectorate for so many years that any political change that does not have our sanction seems intolerable. This is a self-delusion we can no longer tolerate. There are vital areas on which our security hinges. Central America is not one of them. Nor, for that matter, is Cuba, and it is time we broke that obsession.

Further, it must be said that we no longer have the power

to dictate a political settlement in Central America. The old balance has been undermined too much to be restored simply by US support for the extreme right. If the left has nowhere to turn for support but to Cuba and the Soviet Union, that is where it will turn. Then the polarization that our own fundamentalists already see will have taken place precisely because of their own actions. Theirs will have been a self-fulfilling prophecy.

There are no easy answers in Central America. Decades of oppression, with US approval and complicity, have triggered forces that cannot be contained easily. This is an area which, like Mexico nearly three-quarters of a century ago, is going to have to go through its own social revolution. What happens there cannot affect American security. But an obsessive effort by Washington to prop up rightist dictatorships likely will lead to civil war and decades of turbulence. The false assumptions of our Vietnam disaster should not be forgotten so easily.

What if, to raise the liberals' dilemma, there is no middle ground? What if the choice is between a Somoza and a Cuban-backed Sandinista movement? Several weeks ago a . . . [*New Republic*] editorial concluded that in such a case the US, in its own interest, would have no choice but to back Somoza ("Rights and Reagan," . . . November 29). That, to my mind, is both a serious misreading of American interests and a prime example of how, when the chips are down, so many liberals collapse into the arms of the militant right. The anti-liberalism of the right is at least a coherent position. What so often passes for liberalism is merely expediency tempered by wishful thinking.

A concern for human rights is not a sentimental self-indulgence for a country like the United States. Rather it is a direct expression of its basic values and a realization of where its true interests lie. Those who claim to speak for president-elect Reagan are doing him, and the nation, no service by promoting rightist dictatorships and viewing with bemused indifference flagrant abuses of human rights by allied regimes. Politics makes strange bedfellows, and we cannot, it is true, always choose our friends.

But we can choose some of them, and we can help them avoid mistakes likely to be disastrous to them, and to our own interests as well. One hopeful sign is that Reagan's foreign policy advisers have warned the South Korean government against carrying out the death sentence imposed upon the liberal opposition leader, Kim Dae Jung. The reason is not sentimental. Kim's execution on the trumped-up charges brought against him could trigger the uprising, or a North Korean incursion, that Seoul and Washington both fear.

There are other areas, too, where any US administration, however avowedly rightist, cannot express a disinterest in human rights abuses. Among them is South Africa. The stakes there are too high to indulge in such misanthropy. Only in Central and South America is it still possible to maintain the illusion that America's security and well-being can be anchored on a contemptuous disregard for the miseries of others. The reason why such disregard is pharisaical is, of course, because right-wing regimes can be influenced by American pressure. In some cases they remain in power only at American sufferance.

A realpolitik that fails to take human rights into account is not tough-headed; it's just simple-minded.

CRACKDOWN ON THE LEFT?[7]

Reprinted from *U.S. News & World Report.*

Explosive Latin America will pose a crucial early test for the Reagan Presidency.

Military leaders and right-wing politicians expect Reagan to dump Carter's human-rights policies, to actively combat Cuban and Soviet meddling south of the border and to help weaken leftist strength throughout Latin America.

From Guatemala's President, Gen. Fernando Romeo Lucas, to the military chiefs running Argentina, Brazil and

---

[7] Excerpt from article entitled "Foreign Policy: An Acid Test for Reagan." *U.S. News & World Report.* 89:46–7. D. 29, '80/Ja. 5, '81.

Chile, the assumption is that Reagan will ease pressure for social and political reforms, will stress hemispheric security against radical forces and will end the curb on sales of sophisticated U.S. weapons to anti-Communist neighbors.

For their part, there is fear among Latins on the left that Washington will return to the policy of the Big Stick, using its military muscle and secret operations to support regimes of an antileftist stripe.

Right or wrong, the expectations threaten to involve the U.S. in a wave of skyrocketing violence in Central America.

Virtual civil war engulfs bloodied El Salvador, with more than 9,000 dead over the past 12 months. Right-wing paramilitary armies have stepped up attacks in Guatemala. The Marxist-led Sandinista regime in Nicaragua is girding to repulse a takeover bid by forces loyal to the ousted Somoza dictatorship. The fighting between left and right threatens to spill into Honduras and Costa Rica.

Spreading turmoil will call for shrewd and delicate diplomacy by Reagan. All-out backing for the right could unleash a fresh wave of anti-Americanism and open the door for Cuban President Fidel Castro to win new followers.

Castro himself will adopt a wait-and-see stance toward the President. But he clearly fears start of a new round of confrontation with the U.S. and stronger American efforts to deter Communist and Marxist influence in the hemisphere.

Copyright 1980 U.S. News & World Report, Inc.

U.S. FOREIGN POLICY:
THE REVIVAL OF INTERVENTIONISM[8]

To understand U.S. policy toward a particular region like Latin America at any given time, one must analyze the country's global situation and the specific conjuncture out of which

[8] Reprint of article by James Petras, professor of sociology at the State University of New York at Binghamton, member of the Bertrand Russell Tribunal on Repression in Latin America, and author of books and articles on Latin America. *Monthly Review*. 31:15–27. F. '80. Copyright © 1980 by Monthly Review Inc. Reprinted by permission of Monthly Review Press.

it emerges, as well as U.S. historic interests and policies. By "global situation" we mean the successes and failures of recent political, military, and diplomatic encounters abroad; the degree of internal opposition to, or support for, differing foreign policies; and the kind of backing provided by allies and supporters.

The importance of analyzing the "specific conjuncture" out of which U.S. policy emerges becomes clear when we attempt to understand the forms through which policies are presented. For example, as we shall examine in more detail below, the defeats suffered by the United States in Indochina and the diplomatic isolation that accompanied U.S. intervention defined a global situation of relative weakness. The high levels of opposition to U.S. interventionism—both internal and external—dictated an approach emphasizing "human rights" (non-intervention) as the theme of U.S. policy within that specific conjuncture, while at the same time pointing up the desirability of caution in any steps taken toward defusing opposition or recreating the capacity for intervention.

Among many Marxists, U.S. policy is perceived largely as a product of economic developments, as a constant pursuit of economic interests which takes no account of the different levels of activities, the varying policy instruments, and the barriers that must be utilized or overcome in the realization of those interests. Apart from being largely economic-reductionist in content, the arguments advanced usually exaggerate the capacity of the state to realize its interests independently of the political conjuncture. In opposition to such reductionist and simplistic approaches, we propose an analysis which considers imperialism not only as an economic phenomenon but also as a set of class relations that both sustain and oppose it, and as a state structure possessing a capacity which varies over time to promote and defend what it considers to be its interests. Imperialism, in other words, involves not only a static set of interests derived from an economic structure, but reflects a dynamic set of processes that shape the capacity to pursue those interests.

U.S. imperial interests require different policies in changing circumstances, reflecting both internal and external factors. The massive mobilization of humanpower and economic resources behind the large-scale interventionist policies in Asia in the 1960s and early 1970s was followed by the "human rights" policies of the mid- and late-1970s; and these in turn have been followed by the revival of the interventionist preparations at the close of the decade. To elucidate these policy changes, we will analyze their socio-political basis in imperialism and the global context in which they occur. We will then proceed to a more detailed analysis of the rise and demise of the "human rights" policy—its purposes, impact, and necessarily transitory nature. In the last half of our discussion, we will identify the elements behind the interventionist revival, some of the continuing constraints, the emerging mass democratic challenges, and the complex policies that are evolving from a situation of interventionism and limited options.

Overall Context of U.S. Policy

Long-term, large-scale U.S. foreign policy is determined by the imperatives of overseas expansion and the power to respond to those imperatives. This is now even more the case than it was several years ago, since with each year more and more major U.S. corporations derive an ever larger proportion of their profits from their overseas undertakings. The flows of capital and profits, however, are premised on three crucial operating conditions: (1) exercise of hegemony over subordinated classes in the metropolitan countries (i.e., their support for or acquiescence in imperialism) to sustain overseas involvement; (2) a worldwide armed force with capacity to defend these economic interests; and (3) an international network of loyal and supportive allies and clients among the advanced and Third World capitalist countries capable of collaborating in meaningful joint activity.

In summary, the capacity of U.S. imperialism to intervene in defense of its economic interests is dependent on internal political stability, discipline and cohesion within the armed forces, and the cooperation of allied powers.

The Conjuncture of the Mid-Seventies

Three events detonated massive opposition to U.S. foreign policy, severely undermining the capacity of the state to pursue the interests of U.S. corporations. The defeat in the Indochina War and its enormous cost in human and economic terms had the direct consequence of polarizing U.S. society in a fashion detrimental to any effort at outside intervention. Two other factors were equally important in undermining the capacity of the state: widespread demoralization within the armed forces and the alienation of allies in Europe and the Third World, activating substantial sectors within each region. In addition to the Indochina War's erosion of the interventionist capacity of the state, the Watergate affair led to the discrediting of the existing political establishment—Congress, executive, the two parties, etc. Finally, the press and Congressional exposés in the media and Congress of the Kissinger-Nixon-CIA efforts to overthrow the democratically elected Allende government in Chile further discredited U.S. policy in the eyes of most European and Third World observers.

These events generated widespread and deepening distrust within the general population, an increasingly polarized citizenry serving as a possible base for a new movement, an immobile military force, and uncooperative and increasingly competitive allies. The overall consequence was a political crisis in which a serious loss of political legitimacy impaired the capacity of the state to act, and in this way endangered the whole network of economic, political, and military interests created in the period since the Second World War.

U.S. policy-makers *in this conjuncture* had to develop a foreign policy tailored to a set of very urgent and immediate needs: the need to overcome popular discontent with interventionism and the illegitimacy of government, to restructure and strengthen the armed forces, and to create a new image internationally, thus ending the country's diplomatic isolation. In coming to terms with these conjunctural elements, however, policy-makers had at the same time to adhere to

long-term imperatives of the U.S. economic system. Without
sacrificing essential economic, military, and commercial linkages, a new set of "values" had to be projected. Before the
United States could intervene directly in the Third World
again, it needed to defuse the opposition and reconsolidate its
position. Between the demise of the old interventionism and
the revival of the new, Third World revolutionary movements had a brief breathing space to press forward with their
historic tasks.

"Human Rights": A Transitional Policy

In historical retrospect, it is abundantly clear that President Carter's "human rights" policy was essentially directed
at overcoming internal and external opposition and recreating the country's capacity to intervene. The right-wing critics
who opposed his policies completely overlooked the severe
weakness in the fabric of U.S. society and state. Most of their
demands for direct action were purely demagogic since they
were never able to specify any clear line of action, let alone to
rebuild the political and social basis necessary to sustain a
substantial interventionist action. Right-wing calls for intervention prior to political consolidation endangered the political order which the Carter administration was refashioning as
a prerequisite for a more activist role in the proximate future.
Thus at bottom the differences between the "security through
strength" types and the "human rights" policy people in the
Carter administration were over matters of timing: the latter
felt that the former were premature.

The "human rights" foreign policy was expressed in both
symbolic and substantive forms. At the symbolic level, policy
speeches and public rhetoric criticized *past* U.S. intervention
and the excesses of dictatorial allies (and of course of Communist and nationalist adversaries). At the more substantive
level, diplomatic and legislative pressure was applied to liber-
alize military regimes through such measures as legalizing
conservative civilian opposition. In contexts of increasing
military-civilian polarization, where support was sharply

skewed against military incumbents, the United States even went so far as to favor a shift from dictatorial to parliamentary forms of rule.

Nevertheless, and despite the sometimes sharp tone with which some dictatorial regimes were criticized, economic ties were maintained and in many cases expanded. While the Carter administration focused on specific techniques of governing (torture, arbitrary arrest, and disappearances), the regimes as such were not challenged. Washington continued the previous Nixon-Ford policy of cutting back on public loans in favor of private, now giving to this policy a virtuous twist. While a few military-aid programs were cut back selectively, private investment flowed into the repressive countries in greater amounts than ever. The lack of seriousness with which big business considered the rhetoric of human rights was best expressed by the manager of a $34-million Goodyear plant in Chile: "I don't think we spent five minutes talking about human rights when the board made the decision to invest in Chile." Corporate leadership understood from the beginning the superficial nature of the conflict generated by Carter's policy changes and concentrated on making the most of the "free market" policies promoted by the repressive regimes and backed by the U.S. government. Anaconda's president, commenting on their new investments, noted: "We have come back to Chile not only because of mining prospects but because the government has created a climate of confidence for investment."

U.S. policy toward social upheavals was to rely on third parties, encouraging Zaire to back the anti-MPLA forces in Angola, the Moroccans and Egyptians in Shaba (Zaire), etc. Likewise, Israel provided military support and channeled U.S. military supplies to several Central American dictatorships, while Washington was admonishing them to lessen their repressive image. Finally, while the United States criticized certain dictatorial methods, this policy was clearly subordinated to its opposition to social revolution: either it supported the threatened dictatorship; or if the situation looked hopeless, as in Iran and Nicaragua, it attempted a cosmetic change to head off revolutionary victory.

Impact of "Human Rights" Policy

Many observers have mistakenly attempted to evaluate Carter's "human rights" policies according to the publicly stated rhetoric of upholding human values. Some argue that the changes have been insignificant, while others defend the policy in terms of specific results (release of prisoners, opening of newspapers, etc.). From a historical vantage point, most of this debate is beside the point: the central issue to be taken into account in evaluating the "human rights" policy has to do with *its success or failure in reconstituting the capacity of the United States to intervene in the Third World*. And from this standpoint, the policy has been generally successful.

First, the policy has defused internal opposition: many liberals have been co-opted into the administration, while others have developed into lobbyists lending "critical support" to the administration. The anti-interventionist opposition has thus been divided between its radical and liberal wings, weakening its capacity to mobilize supporters. More important, the constant barrage of propaganda and public-relations campaigns effectively shifted public attention away from U.S. involvement and toward what has been happening in the Third World, especially the revolutionary societies. The turnaround in public opinion is particularly striking in the case of Vietnam. The United States has been able to change its image from being the source of destruction and hence internationally isolated to being the virtuous humanitarian saving fleeing refugees. From being attacked for its crimes in Vietnam, the United States has become the accuser of Vietnam over the so-called "boat people." The calls for direct action to save lives is a good example of how "morality" has been put at the service of reconstituting the interventionist capacity.

The "human rights" rhetoric has also led to a reconciliation with allies in Europe and won over some former critics in the Third World. Partly as a result, anti-interventionist movements, especially in Europe, have declined to insignificance.

The image of the United States as a moral leader has been re-floated and has acquired a certain credibility within a broad European public. Meanwhile, as far as the armed forces are concerned, the new professional army is clearly purged of all dissident elements and a strong move is underway to promote an elite interventionist force, a subject to which we return below.

The only area of weakness has been the demise of one of the crucial "regional influentials" (Iran) and serious unrest in another (Brazil). The incapacity of the United States to fashion a regional military force to police the Third World necessitates the organization of U.S. military forces for strategic strikes in "troubled areas." Thus the factors contributing to the deterioration of U.S. interventionist capacity have been largely neutralized by the "human rights" policy, while new policies are emerging in the context of growing popular insurgency in Latin America.

Revolutionary Upsurge and the Non-Interventionist Interlude

While Washington was working on reconstituting its imperial capacity, revolutionary upheavals were taking place in Angola, Ethiopia, Eritrea, Iran, Nicaragua, and Afghanistan. Despite divergences in social base, the common thread was the challenge to Western hegemony and the overthrow of U.S. client regimes. In the absence of sustained U.S. involvement, local power structures were clearly vulnerable. The rapidity with which the various regimes fell, despite massive armaments, training programs, and long-term support, testifies to the political isolation of the regimes in question—their lack of any substantive support. Moreover, each revolutionary upheaval threatened to bring in its wake new uprisings in neighboring countries. The threat of a rising conflagration, especially in the Middle East, Central America, and Southern Africa, affecting large-scale, long-term U.S. interests, created an atmosphere of crisis in Washington. The response has taken essentially two tacks. The right wing clam-

ored for action: there was a desire to convert the political
capital gained from the "human rights" campaign into immediate and massive direct action in the Third World, confrontation with the Russians, and closer military ties with the Chinese. The Carter administration, on the other hand, sought to
avoid premature unilateral intervention in areas of potential
large-scale warfare to avoid undermining the emerging, still
fragile, internal consensus. This approach involved a gradual
shift toward selective involvement, calculating costs and benefits, forming alliances, and working with local elites in client
Third World countries. Whatever the tactical nuances, the
drift of the Carter administration has been toward a more
cautious, yet nonetheless direct, involvement in the internal
conflicts of the Third World.

Elements of Carter's Interventionist Revival

The first cautious step toward a return to interventionism
was U.S. support for the Mobutu regime in Zaire. The airlift
of Moroccan and Egyptian troops, proxies for the United
States and France, suppressed the rebellion in Shaba and preserved Western interests. Beginning in late 1978, human-
rights groups began noticeably to lose influence in Congress
and in the executive branch, a pattern that deepened during
1979. The liberal critics of intervention had no clear answer
to the taunts of their conservative opposition who pointed to
successful revolutionary upheavals as one of the consequences
of past policies. Popular upheavals and their threat to U.S.
economic interests quickly put a damper on the human rights
concerns of U.S. liberalism.

All the campaign promises of 1976 vanished: arms sales
increased, as did the military budget. Military and autocratic
regimes, previously criticized for violation of human rights,
were provided with new military-aid programs—notably in
the Middle East, Southeast Asia, and Central America.

The new aggressive posture toward the Third World also
served to distract attention from internal problems: inflation,
unemployment, declining standards of living, and the energy

crisis were all blamed on OPEC in a major presidential address. Internal problems were transformed into instruments for external confrontation and contributed to the growth of intervention. Political demagogy planted the seeds of recolonizing areas of the Third World—better to intervene against the greedy Arab oil millionaires than to wait in gas lines on Main Street. The externalization of aggression became a tool for sustaining internal cohesion and avoiding potentially divisive cleavages between consumers and corporations.

The first major step toward reactivating the Marines was the effort by the United States within the Organization of American States (OAS) to secure a resolution calling for a joint military force to prevent a Sandinista victory in Nicaragua. The fact that the resolution failed and that the United States was not in a position to intervene unilaterally should not obscure the profound shift in U.S. policy and its important consequences for the immediate future. In the fall of 1979, the Carter administration accelerated efforts to create a 100,000-person Rapid Deployment Force capable of intervening within hours in any part of the world. In his speech on the Soviet military force in Cuba, Carter spelled out the "New Interventionism" very succinctly: "The United States has a worldwide interest in peace and stability. Accordingly, I have directed the Secretary of Defense to further enhance the capacity of our Rapid Deployment Forces to protect our own interests and to act in response to requests for help from our allies and friends. We must be able to move our ground, sea, and air units to distant areas—rapidly and with adequate supplies." (*New York Times*, October 2) Along with this came increasing efforts by the Carter team to promote a Latin American regional force, a proposal which would require a complete reconciliation with the worst dictatorship in the region. On September 29 the *New York Times* reported:

The Carter Administration is consulting with Latin American governments on the creation of a regional military peace-keeping force. . . . Ambassadors have been instructed to sound out the Latin American governments on their willingness to endorse the idea of an inter-American peace-keeping force and to provide troops for it. The force could be called on in emergencies. . . . Washington has made regional security of higher priority for the administration. As a result, the United States is now in the diplomatically awkward position of having to request military cooperation from regimes such as those in Argentina, Chile, and Uruguay that have been denied United States military aid for human rights violations.

These efforts to revive interventionism reached a hysterical pitch with the attempt by the administration to fabricate a Russian military threat in Cuba—an effort so transparently fraudulent that even the mass media and establishment politicians had to reject it. Nonetheless, the incident fell into a singularly bellicose pattern—a drift toward "direct action." In fact, out of this non-threat of Soviet troops Carter was able to create a Caribbean Joint Task Force in Florida to police the region and prepare to intervene. As Carter put it:

I am establishing a permanent, full-time Caribbean Joint Task Force Headquarters at Key West, Florida. I will assign to this headquarters forces from all the military services responsible for expanding and for conducting exercises. This headquarters unit will employ designated forces for action if required. This will substantially improve our capacity to monitor and respond rapidly to any attempted military encroachment in the area. (*New York Times,* October 2)

The moves toward military build-up and intervention go hand in hand. In the fall of 1979, the Carter administration was preparing a budget request for the coming fiscal year that would call for an increase of about 20 billion dollars in military spending. The *Times* (October 26) noted that "part of the increase would go for the development of a 'rapid deployment force' that could be used in a crisis in the Middle East or another region."

In summary, military resources and public opinion are being mobilized to defend imperial interests under the ideology of "defending ourselves against aggression"—i.e., national security. U.S. policy has come full circle since 1976: the policies, rhetoric, and instrumentalities of the 1960s and early 1970s are being refurbished for the 1980s.

In retrospect, one can see that the limits on U.S. intervention in the mid- and late-seventies reflected several factors, some of which are still operative in the eighties, while others grew out of the particular conjuncture. The non-intervention in Angola in 1975 reflected the recency of the defeat in Vietnam, a factor which is obviously no longer relevant. The same was true in the case of Ethiopia and perhaps Afghanistan—though the latter's remoteness from U.S. immediate concerns may have been a factor, as well as the fact that sectors of the Afghan army defected, leaving the U.S. with few internal levers to manipulate. In the case of Iran and Nicaragua the extent of mass support for revolutionary movements within those countries increased the probable cost of direct involvement, threatening to bog U.S. forces down in an endless policing operation. In the case of Nicaragua, U.S. diplomatic efforts failed to secure third-party support (rejection by the OAS of the proposed intervention force), while the opposition of European and Latin American social democratic and liberal governments and parties threatened to undermine efforts to reconstruct alliances within the Western world. Given these conjunctural, as well as long-term, constraints, U.S. policy-makers could not work in a single channel (direct intervention) or with a simple set of alliance partners: in existing circumstances, flexible political tactics in pursuit of deeply rooted economic imperatives characterize U.S. policy.

U.S. Policy: Contextual Determinations

U.S. tactics will be adjusted to contexts in which Washington will not always be able to pursue what it perceives to be an optimal solution. U.S. policy-makers will evidently continue to support viable dictators, those firmly in control of their populations and state apparatuses and willing to promote U.S. economic interests. In periods of emerging instability, the United States may support conservative (civilian) factions of the opposition or "reform" military groups if available. In highly polarized situations, Washington will support reformist-liberal coalitions against revolutionaries if necessary. Finally, in strategic areas the United States will not draw back from direct intervention to prevent social revolution, lacking any of the previous alternatives. The forms of U.S. interventionist activism do not always take the most direct or reactionary (in any absolute sense) form, but rather reflect what leaders take to be the real possibilities in the given context.

U.S. indirect intervention in several recent cases is illustrative: in Iran, faced with an ongoing mass upheaval in an advanced stage, U.S. policy-makers attempted to substitute Bakhtiar for the Shah, thus preserving the state apparatus and maintaining economic ties in exchange for the liberalization of the political regime. This maneuver failed because the struggle was too advanced—and the state apparatus itself was already in a state of disintegration. Subsequently, in a similar case in Nicaragua, the United States attempted to substitute conservative opposition figures for Somoza, preserving the National Guard and forestalling a Sandinista victory. The move occurred, however, on the eve of the popular victory when all but one of the major cities were already in the hands of the revolutionaries.

In these circumstances U.S. policy shifted toward an as yet unsuccessful effort to support a reform coalition against the Marxists. In El Salvador, U.S. policy attempted a preemptive coup: in the face of a profound polarization in which practically all of civilian society was ranged against the Romero regime, the United States promoted a center-right coalition, co-opting liberal Catholics, social democrats, and reformist military, while maintaining the existing state apparatus. The timing of this move in El Salvador was a response to the lesson learned in Nicaragua, where it was impossible to create alternatives in an open insurrectionary situation. The shift in El Salvador from inflexible dictatorial rule, to conservative but "flexible" military control (including openings to the center) clearly reflects a growing recognition in Washington of the importance of timing in directing its activities vis-à-vis the emerging political and social struggles in the Third World.

Conclusion

A proper understanding of U.S. policy must take into account the multiple tracks which it pursues, as well as its capacity to shift from one to another depending on the contextual situation and specifically on the scope and depth of the class struggle. In periods of isolated protests, Washington will continue to collaborate with repressive regimes, occasionally publicly criticizing "excesses." In a situation of escalating opposition, where collective conflicts are still local and uncoordinated, it will continue to work with the regime in power, criticize its lack of tactical flexibility, maintain ties with the civilian conservative opposition, and support repression of the revolutionary left. In periods of mass mobilization, U.S. policy will be to strengthen the conservative, electorally oriented opposition forces and to promote alliances with sectors of the military and even social democrats to isolate the revolutionary left. A coup against the incumbent power-holder may be encouraged, but in any case foreign aid and conciliatory reformist policy declarations are likely to be continued as long as the revolutionary left is effectively kept out of power. If these political maneuvers fail and a social revolutionary victory seems imminent, especially in a country designated as "strategic," the Rapid Deployment Forces would probably be used.

Given rising mass movements, especially in Latin America, and given the increasingly interventionist orientation of U.S. policy, the 1980s promise to be a period of growing confrontation. U.S. interests in preserving, or no more than marginally changing, repressive state apparatuses, and Washington's whole-hearted support of "free market" economic policies in the Third World are inevitably in conflict with the mass pressure for dismantling repressive regimes, nationalizing multinational property, and redistributing income and wealth. As the Third World changes from being a passive "human rights" victim to being an active protagonist of revolution, the United States shifts from being a critic of repression to a promoter of intervention.

HUMAN RIGHTS AND FOREIGN POLICY:
A PROPOSAL[9]

We are all agreed that the movement for human rights, politically expressed, is quite new; that U.S. involvement in that movement has been uneven; that the advent of the United Nations Covenant on Human Rights slightly altered the juridical international picture; that the Soviet Union came recently to a policy of manipulating the West's campaign for human rights; that the Vietnam War brought on a general disillusionment with American idealism. . . .

The United States has had cyclical romances with the notion of responsibility for the rights of extranationals. . . . There were the Fourteen Points of Woodrow Wilson, which he coupled to his antecedent crusade to make the world "safe for democracy." There came then, in 1941, Franklin D. Roosevelt's Four Freedoms. These—in passing—were significant for transmuting human rights into something much more than the negative injunctions on government activity conveyed in the Bill of Rights. FDR did not exactly discover, but he and Winston Churchill gave declamatory voice to positive, but not readily achievable, obligations of government: something called Freedom from Want, which seven years later gave birth to about 30 importunate children (e.g., "Everyone has the right . . . to free choice of employment") in the Universal Declaration and related documents—children who, for the most part, have lived unhappily ever since. But while Woodrow Wilson and Franklin Roosevelt and John F. Kennedy [in his inaugural address] were merely American Presidents, giving voice to an erratic, yet progressively universalist, statement of American idealism, the birth of the United Nations and the subscription by member states to its Charter gave near-universal codification to the notion of the obligation of

[9] Excerpts from article by William F. Buckley, Jr., editor of *National Review. Foreign Affairs.* 58:775–96. Spring '80. Excerpted by permission from *Foreign Affairs,* Spring 1980. Copyright 1980 by Council on Foreign Relations, Inc.

the state to acknowledge the human rights of its own citizens, and hinted at the mutual obligation of states to ensure each other's fidelity to these obligations. Because the Charter itself—and this before the ensuing elaboration in the Universal Declaration and other comments—committed its members to "reaffirm faith in fundamental human rights."

In short, the United Nations transformed human rights into something of an official international paradigm, and began to suggest an obligation by member states to modify their foreign policy accordingly. . . .

My proposal is to separate two questions. The first is: How do human rights fare in a given country? The second: What should the United States do about it? It is the commingling of the two that has brought forth existing confusions and distortions. The question whether we collaborate with the Soviet Union in order to avoid a world war is unrelated to any commitment a civilized nation ought to feel to human rights. Although the avoidance of a world war and the safety of the American state are primary objectives, the ethical imperative requires us as a nation, journeying through history, regularly to remark the brutality of the Soviet system—even if we make no commitment, thereby, to do anything concrete to mitigate those conditions.

On the whole we are better off stating, at all those international conferences, what it is we believe that sovereign states owe to their citizens in the way of recognizing individual rights—and let it go at that—than to collaborate in rituals of efficacy which we know will be without operative meaning. By the same token a constant encephalophonic reading, uninfluenced by distractions of diplomatic concern, of the condition of human rights in a given country, to the extent that this can be accomplished (the difficulty in ascertaining these conditions obviously varies) gives a gyroscopic steadiness of judgment which is the enemy of hypocrisy, dissimulation, and such other inventions as have disfigured the idealism of the human rights movement.

Congress should repeal existing legislation on the question of human rights (although, because of the loopholes, it would not really need to do so in order to promulgate the Commission described below). It should then establish a Commission on Human Rights composed of a Chairman and four members, with provisions for a staff of a dozen persons (approximately the size of the staff of the Assistant Secretary of State for Human Rights and Humanitarian Affairs). For symbolic reasons primarily, but also for practical reasons, the Commission should not be affiliated with the Department of State. It might plausibly be affiliated with the judiciary, or perhaps even with the Department of Justice. What matters most is that its mandate should be distinctive, unrelated to policy-making, whether by the executive or the legislative branches of government.

The Commissioners should be appointed by the President and confirmed by the Senate. The Act should recommend to the President that the Commissioners be selected from a roster of candidates nominated by existing agencies devoted to the internationalization of human rights including—but not restricted to—the International Commission of Jurists, Freedom House, Amnesty International, the Anti-Defamation League, the several religious committees and the Red Cross.

The mandate would most severely restrict the Commission's public role to the reporting of factual conditions: never to the recommendation of policy. Policy would continue to issue from Congress and the Executive. The Commission would report publicly, once a year, to the President and to Congress—in the nature of the event, to the world—on the condition of human freedom in every country, using the Universal Declaration of the United Nations as the paradigm. For administrative purposes, much as Freedom House does in its annual report, these freedoms might be grouped together, e.g., in such a way as to distinguish usefully between the right (Number 5) not to be tortured, and the right (Number 24) to "rest and leisure."

The Commission would be available to the Executive, or to Congress, for such questioning as the government chose to direct to it, e.g., on any special knowledge acquired about human rights in any given country; movements within that country to improve conditions; whatever. However, the tradition should vigorously be nurtured that no policy of the Executive, or of Congress, would flow from any initiative of the Commission, even if that policy resulted from legislative or executive reaction to data collected by the Commission.

The Chairman of the Commission, or any other Commissioner designated by him, would represent the United States government in several relevant posts within the United Nations, occupying there the chair in the Third Committee of the General Assembly. The Commission's restrictions would carry over: i.e., the representative would make the case for human rights, answer questions about human rights in the United States, and describe their findings, insofar as they were relevant. He would leave to the representative of the regular U.S. delegation the exercise of the vote (in favor, against, or abstaining) on any concrete proposal concerning, e.g., the treatment of terrorists, hijackers and so forth. This division of duties would not be so difficult as the reader might suppose. Most of the argumentation before the Third Committee is over trivial points, forgotten the day after they engage the delegates' attentions; and in any event, recommendations of the committees are subject to acceptance or rejection by the General Assembly, where the permanent representative of the United States votes on instructions from the Department of State.

By the same token the Commissioner (or his representative) would sit at the Geneva sessions of the standing United Nations Commission on Human Rights. Once again, his role would be to report on the condition of human rights in any country under discussion; once again, he would decline to vote on recommendations that called for policy decisions. A vote condemning, let us say, racial discrimination, or a condemnation of bondage, or of sex discrimination, or religious persecution is not a vote on U.S. policy toward those countries guilty of such misconduct. The Commissioners would, clearly, be permitted to express themselves in favor of the human rights the very existence of the committee ostensibly seeks to augment.

The Commission would have the right of access to a fixed number of broadcast hours per country per year, for the purpose of factual reporting of its findings. These reports—again, without policy recommendations—would go out over the Voice of America, and affiliated broadcasters in Europe, Asia, Africa and Latin America. Such reports, though unaccompanied by policy recommendations, would not need to go out as dry-as-dust statistics. They could, indeed should, engage the dramatic attention of the listener by, for instance, permitting refugees to tell their own stories. An appropriate term of office for the Commissioners, and for the Chairman, might be seven years.

It should be unnecessary to explain that the existence of a United States Commission on Human Rights could not constitutionally deprive either Congress or the Executive of powers that inhere in those institutions. No one has the power to tell the President he should not make a fool of himself on landing in Warsaw—he would still be free to do so. But the silent, yet omnipresent, countenance of the Commission on Human Rights, with its lapidary findings on the condition of human rights in Poland, would make it less likely that the President, in pursuit of diplomacy, would traduce idealism. Congress can vote to deny arms or soybeans or "Saturday Night Fever" to any country Congress chooses to punish or victimize or bully or wheedle; but the existence of the Commission, with its findings, would provide certain coordinates that might guard against such caprice as nowadays tends to disfigure country-specific legislation.

And—viewed from the other end—for the wretched of the earth, in their prisons, with or without walls, in the torture chambers, in the loneliness they feel as they weigh the distortions of diplomacy, there would be something like: a constant. A Commission mute while the United States collaborates with Stalin in pursuit of Hitler, or Mao in pursuit of Brezhnev, but resolutely unwilling to falsify the record of Josef Stalin or Mao Zedong in their treatment of their own people.

"The great enemy of clear language is insincerity," Orwell wrote, in the same essay in which he lamented that "in our time, political speech and writing are largely the defense of the indefensible." To say the truth—says Solzhenitsyn—is the single most important thing of all. Politicians cannot always say the truth and pursue policies organic to their profession. But the saying of the truth about human rights, as distinguished from the superordination of human rights over all other concerns, is not incompatible with the mechanics of foreign policy.

Finally the question is asked: Would such a Commission, with its yearly findings, its reports to the nation, its testimony before Congress, its international broadcast of its findings— would it enhance human rights? It is quite impossible to assert that it would do so—or that it would not do so. With the best will in the world, Wilsonianism succeeded in making the world most awfully unsafe for democracy. But, as mentioned earlier, there is an encouraging survival, through it all, of the idea of the inviolable individual, and that idea needs watering, not only by the practice of human rights at home, but by the recognition of their neglect abroad. It is a waste of time to argue the inefficacy of telling the truth, the telling of which is useful for its own sake.

EL SALVADOR: THE MILITARY ASPECTS[10]

A Pentagon assessment of El Salvador's Army asserts that it is so ill-prepared to fight Communist-led insurgents that it has "no hope" of defeating them.

Against that background, Secretary of State Alexander M. Haig Jr. has told ambassadors of European allies, as well as the Ambassadors of Australia, Japan, New Zealand and Spain,

---

[10] Reprint of "From Washington and El Salvador, Differing Views on Fighting Rebels: Military Aspects of Crisis Are Underlined by Haig and a Pentagon Study," news story by Richard Halloran, staff correspondent. New York *Times.* p 1+. F. 21, '81. © 1981 by The New York Times Company. Reprinted by permission.

that the Administration's "most urgent objective" is to stop a large flow of arms from Communist nations to guerrillas in El Salvador.

The Pentagon assessment of El Salvador's Army differed somewhat from a comment today by José Napoleón Duarte, President of the country's ruling junta, who said that the armed forces were capable of handling the guerrillas at present if the flow of arms to the insurgents stopped. What his country needed most, he said, was economic aid to counter the guerrilla threat.

A memorandum on Mr. Haig's briefing of the foreign ambassadors on . . . [February 18] quoted Mr. Haig as saying that the United States "will not remain passive" to what he described as a "systematic, well-financed, sophisticated effort to impose a Communist regime in Central America."

He also asserted that the United States would not become engaged in "another bloody conflict," as in Vietnam, but would direct its action toward Cuba, which he declared was the main source of the intervention. This morning Mr. Haig was a little less assertive. He remarked to reporters during a brief conversation that there was "grave concern" over "countries intervening illegally in this hemisphere through provision of arms to a Western Hemisphere nation that is seeking to determine its destiny through due process."

The Pentagon assessment, completed this week on the basis of reports from Central America, asserted that the guerrillas would most likely become stronger by April, when new shipments of arms are scheduled to be finished.

Officials . . . [in Washington] said that the arms, from Vietnam, Ethiopia, Bulgaria, Hungary, and East Germany, were being shipped through Cuba to Nicaragua and Honduras and, finally, to El Salvador. Most of the weapons, ammunition, communications equipment and medical supplies were reportedly bought or captured from Western nations.

The military assessment prepared by the Defense Department said that El Salvador's army numbered 17,000 men, including administrative and support elements, compared with 3,700 full-time guerrillas and 5,000 who take occasional part in actions. With a combat ratio of about 4 to 1, the analysis said, it would be "impossible" for the Government forces to put down the insurgency.

Military experts have long held that a conventional army and police force must outnumber an insurgent force by 10 to 1 because the guerrillas have the advantage of knowing where, when and how they will strike.

The Pentagon study said the Salvadoran Army could not control the infiltration of arms and guerrillas from Honduras on the ground, from Nicaragua by water and from both countries by air. Nor, the study added, were the Government forces capable of rooting the guerrillas out of three pockets along the border with Honduras.

Like '19th Century Constabulary'

The assessment thus concluded that the Salvadoran Army was "not organized to fight a counterinsurgency" battle nor even a conventional war. It was deemed "more like a 19th century constabulary than a 20th-century army" and was said to have "no hope" of winning with the resources at hand.

In an effort to inform allies of that situation and to build up international support for coming Administration actions, Secretary Haig held his briefing in the State Department. Also involved was an intelligence briefing by Ronald I. Spiers, director of intelligence and research.

A report on the briefing said Mr. Haig asserted that the United States had intelligence "which we consider irrefutable" that the Soviet bloc, with Cuban coordination, was "furnishing at least several hundred tons of military equipment to the Salvadoran leftist insurgents."

Only after the foreign intervention, Mr. Haig asserted, did the United States provide additional military assistance, including weapons, to the Salvadoran Government. He said the Administration was considering additions to $63 million appropriated for economic aid this year.

"Our most urgent objective is to stop the large flow of arms through Nicaragua into El Salvador." Mr. Haig said.

"We consider what is happening is part of the global Communist campaign coordinated by Havana and Moscow to support the Marxist guerrillas in El Salvador."

Mr. Haig said the Administration had not yet decided precisely how to deal with the situation but would have to deal "with the immediate source of the problem—and that is Cuba." He said that "I wish to assure you that we do not intend to have another Vietnam and engage ourselves in another bloody conflict where the source rests outside the target area."

Officials said that much of the evidence came from captured documents, in Spanish, with specific references to Soviet financing of arms shipments.

The report said Vietnam was shipping pistols, semiautomatic rifles, machine guns, mortars, antitank rocket launchers and large amounts of ammunition. Officials said that most of those were American-made arms that North Vietnamese soldiers captured from South Vietnamese forces in 1975.

Ethiopia, the report said, had agreed to sell submachine guns, rifles, and ammunition provided by the United States to the Government of Emperor Haile Selassie before his overthrow.

The report said that Bulgaria had agreed to send submachine guns, machine guns, ammunition and medical kits. Officials said most had been made in West Germany and were bought by the Bulgarians openly or in black markets.

THE BEST LONG-TERM SECURITY[11]

The politics of the six coffee-and-banana republics in Central America are not the stuff of which a world crisis should be made. Their combined gross national product is less than Taiwan's and, were they not so infectiously close to Mexico (five times richer than they), their strategic value

[11] Reprint of article entitled "Reagan's Banana Skin," *The Economist*. 278:12–13. F. 7, '81. © The Economist Newspaper Ltd, London, 1981.

would be tiny. But the civil war in El Salvador, which has killed at least 10,000 people in the past year, and the troubles in Nicaragua and Guatemala could yet embroil the United States in a proxy war with the Soviet Union.

In the election campaign, Mr Reagan identified the Cuban threat as the central issue. He argued that Mr Carter had worried too much about ticking off generals and not enough about combating Marxists. Mr Carter's approach to Central America was certainly flawed. He underestimated Cuba's support for the guerrillas in El Salvador, and he agreed to supply weapons to the government only after the guerrillas had launched their main offensive. In neighbouring Guatemala, which is also edging towards a murderous civil war, his attempt to improve the human-rights record of the government led merely to a breakdown in relations. But Mr Carter did understand that arms are not the only weapons that can be used against the revolutionary left. It is not evident that Mr Reagan yet does.

Until a year ago, El Salvador was one of the most unequal states in the world. A small oligarchy controlled the major industries and 263 farmers owned 70% of the cultivable land. Regardless of Cuban policy, it was fertile ground for Marxism. Reform cannot change the hearts of the Marxists who lead El Salvador's guerrillas, but it can change the minds of the democratic-minded who have been alienated by successive regimes to the point of giving succour to the guerrillas.

Since a coup in October, 1979, El Salvador's new junta has gone some way down the road to reform. It has initiated a radical programme of land redistribution—a politically brave act for which it may suffer, like others who have tried it. In the first stage, 15% of the oligarchy's land was expropriated. And it has nationalised the export trade to loosen the leading families' grip on the coffee business. But the junta has faltered under the shadow of the guerrillas' violence. It has delayed further reforms and has allowed the armed forces to retaliate against left-wing brutality with their own, equally vicious, methods.

President Reagan now has a singular opportunity in El Sal-

vador. The right is willing to listen to a man it considers a
friend and the latest guerrilla offensive has failed. As well as
increasing the supply of arms to the junta (to match the sophisticated arms and training that have been supplied by the
Cubans to the rebels), Mr Reagan should insist, discreetly,
that the United States cannot go on supporting the junta unless it gets a grip on the murder squads in its own army, and
commits itself to the creation of an uncorrupted-by-politics
business class and to further social reform.

The danger of an unconditional American commitment to
back this junta is that it would strengthen the hand of the far
right, which wants to block all reform. It would thus increase
the support for the guerrillas and prolong a civil war, which
might then oblige Mr Reagan to send in American troops.
Armed intervention in Central America should never be precluded as a last resort; but to reach the last resort means that
better solutions have failed along the way. An American
Afghanistan in El Salvador would help radicalise the Mexico
it was designed to protect.

How to Handle Nicaragua

President Reagan must also decide whether to continue to
supply economic aid to the increasingly Marxist regime in
Nicaragua. When President Carter signed the aid bill, congress insisted that the money should be withdrawn, if the
president found that the Nicaraguans had supported Marxist
revolutions abroad.

American intelligence had until now failed to determine
for sure whether the Nicaraguan government has supported
guerrillas in El Salvador. Now the evidence of Nicaraguan
complicity seems to be too strong to ignore. It was good
enough to convince Mr Edmund Muskie, the outgoing secretary of state. If Mr Reagan is also convinced, he is obliged to
cut off American aid. But if the Nicaraguans agreed to stop
arming El Salvador's guerrillas, then he should enthusiasti-
cally resume it. Nicaragua's exchange reserves are near to ex-

haustion: it has some reason to bow to American conditions, suitably expressed.

Left-wing regimes in Central America—or in the Caribbean—are not necessarily a threat to the United States. Nor, as Mr Edward Seaga has shown in Jamaica, is the trend all to the left. The United States should certainly not try to crush every political movement left of General Somoza, as many of the ideologues around President Reagan seem to want to do. It must, however, show that it is willing to match every Cuban attempt to disrupt established governments, rocket-launcher for rocket-launcher. And it must accompany its arms shipments with quiet injunctions that freedom and pluralism are the best long-term security against Marxism.

BIBLIOGRAPHY

An asterisk (*) preceding a reference indicates that the article or part of it has been reprinted in this book.

BOOKS AND PAMPHLETS

Beals, Carleton. Latin America: world in revolution. Abelard-Schuman. '63.

Burr, R. N. Our troubled hemisphere; perspectives on United States-Latin American relations. Brookings. '67.

Clark, Gerald. The coming explosion in Latin America. McKay. '63.

Collier, David, ed. The new authoritarianism in Latin America. Princeton University Press. '80.

Corbett, C. D. The Latin American military as a socio-political force: case studies of Bolivia and Argentina. Center for Advanced International Studies, University of Miami. '72.

Douglas, W. O. Holocaust or hemispheric co-op: cross currents in Latin America. Random House. '71.

Etchison, D. L. The United States and militarism in Central America. Praeger. '75.

Fitzgibbon, R. H. and Fernandez, J. A. Latin America. Prentice-Hall. '81.

* Foreign Policy Association. Great decisions '81. The Association. '81.

* Lernoux, Penny. Cry of the people. Doubleday. '81.

Linz, J. J. and Stepan, Alfred, eds. The breakdown of democratic regimes: Latin America. Johns Hopkins University Press. '78.

Lowenthal, A. F. and Fishlow, Albert. Latin America's emergence: toward a U.S. response. (Headline Series 243) Foreign Policy Association. '79.

Sigmund, P. E. Multinationals in Latin America: the politics of nationalization. University of Wisconsin Press. '80.

* Smith, P. H. Mexico: the quest for a U.S. policy. Foreign Policy Association. '80.

Wendt, Herbert. The red, white, and black continent: Latin America, land of reformers and rebels. Doubleday. '66.

PERIODICALS

America. 142:485. Je. 7 '80. Human rights in the Americas. J. R. Brockman.

* America. 143:262–6. N. 1. '80. El Salvador between two fires. R. A. White.

Américas. 31:35–7. O. '79. Meeting today's human needs. J. J. Del Pino.

* Américas. 32:9–10. Ja. '80. Hemisphere trends: in defense of human rights. Michael Morgan.

Américas. 32:39–41. Ja. '80. Development in transition. F. X. Gannon.

Américas. 32:9. My. '80. Hemisphere trends: growth despite inflation. Michael Morgan.

Américas. 32:40–4. My. '80. Traditions in conflict. G. R. Pérez.

Américas. 32:9. S. '80. Hemisphere trends: Andean Parliament.

* Américas. 33:12. Ja. '81. Hemisphere trends: U.S. stake in Latin America.

* Armed Forces and Society. 6:614–24. Summer '80. The military withdrawal from power in South America. M. C. Needler.

Atlantic. 246:6+. Jl. '80. Latin America: the revolutionary bishops. Penny Lernoux.

Business Week. p 50. Ap. 14, '80. The growing Communist threat in Central America. S. W. Sanders.

Commonweal. 108:14–16. Ja. 16, '81. Green light for terror [in El Salvador]. R. A. White.

Current History. 78:49–88+. F. '80. Latin America, 1980 [symposium].

Current History. 80:49–90. F. '81. Latin America, 1981 [symposium].

* Daedalus. 109:115–33. Fall '80. The United States and its regional security interests: the Caribbean, Central, and South America. J. I. Domínguez.

Daedalus. 110:1–22. Winter '81. Toward an American conception of regional security. Michael Nacht.

Department of State Bulletin. 79:13–16. N. '79. Currents of change in Latin America; address. C. R. Vance.

Department of State Bulletin. 80:58–65. Ja. '80. Central America at the crossroads. V. P. Vaky.

Economic Development and Cultural Change. 28:267–91. Ja. '80. Market-oriented economic policies and political repression in Latin America. John Sheahan.

Economist. 277:13. D. 20, '80. Hombre no!

Economist. 278:39–40. Ja. 24, '81. El Salvador: tragedy trap.

* Economist. 278:12–13. F. 7, '81. Reagan's banana skin.

Economist. 278:30. F. 21, 81. El Salvador: tell the Europeans where it is.

Economist. 278:33. Mr. 14, '81. A gleam or two of light over Central America.

Economist. 278:30. Mr. 21, 81. El Salvador: last statement inoperative.

Forbes. 125:6, 41–6+. Mr. 31, '80. More Cubas in the making. Jerry Flint.

Foreign Affairs. 58:449–84. Special Issue '80. America in decline: the foreign policy of maturity. R. W. Tucker.

Foreign Affairs. 58:485–514. Special Issue '80. Regionalism as geopolitics. Peter Jay.

Foreign Affairs. 58:659–92. Special Issue '80. The United States and Latin America: vital interests and the instruments of power. Alfred Stepan.

* Foreign Affairs. 58:775–796. Spring '80. Human rights and foreign policy: a proposal. W. F. Buckley, Jr.

* Foreign Affairs. 58:1084–1103. Summer '80. Oligarchs and officers: the crisis in El Salvador. W. M. LeoGrande and C. A. Robbins.

* Foreign Policy. no 39, p 99–117. Summer '80. Central American paralysis. Richard Millett.

Harper's. 262:31–50. Mr. '81. Rising to rebellion. T. D. Allman.

Monthly Review. 31:26–37. Je. '79. Political change, class conflict, and the decline of Latin American fascism. James Petras.

* Monthly Review. 31:15–27. F. '80. U.S. foreign policy: the revival of interventionism. James Petras.

* Multinational Monitor. 1:12–16. Mr. '80. Multinationals, development and democracy; interview with Henry Geyelin.

Nation. 231:172–3. Ag. 30–S.6, '80. Red-scare tactic.

Nation. 232:289+. Mr. 14, '81. The new counterinsurgency. M. T. Klare.

* Nation. 232:304–7. Mr. 14, '81. Background to repression: Guatemala's Indian Wars. Clifford Krauss.

Nation. 232:361–2. Mr. 28, '81. The Kirkpatrick doctrine for Latin America. Penny Lernoux.

National Catholic Reporter. 16:2. Ja. 11, '80. Pilate was fairer [South America's military regimes]. Penny Lernoux.

National Catholic Reporter. 16:1+. Mr. 28, '80. Rights court to start slowly. Stephanie Russel.

National Catholic Reporter. 16:2+. Je. 20, '80. The crime of machismo politics. Penny Lernoux.

National Review. 31:920-1+. Jl. 20, '79. Moscow reaches for America's slim waist. Robert Peter.

National Review. 31:1481. N. 23, '79. Targets of opportunity. Brian Crozier.

National Review. 32:600-1. My. 16, '80. Why not a new Monroe doctrine? H. E. Catto, Jr.

* National Review. 32:1068. S. 5, '80. Caribbean rot. Brian Crozier.

National Review. 33:148-50+. F. 20, '81. Nation in our midst: the Cuban diaspora. F. X. Maier and R. B. McColm.

National Review. 33:153+. F. 20, '81. Huber Matos the undefeated [interview]. Lorrin Philipson.

National Review. 33:228. Mr. 6, '81. The moral minority and the Savior. Michael Novak.

* New Republic. 183:5-6+. N. 29, '80. Rights and Reagan.

* New Republic. 183:14+. D. 27, '80. Are human rights passé? Ronald Steel.

New Republic. 184:5-7. Ja. 17, '81. Latin lessons.

New Republic. 184:15-17. Mr. 14, '81. Salvadoran quagmire. Ronald Steel.

New Republic. 184:5-7. Mr. 21, 81. Salvaging El Salvador.

* New York Times. p A1+. F. 21, '81. From Washington and El Salvador, differing views on fighting rebels; military aspects of crisis are underlined by Haig and a Pentagon study. Richard Halloran.

New York Times. p A1. Mr. 4, '81. President doubtful of U.S. intervention. Edward Schumacher.

New York Times. p A2. Mr. 5, '81. Nicaragua, attacked on rights, defends its record. Alan Riding.

New York Times. p A6. Mr. 6, '81. Reagan aides meet sharp attack in House on new Salvadoran aid. Juan de Onís.

New York Times. p E2. Mr. 8, '81. Arms aid and advisers; debating the new policy on El Salvador [colloquy between Jeane J. Kirkpatrick and Robert E. White].

New York Times. p A1. Mr. 12, '81. U.S. aides hint Cuba cuts arms to Salvador left. Bernard Gwertzman.

New York Times. p A2. Mr. 19, '81. Mexico, crushing a maverick, razes a neighborhood. Alan Riding.

New York Times. p A11. Mr. 19, '81. Use of force against Cuba an option, senators told. Judith Miller.

New York Times. p A3. Mr. 25, '81. Protests on Salvador are staged across U.S. Raymond Bonner.

New York Times. p A27. Mr. 27, '81. Salvador: who's who, and what. Bennett Poor.

New York Times. p A3. Mr. 30. '81. Viola takes his turn as the president of Argentina.

New York Times. p A14. Mr. 31, '81. Costa Rica buffeted by regional unrest. Alan Riding.

New York Times. p A3. Ap. 2, '81. U.S. halts economic aid to Nicaragua.

New York Times. p A14. Ap. 9, '81. Mexico and Venezuela try to ease tensions in Caribbean. Alan Riding.

New York Times. p A7. Ap. 13, '81. Argentine defends human rights stand; foreign minister asserts approach won't be changed to improve relations with the U.S. Edward Schumacher.

° Newsweek. 95:38–9+. Ap. 14, '80. Dominoes in Central America? Steven Strasser and others.

Newsweek. 96:50. Ag. 18, '80. Back to square one with Reagan? Steven Strasser and others.

Newsweek. 96:78. O. 27, '80. Peace prize: why him? [Argentine Nobel laureate Adolfo Pérez Esquivel]. John Brecher and Larry Rohter.

Newsweek. 97:36–7. Ja. 12, '81. Reagan's Mexican overture. Bob Levin and others.

Newsweek. 97:42+. Ja. 19, '81. El Salvador's short fuse. Bob Levin and others.

Newsweek. 97:45–6. F. 9, '81. Reagan changes the rules. Tom Mathews and Fred Coleman.

Newsweek. 97:41+. Mr. 2, '81. Salvador's arms pipeline. Bob Levin and others.

Newsweek. 97:37–9. Mr. 9, '81. El Salvador: the U.S. gets tougher. Bob Levin and others.

Newsweek. 97:34–8. Mr. 16, '81. Storm over El Salvador. Bob Levin and others.

Newsweek. 97:43–6. Mr. 16, '81. The ferment in Central America. Tom Mathews and others.

Newsweek. 97:47. Mr. 16, '81. Argentina: a crackdown on rights. John Brecher.

Newsweek. 97:37. Mr. 23, '81. El Salvador: the Americans on the spot. Bob Levin and others.

Politics Today. 7:51–4. Ja./F. '80. The one-man band of the human rights fight. Michael Massing.

Senior Scholastic. 112:22. S. 20, '79. Democracy in South America? It might be a trend. P. M. Jones.

Time. 113:88. My. 7, '79. The Church of the poor *comunidades de base* (base communities).

Time. 116:75. O. 27, '80. Light in the Latin darkness.

U.S. News & World Report. 88:21–7. My. 19, '80. Powderkeg at
our doorstep. C. J. Migdail.

* U.S. News & World Report. 89:51–3. Ag. 18, '80. Military's tight
grip on South America.

* U.S. News & World Report. 89:37. S. 15, '80. Why Latins are
losing respect for the U.S. C. J. Migdail.

U.S. News & World Report. 89:37–8. D. 1, '80. Where Castro still
threatens in Caribbean. Dennis Mullin.

* U.S. News & World Report. 89:45–7. D. 29, '80/Ja. 5, '81. Foreign policy: an acid test for Reagan.

U.S. News & World Report. 90:37–8. Ja. 26, '81. El Salvador's future—and how U.S. can influence it; interview with Ambassador R. E. White.

U.S. News & World Report. 90:37–9. Mr. 9, '81. Strains on U.S.-
Mexican ties: oil, migrants, Castroism. C. J. Migdail and J. L.
Benham.

U.S. News & World Report. 90:28–32. Mr. 16, '81. El Salvador:
will it be another Vietnam?

U.S. News & World Report. 90:25–6. Mr. 23, '81. Nicaragua blinks
in showdown with U.S. [on arming leftist rebels in El Salva-
dor]. C. J. Migdail.

USA Today. 109:3–4. O. '80. Central America may be next Iran.

* World Press Review. 27:50. Ja. '80. 'Liberating' Latin America.
Conrado Contreras.

DATE DUE

OCT 2 8 1982		